GO PROGRAMMING FOR ABSOLUTE BEGINNERS

Your Ultimate Guide To Go Programming,No Experience Needed

KRISTINE ELLIS

INTRODUCTION

Welcome to Go Programming

Welcome to the exciting world of Go programming! If you are reading this, you've taken the first step toward mastering one of the most powerful yet beginner-friendly programming languages available today. Whether you're just starting out in programming or are looking to expand your skillset, this book will guide you through every concept, step-by-step, ensuring you build a solid foundation in Go.

Go, also known as Golang, was created by Google in 2007 and publicly released in 2009. It was designed with the aim of simplifying complex systems programming while ensuring high performance. While Go is still a relatively young language compared to established ones like Python or Java, it has quickly become one of the most popular languages among developers, particularly for tasks involving web servers, cloud computing, and data processing.

In this book, we will take a hands-on approach, introducing you to Go's simplicity and power, helping you learn how to write clean, efficient, and scalable programs. By the end of this journey, you'll not only understand the syntax of Go but also be comfortable with concepts like error handling, concurrency, and deploying Go applications in real-world scenarios.

Go is built with simplicity and efficiency in mind, and as we walk you through the language, you'll realize that these principles make Go exceptionally well-suited for beginners and experienced developers alike. The key to success with Go, like any language, is consistent practice and a desire to solve real problems. Through this book, we will equip you with the knowledge and confidence to start writing functional and production-ready Go applications.

Let's dive in and start learning Go!

What is Go?

Go is an open-source programming language designed for simplicity and high performance. Its primary creators, Robert Griesemer, Rob Pike, and Ken Thompson, initially set out to create a language that could tackle the complexity of modern software development while also being intuitive and easy to learn. The result was Go—an elegant, powerful, and expressive language that combines the best features of some of the world's most popular programming languages, like C, Python, and Java.

The Key Features of Go

Go stands out for its simplicity, speed, and effectiveness. Let's break down some of its key features:

1. Simplicity and Minimalism

One of the biggest draws of Go is its simplicity. Unlike many programming languages that come with a myriad of features and complexities, Go follows a minimalist design philosophy. This doesn't mean that Go lacks power—it's quite the opposite. Go keeps things clean and concise, removing unnecessary features that often make other languages harder to grasp for beginners.

For example, Go eliminates the need for complex inheritance structures found in other object-oriented languages, such as Java or C++. Instead, Go uses **composition** as its primary method for reusing code, which is easier to understand and implement.

With Go, you won't find yourself overwhelmed by complicated syntax or confusing constructs. Instead, you can focus on learning core programming concepts, writing effective algorithms, and building applications.

2. Compiled Language

Go is a compiled language, meaning that code written in Go is directly translated into machine code that the computer can execute. This gives Go a significant performance advantage over many interpreted languages, such as Python or Ruby, which require an interpreter to execute the code at runtime.

By compiling your code into a standalone executable, Go ensures that your programs are fast and efficient, a key reason why Go is so popular for building highly scalable and performance-sensitive applications, such as web servers and cloud-based systems.

3. Concurrency Made Simple

One of Go's standout features is its built-in support for **concurrency**—the ability to run multiple tasks at the same time. This is an increasingly important concept in modern programming, especially when building scalable systems or handling multiple user requests at once.

2

In most programming languages, dealing with concurrency involves complex concepts like threads and locking mechanisms. However, Go simplifies concurrency with **goroutines** and **channels**. Goroutines are lightweight threads that can run concurrently without the need for extensive memory or CPU resources. Channels are used to communicate between goroutines, ensuring that data is safely shared between them.

This makes it incredibly easy to write programs that can handle multiple tasks simultaneously, which is particularly useful when building web servers or handling large amounts of data.

4. Garbage Collection

Memory management can be a complex and error-prone part of programming, especially in languages like C or C++, where developers need to manually allocate and deallocate memory. Go handles memory management for you with a built-in **garbage collector**.

The garbage collector automatically frees up memory that is no longer in use, which reduces the likelihood of memory leaks and improves the stability and performance of Go applications. This allows you to focus on writing code rather than worrying about memory allocation, making Go a great choice for beginners who don't yet have experience with complex memory management.

5. Strong Standard Library

Go comes with an extensive standard library that provides everything you need to build robust applications. Whether you're handling HTTP requests, working with files, parsing JSON, or building databases, Go's standard library covers most of the tools you'll need to get started.

For beginners, this is a huge advantage. You won't have to waste time searching for third-party libraries or tools. The Go standard library is well-documented, easy to use, and highly optimized, which makes building applications much faster and simpler.

6. Cross-Platform Compatibility

Go is a cross-platform language, meaning that programs written in Go can run on various operating systems, including Windows, macOS, and Linux, without requiring any changes to the source code.

In fact, one of the features that makes Go especially attractive for developers is its **cross-compilation** capabilities. You can write your Go code on one platform, compile it, and deploy it to another platform without any issues. This is ideal for building applications that need to run on different servers or environments, as Go simplifies the process of developing and deploying cross-platform applications.

7. Easy Deployment

Once you've written your Go program, deploying it is straightforward. Since Go is compiled into a single binary, you don't need to worry about installing dependencies or setting up a runtime environment. You simply compile your code, and the result is an executable that can run on any machine.

This makes Go an excellent choice for building applications that need to be quickly deployed or distributed to multiple servers or environments.

8. Fast Compilation Time

One of the things that developers love about Go is its extremely fast compilation time. While many languages take a long time to compile, Go was specifically designed to be compiled quickly, even for large applications. This makes the development process more efficient, as you can spend more time writing code and testing it rather than waiting for the compiler to finish.

Why Beginners Should Learn Go

As a beginner, Go offers several compelling reasons to choose it as your first programming language:

- **Ease of Learning:** Go's minimalist syntax makes it easy to get started with, even if you have no prior programming experience. The language is designed to be intuitive and clear, which makes it an excellent starting point for anyone new to programming.
- **Practical and Powerful:** Go allows you to build real-world applications quickly, from web servers to network applications, all with relatively simple code. Its simplicity doesn't limit its capabilities, and you can build powerful software with minimal effort.
- **Great for Building Scalable Applications:** Whether you're looking to build a web server, an API, or a cloud-based system, Go's concurrency model and performance make it an excellent choice for developing applications that can handle high traffic and large amounts of data.

- **Strong Community Support:** Go has a vibrant community of developers, and there are plenty of online resources to help you as you learn. Whether you're seeking tutorials, examples, or advice from experienced developers, Go's community is always ready to help.
- **Demand in the Job Market:** Go's popularity is growing rapidly, and many companies, including Google, Uber, and Dropbox, use Go for production systems. By learning Go, you'll be entering a job market with plenty of opportunities.

Go is a powerful and versatile programming language that is perfect for beginners. With its clean syntax, fast performance, and support for building scalable applications, Go is an ideal choice for anyone looking to break into software development. Whether you want to build web servers, data-processing systems, or anything in between, Go gives you the tools to get started quickly and effectively.

In the next section, we will explore the basics of programming, and how Go fits into the broader landscape of modern software development. Let's continue this journey and dive deeper into the world of Go!

Why Choose Go as a Beginner?

When it comes to choosing your first programming language, you want something that is both approachable and powerful. Go (or Golang) stands out as an excellent choice for beginners, and here's why.

1. Simplicity and Clarity

Go is designed with simplicity in mind, making it incredibly easy for newcomers to pick up. Unlike other languages that may have complex syntax or a steep learning curve, Go uses clean, minimalistic syntax that makes it easier to understand.

There are no confusing concepts like classes or inheritance that can overwhelm beginners, yet it still allows you to write highly functional and efficient code. Go doesn't require deep knowledge of complex language features to get started, so as a beginner, you can focus on the fundamentals of programming, like data types, control flow, and basic algorithms, without worrying about intricate language details.

With fewer lines of code required to achieve the same functionality, Go allows you to see results faster. This immediate feedback loop is ideal for beginners, providing a satisfying experience that motivates them to continue learning.

2. Clear, Readable Code

Go enforces a clean, readable code style. The language has a built-in tool, gofmt, which automatically formats your code according to a standard style. This means that, regardless of who writes the code, it will always look the same—easy to read and consistent. This is especially helpful for beginners who are learning how to structure their code. When you write Go code, it looks clear and understandable, which minimizes confusion as you learn.

3. Built-in Features for Concurrency

Concurrency, or the ability for multiple tasks to run simultaneously, can be a difficult concept to grasp in other programming languages, especially for beginners. However, Go makes concurrency easy with its built-in features, such as **goroutines** and **channels**. These features let you write concurrent code with minimal effort.

Go allows you to work on multiple tasks at once, which is crucial for modern applications like web servers, data processing, and network programming. With Go's goroutines and channels, you won't need to dive into complicated concepts like threads or mutexes early on. Instead, Go abstracts away the complexity, so you can learn how to work with concurrency without getting bogged down in the technicalities.

4. Powerful Yet Beginner-Friendly

Even though Go is simple enough for beginners, it is also incredibly powerful. It is used by large companies like Google, Dropbox, and Uber to build scalable, high-performance systems. As a beginner, this means you can trust that the tools you're learning today will allow you to build real-world applications tomorrow. The language is robust enough to handle projects of all sizes, so you can start small and continue growing as you build your skills.

Additionally, Go is a statically typed language, which means that types are explicitly declared, reducing errors. If you accidentally try to perform an operation on the wrong type of data, Go will alert you before running the program. This feature is incredibly useful for beginners, as it helps prevent many common mistakes that are harder to debug in dynamically typed languages.

5. Fast Compilation and Execution

Go's compilation is fast, and it produces highly efficient code. For beginners, the fast compilation process ensures that you spend more time coding and less time waiting for the computer to build your programs. When you make changes to your code, you can see the results quickly, which is a great advantage when you're learning. Additionally, Go's performance is on par with lower-level languages like C and C++, but with much simpler syntax and fewer complexities.

6. Excellent Documentation

Go comes with extensive and easy-to-understand documentation, which makes learning the language more straightforward. The official Go website (https://golang.org) has a wealth of tutorials, examples, and resources to guide you. Plus, Go's standard library is well-documented and full of useful tools to help you write powerful applications without needing to rely on external libraries.

When you run into issues or have questions, you can easily access the Go documentation and quickly find solutions. The documentation is designed to be beginner-friendly, so you won't get lost in overly technical details.

7. Large and Supportive Community

Go has a strong and growing community that's actively supporting learners. Whether through forums, user groups, or open-source projects, the Go community provides a wealth of resources to help beginners. The community's culture is friendly and welcoming, which makes it easier for you to find answers to your questions, learn from others, and contribute to projects.

When you start writing Go code, you'll find plenty of tutorials, blogs, YouTube videos, and books—like this one—that will guide you through every step. Additionally, as you progress, you can connect with other Go enthusiasts who are eager to help newcomers grow and succeed.

8. Great for Real-World Applications

Go is used in many real-world applications, particularly in web development, cloud computing, and data science. As a beginner, learning Go will equip you with skills that are directly applicable in industry, which increases the value of your learning experience. The language is used to create APIs, microservices, distributed systems, and even mobile applications, so you'll be able to see the direct impact of your learning on real-world projects.

How This Book Will Help You

This book is designed to help you become proficient in Go programming, even if you have no prior experience in coding. Whether you are learning Go as your first language or transitioning from another programming language, this book will provide a clear, structured path to mastering Go, making it the ideal guide for beginners.

1. Step-by-Step Learning Path

We've organized this book in a way that breaks down complex concepts into manageable chunks. Each chapter builds upon the previous one, so you never feel overwhelmed. We'll start by explaining the core programming principles, such as variables, data types, and control flow, before introducing you to Go-specific features like concurrency and the Go runtime.

Every concept is introduced with simple, practical examples, followed by exercises that will help you apply what you've learned. This step-by-step progression ensures that you don't just memorize the syntax, but truly understand the logic behind how Go works.

2. Hands-On Approach

Programming is best learned through practice. That's why this book emphasizes **learning by doing**. You'll be encouraged to write your own code alongside the examples we provide. Each chapter contains practical exercises that will help you apply what you've learned, and by the end of the book, you will have built several functional Go programs.

You won't just be reading theory; you will be writing code, debugging it, and seeing the immediate results of your work. This hands-on approach makes learning more engaging and ensures you retain the information better.

3. Real-World Examples

Throughout the book, we will guide you through building real-world applications. Whether you're writing a simple command-line program or learning how to work with web servers and APIs, you will be building projects that have practical, real-world applications. This approach makes Go relevant to your goals and gives you the tools to start building your own software projects as soon as you feel comfortable.

4. Code Walkthroughs and Explanations

In addition to exercises, each section contains detailed code walkthroughs, where we explain how the code works, step by step. We'll break down complex code snippets and highlight what each part of the code does, helping you understand not just the syntax but also the logic behind it.

This approach ensures that, even when you encounter unfamiliar code, you'll be able to grasp its meaning and implement similar solutions on your own in the future.

5. Troubleshooting and Debugging Tips

One of the most important skills in programming is learning how to debug your code. As you go through the book, you will inevitably run into issues, and we will help you troubleshoot them. Each chapter includes debugging tips and common errors that beginners often face, ensuring you don't get discouraged if things don't work on the first try.

We'll also cover **best practices** for writing clean, maintainable code and how to structure your projects to make them easy to read and extend. Learning how to write clean code from the start will pay off as you continue to develop your skills.

6. Continued Support After the Book

This book is just the beginning of your Go programming journey. At the end of each chapter, we will direct you to additional resources where you can deepen your understanding and keep learning. We will also introduce you to Go's broader ecosystem, such as open-source libraries, frameworks, and communities, where you can continue to grow as a Go developer.

By the end of this book, you'll have a solid understanding of Go and be able to write production-quality programs. You will also have the confidence to continue exploring more advanced Go concepts and to contribute to the Go community.

A Quick Overview of Go's Simplicity

Go is a simple language, and its simplicity is one of the reasons it has become so popular. It was designed to eliminate unnecessary complexity while still providing powerful features that allow developers to build robust software. Let's take a closer look at why Go is known for its simplicity:

1. Minimalist Syntax

Go's syntax is minimalistic yet expressive, meaning that you can get a lot done with just a small amount of code. Unlike some other programming languages, Go does not have extraneous keywords or syntax rules. It avoids the need for things like semicolons or curly braces in places where they're not needed. This simplicity allows you to focus on the logic of the program rather than the language itself.

2. No Unnecessary Abstractions

In Go, the abstractions are kept to a minimum. For example, Go avoids complex features like inheritance, which can make object-oriented programming difficult to grasp for beginners. Instead, Go focuses on composition, making code easier to understand and maintain. This approach also prevents unnecessary complexity in your codebase, helping you avoid problems that can arise from overly complex structures.

3. Straightforward Error Handling

One area where Go differs from many languages is in how it handles errors. Rather than relying on exceptions or complex error handling mechanisms, Go uses a simple pattern where functions return error values explicitly. This makes error handling clear and easy to understand, which is especially useful for beginners.

4. Easy to Learn, Hard to Outgrow

Go's simplicity doesn't mean it lacks depth. While the language is beginner-friendly, it's also powerful enough to handle complex software projects. As you grow as a programmer, you'll be able to use Go for more advanced tasks without needing to switch to a different language. Go allows you to learn and grow at your own pace.

By focusing on what really matters and leaving out unnecessary complexity, Go provides a clean and streamlined environment for learning programming. As you dive deeper into Go, you'll appreciate how its simplicity allows you to focus on solving problems without getting bogged down in language intricacies.

Go's Key Features

Go is not only powerful but also remarkably simple, which is why it has gained such a wide following. Understanding its key features is crucial to appreciating why it is ideal for beginners, as well as why it's so widely adopted for large-scale production systems. Let's explore some of the most important features of Go that make it stand out from other programming languages.

1. Static Typing with Type Inference

One of Go's fundamental features is its **static typing**. In static typing, the type of a variable (such as int, string, or float64) is known at compile time. This leads to greater performance and early detection of errors, which is beneficial for both debugging and optimization. Static typing ensures that the types of variables are consistent, preventing many bugs that occur due to type mismatches.

However, Go also supports **type inference**, which makes it easier to write concise code. When you declare a variable using the short assignment (:=) operator, Go automatically infers the type based on the assigned value. This means you don't have to explicitly declare the type, but Go still ensures that it's safe. For example:

go

Copy

```
age := 25  // Go infers that 'age' is of type int

name := "John"  // Go infers that 'name' is of type string
```

This combination of static typing and type inference helps to keep Go both simple and efficient.

2. Garbage Collection

In programming, managing memory manually can be both error-prone and time-consuming, especially in languages like C or C++. Go, however, handles this issue with its built-in **garbage collector**. The garbage collector automatically frees up memory that is no longer in use, which eliminates the need for manual memory management.

11

This simplifies development, as it allows you to focus more on writing functional code and less on worrying about memory allocation and deallocation. Go's garbage collection is designed to be low-latency and efficient, even in high-performance applications.

3. Concurrency with Goroutines and Channels

Go shines when it comes to **concurrency**—the ability to run multiple tasks simultaneously. While many languages have concurrency mechanisms, Go makes it simple and elegant with **goroutines** and **channels**.

- **Goroutines**: A goroutine is a lightweight thread of execution. Creating a goroutine in Go is as simple as adding the go keyword in front of a function call. This allows you to run multiple operations concurrently without dealing with complex thread management. Goroutines are extremely efficient, using only a fraction of the memory that traditional threads would require.

go

Copy

```
go func() {

    fmt.Println("Running concurrently")

}()
```

- **Channels**: Channels provide a way for goroutines to communicate safely and efficiently. They allow one goroutine to send data to another goroutine, helping to synchronize and share information. This mechanism simplifies the writing of concurrent programs by abstracting away the complexities typically associated with multithreading, like mutexes and locks.

go

Copy

```
ch := make(chan string)

go func() {
```

```
    ch <- "Hello from goroutine"
}()

message := <-ch  // Receive the message from the channel
fmt.Println(message)
```

With Go's goroutines and channels, developers can write concurrent applications easily, without the complexity found in other languages like Java or Python.

4. Cross-Platform Support

Go is designed to be **cross-platform** from the ground up. This means that you can write Go code on one operating system (OS) and compile it to run on a variety of others, including Linux, macOS, and Windows. The Go compiler supports a wide range of platforms, allowing developers to write code that is portable without having to worry about platform-specific details.

Moreover, Go's easy cross-compilation capabilities make it ideal for building applications that need to run on different environments or devices. For example, you can develop and compile an application on your local machine (Linux), then compile it for Windows or macOS with minimal effort.

5. Standard Library

Go comes with a powerful and comprehensive **standard library** that simplifies development. The standard library includes packages for everything from handling I/O, working with strings, and manipulating data structures, to implementing web servers and networking protocols.

You don't have to worry about finding third-party libraries for many common tasks, as Go's standard library already provides robust solutions. This makes Go an ideal choice for beginners because they can focus on learning core programming concepts without getting bogged down by external dependencies.

Here are some examples of tasks that Go's standard library handles:

- **HTTP Servers**: Go has an in-built net/http package to easily create web servers.
- **JSON Parsing**: The encoding/json package simplifies working with JSON data.
- **File Handling**: The os and io/ioutil packages allow easy manipulation of files and directories.

The standard library is not only extensive but also well-documented, providing beginner-friendly examples for each package.

6. Simplicity in Code and Structure

Go encourages simple and clear code. Unlike other languages that encourage complex patterns and features (like multiple inheritance or generics), Go promotes a minimalist approach. For example, Go uses **composition** instead of inheritance for object-oriented principles, which results in simpler, more understandable code.

Additionally, Go's **gofmt** tool automatically formats your code to a consistent style. This reduces the need for worrying about code style, making it easy for teams to collaborate on projects. It ensures that all Go code, regardless of who wrote it, looks consistent and is easier to read.

7. Error Handling as a First-Class Concept

Unlike languages that use exceptions for error handling, Go uses a more straightforward and predictable method: the explicit **error type**. Functions in Go that might produce an error explicitly return an error value, allowing the caller to handle it directly.

This approach forces you to handle errors right where they occur, reducing the chance of missed errors and improving the robustness of your code. While some developers initially find this method tedious, many later appreciate its clarity and control.

go

Copy

```
result, err := someFunction()

if err != nil {

    fmt.Println("Error:", err)
```

```
return

}
```

8. Fast Compilation

Go is known for its **fast compilation** times. It was designed to be quick both in terms of execution and compilation, which greatly speeds up the development process. When you make changes to your code, Go can compile and run it in a matter of seconds. This makes it much easier to test and iterate on your programs without losing valuable time waiting for the compiler.

What Makes Go Ideal for Beginners

Go has a reputation for being a beginner-friendly language, and for good reason. Let's explore some of the features and qualities that make Go an excellent choice for newcomers to programming.

1. Simple and Minimalistic Syntax

Go was designed to be easy to read and understand, even for those who are new to programming. Its syntax is minimal, with fewer complex keywords and features compared to other languages like C++ or Java. This simplicity makes Go an excellent starting point for beginners who want to learn core programming concepts without getting lost in complicated syntax rules.

For example, Go eliminates features such as classes and inheritance that can confuse beginners, opting instead for simpler approaches like structs and composition. This makes the language easier to pick up and use.

2. Clear and Readable Code

One of Go's core philosophies is **simplicity**. Code written in Go is easy to understand and follow, even for someone with little programming experience. Its concise and consistent syntax helps beginners write code that is clean, readable, and maintainable.

Go's **gofmt** tool enforces this simplicity by formatting code automatically, making it easy to work in teams and collaborate with others. This means beginners don't need to spend time worrying about indentation or code style, allowing them to focus on the content of the code itself.

3. Quick to Learn and Use

Go's learning curve is shallow, which is great for beginners. With minimal setup, Go allows you to write, compile, and run code quickly. The language has a small number of keywords and concepts, so you can start writing your first program right away without feeling overwhelmed by advanced features. Go's simplicity ensures that you can get productive almost immediately.

Additionally, Go's strong documentation, combined with a large online community, makes it easy to find answers to your questions and continue learning at your own pace.

4. Real-World Use Cases

Unlike many other beginner programming languages, Go is not just a "toy language." It's widely used in production systems, including large-scale applications at companies like Google, Uber, and Dropbox. As a beginner, learning Go gives you skills that are immediately applicable in the real world.

Go is commonly used for web development, cloud computing, distributed systems, and more. This means that, as you learn Go, you're not only gaining valuable coding skills but also developing expertise in building robust, scalable applications.

5. Strong Community Support

Go has a vibrant, growing community of developers. Whether you need help debugging code, learning new techniques, or discussing best practices, the Go community is welcoming and supportive. You can easily find resources like tutorials, articles, and forums that will help you along your journey.

This community-driven aspect of Go ensures that beginners have access to a wealth of knowledge and experience, making it easier to get started and overcome common learning hurdles.

Go's combination of simplicity, power, and efficiency makes it an ideal choice for beginners. It allows you to start writing meaningful programs quickly, while providing the depth you need to scale up as you grow in your programming journey. With its clean syntax, clear error handling, and built-in concurrency support, Go strikes the perfect balance between beginner-friendliness and advanced functionality, making it the perfect starting point for anyone learning to program.

In the next chapters, we will dive deeper into Go's core concepts and start writing your first Go programs!

Chapter 1: The Basics of Programming

1.1 Understanding Code and Computers: What is Programming?

Before diving into the world of Go programming, it's essential to have a solid understanding of the fundamental concepts that underpin all programming languages. To begin, let's break down what programming actually is, and how it connects to the computers we use daily. This foundational knowledge will set you up for success as you learn Go and any other programming language in the future.

What is Programming?

Programming, at its core, is the process of giving a computer a set of instructions to perform a task. These instructions, written in a language that the computer can understand, are called **code**. Programming is not just about writing lines of text—it's about solving problems and automating tasks through logical thinking and precise instructions.

Just as we use spoken or written language to communicate ideas to other humans, programming languages allow us to communicate our ideas to computers. However, unlike natural languages, programming languages are highly structured and formal, with strict rules and syntax that the computer must follow to execute the instructions correctly.

When you write code, you are essentially telling the computer, "I want you to do this," and the computer then interprets those instructions and carries them out. This process might involve simple tasks, like adding two numbers together, or more complex tasks, like creating a website or building an application that can communicate with users in real-time.

How Computers Understand Code

Computers, as powerful as they are, don't inherently understand human language. In fact, they only understand **binary**, a system made up of two numbers: 0 and 1. This is because the underlying hardware in a computer (its processors and memory) can only recognize two states: on (1) or off (0).

However, it would be impractical for programmers to write in binary. Imagine writing a program by typing out long strings of 1s and 0s. Instead, **programming languages** provide a more human-readable way of writing instructions that can be translated into machine language (binary). These programming languages act as an intermediary between humans and computers.

When we write code in a programming language like Go, it's eventually translated by a **compiler** into machine code that the computer can execute. Think of the compiler as a translator between the human-readable programming language and the computer-readable binary code.

The Process of Programming: A Step-by-Step Breakdown

Here's a simplified version of how programming works:

1. **Writing the Code**: You start by writing instructions using a programming language like Go. These instructions can be simple or complex, depending on the task you want the computer to perform.
2. **Compiling**: Once the code is written, it needs to be compiled. A **compiler** takes your human-readable code and translates it into machine code (binary), which is understandable by the computer's processor. This step is important because computers only execute machine code.
3. **Executing**: Once the code has been compiled into machine code, the computer runs the program, performing the tasks or operations specified in the code. This could involve performing calculations, retrieving data from a database, displaying text on a screen, or interacting with the user.
4. **Feedback and Debugging**: As the program runs, the computer executes each line of code in the sequence you've written. If the code contains errors, the computer will usually produce feedback, either in the form of an error message or unexpected behavior. This is where debugging comes in: developers often need to examine their code, find mistakes, and correct them.

Types of Programming Languages

Programming languages can be broadly categorized into two types based on their level of abstraction: **high-level** and **low-level** languages.

1. **High-Level Languages**: These are designed to be easy for humans to read and write. They use more natural language-like syntax and abstract away the complexities of the computer's hardware. Examples of high-level languages include Go, Python, Java, and C#. These languages are user-friendly and often come with built-in functions and libraries that make complex tasks much easier to implement.

2. **Low-Level Languages**: These are closer to the machine code and provide less abstraction. Low-level languages allow developers to control the hardware directly, which can lead to more efficient programs but at the cost of greater complexity. **Assembly language** and **C** are examples of low-level languages. While these languages offer more control, they are harder to learn and use effectively, especially for beginners.

Translating Code into Machine Language

While Go, like other high-level languages, is much easier to write and understand than low-level languages, it still eventually needs to be converted into machine code for the computer to execute it. The process of converting code into something the computer can understand involves two main steps: **compiling** and **linking**.

1. **Compilation**: The code you write is first processed by a **compiler**, which translates it into intermediate machine code. This intermediate code isn't yet ready to be run but is a step closer to the final executable.
2. **Linking**: After compilation, the code may depend on external libraries or resources. The **linker** comes in here, connecting your code to these libraries or other resources, ensuring everything is in place for the program to run smoothly.

Once the compilation and linking processes are complete, your program is turned into an executable file that the computer can run directly, performing the tasks you've programmed it to do.

Algorithms: The Heart of Programming

At the core of every program lies the **algorithm**—a step-by-step procedure or a set of instructions to solve a specific problem. Algorithms are what make programs functional; they define the logic of how a program should process data or interact with users.

An algorithm can be simple, like sorting a list of numbers, or more complex, like processing a payment transaction. In Go, you'll learn how to develop and implement algorithms efficiently using the language's simple syntax and powerful built-in functions.

Example of an Algorithm: Sorting a List

Let's say we need to sort a list of numbers from smallest to largest. A simple algorithm to accomplish this might involve repeatedly comparing adjacent numbers in the list and swapping them until the list is in the correct order.

Here's how the algorithm might look in pseudocode:

vbnet

Copy

1. Start with the first number in the list.

2. Compare it to the next number.

3. If the first number is larger, swap them.

4. Move to the next number and repeat steps 2-3 until the entire list is sorted.

This is a simple **sorting algorithm**, but more complex algorithms can be used to solve different problems, like finding the shortest path in a graph, processing user input, or performing data analysis.

As a programmer, you'll write algorithms that allow your software to function effectively, whether you're building simple applications or complex systems. In Go, understanding how to write efficient algorithms will be a key skill.

What is Logic in Programming?

Programming is not just about writing code—it's also about thinking logically and breaking problems down into manageable steps. **Logic** in programming refers to the rules and reasoning that determine how a program operates, makes decisions, and solves problems.

There are several key aspects of logic in programming:

- **Conditionals**: These are used to make decisions in a program. If certain conditions are met, the program will execute a specific action. In Go, you can use if, else, and switch statements to handle decision-making.
- **Loops**: These allow a program to repeat a set of instructions multiple times. For example, you could loop through a list of items, performing the same action on each item.
- **Boolean Logic**: Boolean logic, using true/false values, forms the foundation of decision-making in programming. Expressions like $x > 5$ && $x < 10$ (which

checks if x is between 5 and 10) are examples of Boolean logic that determine how the program behaves.

Example of Logic: Checking User Input

Here's an example of logic in a Go program that checks whether a user has entered a valid number:

go

Copy

```go
var number int

fmt.Println("Please enter a number:")

fmt.Scan(&number)


if number >= 0 {

    fmt.Println("You entered a positive number!")

} else {

    fmt.Println("You entered a negative number!")

}
```

In this example, the logic is based on a simple if-else decision: the program checks if the number entered by the user is greater than or equal to zero. Based on that condition, it prints out one of two possible messages.

Why Understanding Programming Basics is Essential

Having a strong grasp of programming fundamentals, including how computers interpret code, understanding algorithms, and mastering logic, will make you a more effective Go programmer. These concepts are applicable not only in Go but in any programming language you learn in the future.

Programming is not just about writing code; it's about thinking critically and logically to solve problems. By building a solid foundation in programming concepts, you will be able to approach coding challenges with confidence and find solutions more easily.

In this section, we have laid the groundwork for understanding the essential concepts of programming. We've explored what programming is, how computers interpret code, and how algorithms and logic form the basis of every program. By understanding these fundamentals, you are now prepared to begin your journey with Go.

As we continue through this book, we'll build on these concepts, teaching you how to implement them in Go. From there, you'll move on to writing your own programs, solving real-world problems, and gaining the skills necessary to become a proficient programmer. Let's get started with the first steps in Go programming, beginning with the installation process and writing your first Go program

How Computers Understand Code

As mentioned earlier, computers fundamentally operate in a world of **binary**, meaning they can only process two states: **on** and **off**, represented as **1** and **0**. This is the language of the hardware that powers computers, known as **machine language** or **machine code**. However, as programmers, we do not write directly in binary, because it is impractical and extremely difficult for humans to understand.

To bridge the gap between human-readable code and machine-readable code, we use **programming languages**. These languages allow us to write instructions that are closer to human language, which are then translated into machine code so the computer can execute them.

When you write a program, you're writing instructions in a language that the computer must interpret, so it can understand what you want it to do. The process of translating human-readable instructions into something the computer understands happens in two main steps:

1. **Compilation (for compiled languages like Go)**: The **compiler** takes your source code written in a programming language (like Go) and translates it into

machine code all at once. The result is an executable file that can run directly on the machine.

2. **Interpretation (for interpreted languages)**: In interpreted languages, there's no direct compilation. Instead, the code is run line-by-line by an **interpreter**, which translates each instruction into machine code as it's needed. While this can slow down execution, it allows for more flexibility, especially during the development process.

In Go, the process is generally compilation, where you write code in Go, compile it, and the computer runs the resulting executable. The beauty of Go's design is that it abstracts away many of the complexities of writing machine code, yet it allows the programmer to have more control over performance than languages like Python or JavaScript.

Code Structure and Syntax: Writing Instructions for a Computer

Code structure refers to how the instructions in a program are organized and written. **Syntax** refers to the rules that govern how these instructions should be written. Every programming language has its own syntax and rules for how code must be structured to be understood by the compiler or interpreter. If the syntax is not followed properly, the code won't work, and the compiler or interpreter will throw an error.

Let's break down some important aspects of code structure and syntax that are important to understand when you start writing programs:

1. Statements

A **statement** is a single line of code that performs an action. In Go, like most other programming languages, statements are written one after another to instruct the computer to perform a specific task.

For example, in Go, a statement might look like this:

go

Copy

```
fmt.Println("Hello, World!")
```

This statement instructs the computer to print "Hello, World!" to the console. It tells the computer to invoke the fmt.Println() function and pass the string "Hello, World!" as an argument.

2. Variables

Variables are used to store data that your program can use and manipulate. A variable has a **name** (to identify it) and a **type** (to define what kind of data it holds, such as a number or a string).

In Go, a variable declaration looks like this:

go

Copy

```
var age int

age = 25
```

In this example, age is a variable of type int (integer), and we assign it the value 25. Alternatively, Go allows you to use **short declaration syntax**, which lets you declare and initialize a variable in one step:

go

Copy

```
age := 25
```

3. Functions

A function is a block of code that performs a specific task. Functions help break down code into smaller, reusable chunks, which makes programs easier to understand and maintain.

In Go, a simple function might look like this:

go

Copy

```
func greet(name string) {
```

25

```go
    fmt.Println("Hello, " + name)

}
```

In this example, greet is a function that takes a parameter name of type string and prints a greeting to the console.

4. Control Flow

Control flow refers to the order in which individual statements, instructions, or function calls are executed in a program. Go has several control flow mechanisms, including:

- **Conditionals** (e.g., if, else, and switch): These allow the program to make decisions and execute different sections of code based on specific conditions.
- **Loops** (e.g., for): Loops allow the program to repeat a set of instructions until a condition is met, making it possible to work with collections or perform repetitive tasks.

Example of a conditional statement in Go:

go

Copy

```go
if age >= 18 {

    fmt.Println("You are an adult.")

} else {

    fmt.Println("You are a minor.")

}
```

Here, the program checks if age is greater than or equal to 18. If true, it prints "You are an adult."; otherwise, it prints "You are a minor."

26

5. Indentation and Formatting

Indentation refers to the spaces or tabs used at the beginning of a line to show the logical structure of your program. In Go, consistent indentation is vital for readability, though unlike Python, Go doesn't enforce indentation rules as part of the syntax. The **gofmt** tool automatically formats Go code to a standard style, ensuring that code remains clean and easy to read.

Example of indented code in Go:

go

Copy

```go
if age >= 18 {
    fmt.Println("You are an adult.")
} else {
    fmt.Println("You are a minor.")
}
```

Using indentation makes it easy to see which statements are part of the same block, especially when you have nested conditionals or loops.

High-Level vs. Low-Level Languages

Now that you understand the basic structure of code, it's important to know that there are different kinds of programming languages, classified based on how close they are to machine code. These are known as **high-level** and **low-level** languages.

1. High-Level Languages

High-level languages are designed to be easy for humans to read and write. They are more abstract and provide more powerful features to help developers write code more efficiently. High-level languages are designed to be portable across different systems, meaning that you can write code on one machine and run it on others without needing to make changes.

Go is a high-level language, and it shares many characteristics with other languages in this category, such as Python, Java, or JavaScript. Some key features of high-level languages include:

- **Abstraction from hardware**: High-level languages hide the complexities of managing memory, interacting with hardware, or dealing with system-specific issues.
- **Readable syntax**: These languages use syntax that is closer to human language, making it easier to understand and use.
- **Portability**: Code written in high-level languages can often be run on multiple platforms without modification.

Go's high-level nature means that you don't have to manage low-level system details, such as memory management or direct hardware interaction, while still benefiting from powerful programming tools and libraries. For a beginner, this is a huge advantage, as you can focus on learning how to solve problems with code, not how the computer's hardware works.

2. Low-Level Languages

Low-level languages are closer to the computer's machine code, meaning they offer less abstraction and give developers more control over system resources like memory and hardware. These languages are harder to learn and use but offer more flexibility and can achieve higher performance in certain contexts.

- **Assembly Language**: This is a step up from pure binary machine code, using human-readable mnemonics to represent machine-level instructions. Assembly language is specific to a computer's architecture and needs to be compiled into machine code.
- **C Language**: C is another low-level language that allows direct manipulation of memory and hardware resources. While it provides more control over performance, it requires the programmer to handle things like memory management manually, which can lead to bugs and security vulnerabilities.

Low-level languages like C or Assembly give the programmer more control over the hardware but at the cost of increased complexity. They are often used in systems programming, embedded systems, or applications that require high performance and direct access to hardware.

28

Understanding how code works and how computers understand and execute it is fundamental to becoming a proficient programmer. In this section, we explored the relationship between high-level and low-level programming languages, the structure and syntax of Go code, and how Go abstracts away many of the complexities of low-level programming to make development faster and easier.

As you continue through this book, you'll deepen your understanding of how to write clean, efficient code in Go, and you'll start building real-world applications. But first, let's move on to installing Go and setting up your development environment so you can start writing your first Go program.

Introduction to Algorithms and Logic

As you begin your journey in programming, understanding **algorithms** and **logic** is crucial. These two concepts form the backbone of every program, from the simplest to the most complex. In this section, we'll explore the fundamentals of algorithms and logic, explaining how they work together to solve problems in code. Understanding these concepts will not only help you write more effective programs but also give you the problem-solving mindset that every great programmer develops over time.

What is an Algorithm?

An **algorithm** is a set of well-defined, step-by-step instructions used to perform a task or solve a problem. The word "algorithm" may sound technical, but at its core, an algorithm is simply a method for achieving a specific goal, broken down into manageable steps.

For example, if you want to sort a list of numbers from smallest to largest, you might use a sorting algorithm. Algorithms can be simple, like adding two numbers, or complex, like finding the shortest path in a graph of cities.

An algorithm needs to be:

1. **Clear and unambiguous**: Each step should be simple and precise so that there's no confusion about how it should be executed.

2. **Finite**: It must have a definite ending point; it cannot run indefinitely.
3. **Effective**: It should be capable of solving the problem within a reasonable amount of time and resources.

Why are Algorithms Important?

Algorithms are the foundation of any program, no matter what language you're using. Every task a computer performs, whether it's processing data, handling user input, or even performing calculations, is guided by an algorithm. The better the algorithm, the more efficient and effective the program will be.

By understanding how to design and implement algorithms, you'll be able to solve problems logically and efficiently, which is at the heart of programming. Go, like many other languages, offers several built-in tools and libraries to help you implement these algorithms with ease, but the core idea of breaking down a problem into steps remains constant.

Basic Algorithm Examples

Here are a couple of simple algorithms to help clarify the concept:

Example 1: Finding the Maximum Number in a List

Let's say you have a list of numbers, and you want to find the maximum number. An algorithm for this task might look like this:

1. Start with the first number in the list. Assume it's the largest.
2. Compare it with the next number in the list.
3. If the next number is larger, update your assumption.
4. Continue comparing the assumed largest number with each remaining number in the list.
5. When you reach the end of the list, the last assumed number is the largest.

This algorithm runs through the list, comparing each number to find the maximum.

Example 2: Sorting a List of Numbers (Bubble Sort)

Another common algorithm is **Bubble Sort**, which arranges numbers in order by repeatedly swapping adjacent elements if they are in the wrong order. The algorithm works as follows:

1. Start at the beginning of the list.
2. Compare the first two numbers. If the first is greater than the second, swap them.
3. Move to the next pair of numbers and repeat the process until you reach the end of the list.
4. Once you reach the end, repeat the process for the entire list, excluding the last number (as it's already sorted).
5. Repeat until no more swaps are needed.

Here's a quick visualization of how the list looks during sorting:

css

Copy

[5, 3, 8, 4] → Compare 5 and 3 → Swap → [3, 5, 8, 4]

[3, 5, 8, 4] → Compare 5 and 8 → No swap → [3, 5, 8, 4]

[3, 5, 8, 4] → Compare 8 and 4 → Swap → [3, 5, 4, 8]

...

At the end of the process, the list is sorted in ascending order.

Both of these examples—finding the maximum number and sorting a list—are simple algorithms, but they lay the groundwork for more complex solutions. As you progress in Go, you'll learn how to implement these and more advanced algorithms.

What is Logic in Programming?

While algorithms define the steps to solve a problem, **logic** determines the flow of control within the program. Logic is how we make decisions in code: when to run a block of code, when to repeat actions, and how to respond to different conditions.

31

In programming, logic is implemented through:

Conditional Statements: These allow the program to make decisions based on certain conditions. The most common type of conditional is the if statement, which allows you to execute a block of code if a condition is true, or execute another block if it's false. Example:

go
Copy

```
if age >= 18 {

    fmt.Println("You are an adult.")

} else {

    fmt.Println("You are a minor.")

}
```

1. **Loops**: Loops enable the program to repeat a block of code multiple times. There are several types of loops, such as the for loop, which can iterate over a range of values or repeat actions until a specific condition is met.
   Example:
   go
   Copy

```
for i := 0; i < 10; i++ {

    fmt.Println(i)  // Prints numbers 0 to 9

}
```

2. **Boolean Logic**: **Boolean values** are either true or false, and they form the basis of most decisions in a program. By combining Boolean values with logical operators (like && for "and", || for "or", and ! for "not"), you can create complex conditions for control flow.
   Example:
   go
   Copy

```
if age >= 18 && country == "USA" {

    fmt.Println("You are eligible to vote.")
```

}

3. **Switch Statements**: Switch statements are an elegant way of handling multiple conditions without using several if-else blocks. They allow you to match a value against a list of possibilities and execute the corresponding code.
Example:
go
Copy

```
switch dayOfWeek {

case "Monday":

    fmt.Println("Start of the workweek.")

case "Friday":

    fmt.Println("End of the workweek.")

default:

    fmt.Println("Midweek day.")

}
```

Logical Flow in a Program

When you write a program, you often need to make decisions based on the input or data being processed. Logic determines how these decisions are made. For instance, when writing a login system, you might check if the username and password match a database record. If they do, the user is granted access; if they don't, the program could ask for the credentials again.

This process of logical decision-making allows the program to behave dynamically, reacting differently depending on input or other variables.

How Algorithms and Logic Work Together

Algorithms and logic are inseparable. Algorithms define the process for solving a problem, while logic dictates the specific decisions and steps taken within the algorithm. In simple terms:

- **Algorithms** provide the roadmap for solving problems (i.e., the sequence of steps).
- **Logic** directs how those steps should be carried out based on conditions and repetition.

Let's consider an example of using both together to find the sum of even numbers from a list:

1. **Algorithm**: Loop through the list of numbers, check if the number is even, and if so, add it to a running total.
2. **Logic**: Use an if statement to check if each number is even, and then use a for loop to repeat the action for each number.

Here's how the code might look in Go:

go

Copy

```go
numbers := []int{1, 2, 3, 4, 5, 6, 7, 8, 9, 10}

sum := 0


for _, number := range numbers {

    if number%2 == 0 {  // Check if the number is even

        sum += number   // Add the even number to the sum

    }

}
```

```
fmt.Println("The sum of even numbers is:", sum)
```

In this example, the **algorithm** involves looping through the list and adding the even numbers, while the **logic** is the use of the if statement to determine if a number is even, and the for loop to repeat the check for each number.

Algorithms and logic form the core of programming. Algorithms provide a structured way to solve problems by breaking them into smaller, manageable steps, while logic controls the flow of these steps, making decisions and repeating actions as necessary. Whether you are building a simple application or developing complex systems, these concepts will guide you through writing effective and efficient code.

As you continue to learn Go, you'll become more adept at designing and implementing algorithms, applying the right logic at each stage of the program. These foundational skills will serve you well as you tackle increasingly complex problems in software development. Next, we will explore Go's basic features and syntax, and begin writing your first program!

1.2. Algorithms and Logic

Now that we've covered the basics of programming and the foundational role of logic, let's dive deeper into **algorithms** and how they relate to **logic** in programming. Understanding these concepts is key to solving real-world problems through code, and mastering them will improve your ability to write efficient, effective software.

What is an Algorithm?

In the simplest terms, an **algorithm** is a sequence of instructions or steps used to perform a specific task or solve a problem. You can think of an algorithm as a recipe that outlines how to achieve a particular goal.

For example, when you make a cup of tea, the steps (or algorithm) might look something like this:

1. Boil water.
2. Put tea leaves or a tea bag in a cup.
3. Pour the boiling water into the cup.
4. Let it steep for a few minutes.
5. Add sugar or milk if desired.

This process of boiling water, steeping tea, and serving it is an algorithm. Similarly, in programming, an algorithm describes a step-by-step procedure that a program follows to process input and generate the desired output.

In computer science, algorithms are used to perform tasks like searching through data, sorting data, or making decisions based on certain conditions. They help us break complex problems down into manageable steps, allowing us to write code that can perform sophisticated tasks in a controlled and predictable way.

Why Are Algorithms Important?

Algorithms form the foundation of computer programs. Every task that a program performs, whether simple or complex, is driven by an algorithm. Whether you're building a web application, analyzing data, or automating processes, algorithms are at the heart of it all. Understanding how to write efficient algorithms is a key skill in programming, as it directly impacts the performance and scalability of your software.

For example, consider a task like **searching for an item in a large list of data**. There are many ways to approach this problem, but the algorithm you choose determines how fast the program can find the item. A simple algorithm might involve checking each item in the list one by one, but more efficient algorithms can significantly reduce the time it takes to find the item, especially when dealing with large amounts of data.

In Go, you will often need to implement algorithms for tasks such as sorting, searching, and processing data, and you'll rely on the language's powerful built-in libraries to help you do this. But the underlying concept of algorithms—the idea of breaking down a task into smaller, manageable steps—remains the same.

Key Properties of an Algorithm

Not all sets of instructions are algorithms. For something to be an algorithm, it must satisfy certain properties:

1. **Finiteness**: An algorithm must have a clear stopping point. It should not run indefinitely unless there is a clear condition for termination. If an algorithm doesn't eventually finish, it's not an algorithm.
2. **Definiteness**: Every step of the algorithm must be precisely defined. There should be no ambiguity in how each step is executed.
3. **Input**: An algorithm must take input, which is the data that it processes. For example, in a sorting algorithm, the input might be a list of numbers.
4. **Output**: An algorithm must produce output, which is the result of the computations or transformations it performs. For example, in the sorting algorithm, the output would be the sorted list of numbers.
5. **Effectiveness**: An algorithm must be effective, meaning that each step must be basic enough to be carried out exactly and in a finite amount of time.

Example of an Algorithm: Finding the Largest Number in a List

Let's look at a simple example of an algorithm: finding the largest number in a list of integers. Here's how the algorithm might look:

Step-by-step process:

1. Start with the first number in the list. Assume this is the largest number.
2. Compare this number to the next number in the list.
3. If the next number is larger, update the assumed largest number.
4. Repeat this process for every number in the list.
5. When you finish going through the list, the largest number is the final answer.

Algorithm Example in Go:

Here's how this might look in Go:

go

Copy

```
package main
```

37

```go
import "fmt"

func findLargest(numbers []int) int {
    largest := numbers[0]  // Assume the first number is the largest
    for _, number := range numbers {
        if number > largest {
            largest = number  // Update largest if a larger number is found
        }
    }
    return largest
}

func main() {
    numbers := []int{10, 5, 18, 42, 30, 15}
    fmt.Println("The largest number is:", findLargest(numbers))
}
```

In this example:

- The **input** is the list of numbers: [10, 5, 18, 42, 30, 15].
- The **output** is the largest number in the list: 42.
- The algorithm follows a simple set of instructions to find the largest number, going through each element of the list and updating the largest value when it finds a number greater than the current largest.

38

This is a basic example of an algorithm, but even the simplest tasks require well-defined, logical steps. In more complex algorithms, the steps may involve additional logic, like sorting or multiple conditions, but the core concept remains the same.

Types of Algorithms

There are many different types of algorithms that programmers use depending on the problem they're solving. Here are a few key categories:

1. **Sorting Algorithms**: These algorithms arrange data in a specific order, typically ascending or descending. Examples include **Bubble Sort**, **Quick Sort**, and **Merge Sort**.
2. **Search Algorithms**: These algorithms are used to find an element in a data structure. For example, **Binary Search** is a fast algorithm for finding an item in a sorted list, while **Linear Search** checks each element in a list one-by-one.
3. **Greedy Algorithms**: These algorithms make the locally optimal choice at each stage with the hope of finding a global optimum. For example, finding the most efficient way to pack items into a box.
4. **Dynamic Programming**: Used for solving problems by breaking them into subproblems and storing the results of already-solved subproblems to avoid redundant work. It's especially useful in optimization problems.
5. **Graph Algorithms**: These algorithms are used to solve problems involving graphs (i.e., networks). For example, finding the shortest path between two points (using **Dijkstra's Algorithm**) or finding connected components in a network.
6. **Divide and Conquer**: This approach involves breaking a problem down into smaller parts, solving each part, and then combining the results. **Merge Sort** and **Quick Sort** are examples of divide-and-conquer algorithms.

Each of these types of algorithms is useful for different kinds of problems, and Go's efficiency and simplicity make it a great language for implementing all kinds of algorithms.

How Algorithms Work with Logic

In programming, algorithms don't function in isolation—they rely heavily on **logic** to drive decision-making. Logic in programming allows an algorithm to make choices, repeat certain tasks, and branch off into different paths based on conditions.

For example, in the largest number algorithm we discussed, we used **conditional logic** to decide whether the next number in the list was larger than the current largest. This decision-making ability is crucial for more complex algorithms, like sorting or searching, where different paths are taken based on the data and conditions encountered.

To understand how logic enhances an algorithm, let's look at an example of a sorting algorithm: **Bubble Sort**.

Bubble Sort Algorithm:

1. Compare the first two numbers in the list.
2. If the first number is greater, swap them.
3. Move to the next pair of numbers and repeat.
4. Once you've checked all adjacent pairs, start over from the beginning of the list.
5. Repeat until no more swaps are needed.

Here, logic is involved in determining whether two numbers need to be swapped. The algorithm's flow is guided by logical conditions (e.g., is one number greater than the other?).

In this section, we've introduced the concept of **algorithms** and their fundamental role in programming. An algorithm is a series of steps that a computer follows to solve a problem, and it relies on logic to execute decisions and repetitive actions. Understanding algorithms and the underlying logic is essential for writing efficient, effective programs.

As we progress in this book, you'll gain a deeper understanding of how to implement algorithms in Go, explore the best practices for writing efficient code, and learn how to approach problem-solving in a structured, logical way.

With a solid understanding of algorithms and logic, you're well on your way to becoming a skilled programmer, capable of solving complex problems with elegance and efficiency. Now, let's move on to understanding how Go's syntax and features allow you to implement these algorithms effectively!

Basic Logic in Programming (Conditionals, Loops, and More)

Logic plays a crucial role in programming by determining how a program responds to different conditions and how it makes decisions. The ability to express logic in code is essential to creating meaningful, functional applications. Let's break down some of the most fundamental concepts in programming logic: **conditionals**, **loops**, and **more**. These constructs help guide the flow of a program, enabling it to react to different inputs and conditions.

1. Conditionals: Making Decisions in Code

Conditionals are statements that allow your program to make decisions based on certain conditions. With conditionals, you can control the flow of your program by specifying different actions depending on whether a condition is true or false.

In Go, the primary conditional statements are if, else, and switch. Let's take a closer look at how these work:

The if Statement

The if statement is used to execute a block of code only if a specific condition evaluates to true. For example, you can check whether a user is old enough to vote and print a message accordingly.

Example:

go

Copy

```go
age := 20

if age >= 18 {

    fmt.Println("You are eligible to vote.")

}
```

41

In this example:

- The program checks if the age is greater than or equal to 18.
- If the condition is true, the program executes the code inside the curly braces and prints the message: "You are eligible to vote."

The else Statement

The else statement is used in conjunction with an if statement to specify what happens if the condition is false. If the if condition is not met, the else block will be executed.

Example:

go

Copy

```
age := 16

if age >= 18 {

    fmt.Println("You are eligible to vote.")

} else {

    fmt.Println("You are not eligible to vote yet.")

}
```

Here:

- The program first checks if the age is 18 or greater.
- Since age is 16, the condition is false, and the program executes the else block, printing "You are not eligible to vote yet."

The else if Statement

You can also use else if when you need to check multiple conditions. This allows you to evaluate different possibilities sequentially.

42

Example:

go

Copy

```
age := 22

if age < 18 {

    fmt.Println("You are a minor.")

} else if age >= 18 && age < 21 {

    fmt.Println("You are an adult but cannot drink alcohol in some places.")

} else {

    fmt.Println("You are an adult and eligible to drink alcohol.")

}
```

In this example:

- The program checks if age is less than 18. If true, it prints "You are a minor."
- If the first condition is false, it checks if the age is between 18 and 21 and prints the appropriate message.
- If neither condition is true, it prints the final message, "You are an adult and eligible to drink alcohol."

The switch Statement

The switch statement is an elegant way to handle multiple conditions that might have several possible outcomes. It is often used when you have many possible values to check against a single variable.

Example:

go

Copy

```go
dayOfWeek := "Monday"

switch dayOfWeek {
case "Monday":
    fmt.Println("Start of the workweek.")
case "Friday":
    fmt.Println("End of the workweek.")
default:
    fmt.Println("Midweek day.")
}
```

In this example:

- The program checks the value of dayOfWeek and matches it against each case.
- If a match is found, the corresponding block of code runs.
- If no matches are found, the default block is executed.

2. Loops: Repeating Actions

Loops are used to repeat a set of instructions multiple times. Loops are crucial for working with collections of data, processing information, or performing repetitive tasks. Go supports the for loop, which is versatile and can be used in several ways.

The for Loop

The for loop is the most common loop in Go. It allows you to repeat a block of code as long as a specified condition is true. The syntax for a basic for loop in Go is as follows:

go

Copy

```go
for i := 0; i < 5; i++ {

    fmt.Println(i)

}
```

This example will print the numbers 0 to 4. Here's a breakdown of the loop:

- $i := 0$: Initializes the loop variable i to 0.
- $i < 5$: This is the condition that will stop the loop when i is no longer less than 5.
- i++: This increments i by 1 with each iteration.

The for Loop as a While Loop

Go does not have a while loop, but the for loop can function like a while loop by omitting the initialization and increment sections. For example:

go

Copy

```go
count := 0

for count < 5 {

    fmt.Println(count)

    count++

}
```

This loop works similarly to a while loop in other languages. It continues running as long as the condition (count < 5) is true, and the value of count is incremented after each iteration.

The for Loop as an Infinite Loop

You can create an infinite loop by omitting the condition entirely, like this:

go

Copy

```
for {
    fmt.Println("This loop will run forever.")
}
```

While infinite loops can be useful in certain scenarios, such as continuously waiting for user input or handling server requests, they should be used with caution to avoid running your program into an endless loop unintentionally.

3. Breaking and Continuing Loops

Go provides control statements to manage loops further. Specifically, you can use break to exit a loop prematurely, and continue to skip the current iteration and move to the next.

Using break in Loops

The break statement can be used to exit a loop before its normal termination condition is met. This can be useful when a certain condition is met, and you no longer need to process further iterations.

Example:

go

Copy

```go
for i := 0; i < 10; i++ {

  if i == 5 {

    break  // Exit the loop when i equals 5

  }

  fmt.Println(i)

}
```

This will print numbers from 0 to 4, and when i equals 5, the break statement will terminate the loop early.

Using continue in Loops

The continue statement skips the current iteration and moves to the next one. This is useful when you want to ignore certain conditions but continue processing the loop.

Example:

go

Copy

```go
for i := 0; i < 10; i++ {

  if i%2 == 0 {

    continue  // Skip even numbers

  }

  fmt.Println(i)
```

47

In this example, the program skips even numbers, printing only the odd ones: 1, 3, 5, 7, 9.

How Logic Drives Program Execution

Logic is what drives the flow of control in a program. It determines the conditions under which certain actions are taken and defines how a program should respond to various inputs or changes in state.

1. Decision Making

At the core of many programs is decision-making. Logic allows the program to make choices based on specific conditions. For example, whether or not a user is logged in determines which content is displayed in a web application. This decision-making process is handled through conditionals (like if, else, and switch), enabling the program to adapt based on real-time data.

2. Repetition and Efficiency

Without logic, programs would be limited to performing tasks only once. Logic allows programs to repeat certain actions, saving time and ensuring efficiency. Whether iterating through an array of data, checking multiple user inputs, or automating tasks, loops make sure that actions are performed the required number of times. This repetition helps you process large amounts of data efficiently.

3. Flow Control in Complex Programs

In more complex programs, logic plays an even larger role. Consider a web application that performs multiple tasks like fetching data from a database, processing the data, and then displaying results. These tasks need to be executed in a specific order, with some tasks only being performed if certain conditions are met (such as if the user is logged in or if the data fetch is successful). In these scenarios, conditional logic and loops combine to create a fluid and interactive experience for users.

4. Error Handling

One important aspect of logic is error handling. Programs must be able to respond to unexpected events, such as a user entering invalid input, or a network connection failure. Logic helps manage these errors by checking conditions before an operation and reacting appropriately when something goes wrong. For example, a program might display an error message if a file cannot be found, or ask the user to try again if their input doesn't meet the expected format.

In this section, we've introduced you to the essential concepts of **logic** in programming, including conditionals and loops. These basic constructs are the building blocks for controlling the flow of a program, making decisions, repeating actions, and responding to errors. Without logic, your program would be unable to interact dynamically with the user or adapt to changing data.

As you continue learning Go, you'll gain the skills to implement increasingly complex logic in your programs. Whether you're building a simple application or a large-scale system, mastering logic will be crucial to your success as a programmer.

1.3. Input and Output (I/O) in Programming

One of the most important concepts in programming is **input and output (I/O)**. Programs rarely exist in isolation; they need to interact with the outside world in some way. This interaction can involve receiving input from a user, a file, or another program, and providing output in the form of printed results, files, or even sending data over the internet. In this section, we'll look at how input and output work in general programming and specifically how to handle user input and output in Go.

Understanding Input and Output

In every programming task, there is a need for the program to either receive information or send information out. This is typically handled by the concepts of **input** and **output**.

- **Input** refers to any data or information that comes into the program. This could be from a variety of sources:
    - **User input**: When the user types something on the keyboard or interacts with the application in some way.

49

- ○ **File input**: When the program reads data from files stored on the computer.
- ○ **Network input**: When the program receives data from the internet or other networked systems.
- **Output** refers to any data or information that the program sends out. This could be displayed on the screen, written to a file, or sent to another program. Examples of output include:
  - ○ **Displaying text on the screen**: For instance, printing messages or results for the user to see.
  - ○ **Writing to a file**: Saving data for later use or for records.
  - ○ **Sending data over a network**: In client-server applications, sending or receiving data between systems.

I/O operations are essential for making your programs interactive and capable of dealing with real-world data.

Handling User Input in Go

Go provides several ways to handle input and output, particularly through the fmt package. The fmt package allows for formatted input and output, which is essential for reading data from users and printing results.

1. Reading User Input

In Go, user input is typically read using the fmt.Scan() or fmt.Scanln() functions. These functions allow you to gather input from the user during the program's execution.

Here's a simple example that reads a user's name and age:

go

Copy

```
package main

import "fmt"

func main() {
```

50

```
var name string

var age int


fmt.Println("Please enter your name:")

fmt.Scanln(&name)  // Read user input for name


fmt.Println("Please enter your age:")

fmt.Scanln(&age)   // Read user input for age


fmt.Printf("Hello, %s! You are %d years old.\n", name, age)
}
```

Explanation of the code:

- **.fmt.Scanln(&name)**: Reads a line of input and stores it in the name variable. The & symbol is used to pass the variable's address (a reference) to the Scanln function so that it can modify the variable directly.
- **fmt.Scanln(&age)**: Similarly, this reads an integer input and stores it in the age variable.

The program will prompt the user to enter their name and age, then it will print a message including the data they provided.

2. Reading Multiple Inputs

You can use fmt.Scan() to read multiple values in a single line. This function reads input from the user and assigns it to the provided variables.

Example:

go

Copy

```go
package main

import "fmt"

func main() {
    var num1, num2 int

    fmt.Println("Enter two numbers separated by space:")
    fmt.Scan(&num1, &num2) // Read multiple inputs

    sum := num1 + num2
    fmt.Printf("The sum of %d and %d is %d\n", num1, num2, sum)
}
```

In this case:

- The user is prompted to enter two integers in a single line.
- fmt.Scan() reads these values and stores them in the variables num1 and num2.

This technique is particularly useful for handling multiple pieces of data in one go, such as collecting multiple inputs for calculations.

3. Using fmt.Scanf for Formatted Input

Sometimes, you might want to read input in a specific format. For example, you might want to read a string and a number, ensuring that the user inputs the data in a specific order and type. The fmt.Scanf() function lets you do this by specifying a format string, similar to how formatted output is printed with fmt.Printf().

Example:

go

Copy

```go
package main

import "fmt"

func main() {
    var name string
    var age int

    fmt.Println("Enter your name and age (e.g., John 30):")
    fmt.Scanf("%s %d", &name, &age) // Scan formatted input

    fmt.Printf("Hello, %s! You are %d years old.\n", name, age)
}
```

In this example:

- The program expects the user to input their name (a string) followed by their age (an integer) in a single line.
- The format string "%s %d" tells fmt.Scanf() to expect a string followed by an integer.

The fmt.Scanf() function is ideal when you need to enforce a specific input format.

Handling Output in Go

Once you've gathered input from the user or processed data, you typically want to output the result to the user or somewhere else, such as a file or a web server. In Go, the fmt package provides functions to output data in various formats.

1. Printing to the Console

The most basic form of output is printing text to the console. You can use fmt.Println() to print a new line after the output, or fmt.Print() if you want to print without a newline at the end.

Example:

go

Copy

```go
package main

import "fmt"

func main() {
    fmt.Println("This is a simple output with a newline.")
```

```go
fmt.Print("This output does not have a newline.")

}
```

- fmt.Println() prints the provided text and automatically adds a newline after it.
- fmt.Print() prints the text without a newline at the end.

2. Formatted Output with fmt.Printf

To print output in a more controlled way, you can use fmt.Printf(). This function allows you to format the output by embedding placeholders that will be replaced with variable values.

Example:

go

Copy

```go
package main

import "fmt"

func main() {
    name := "Alice"
    age := 25
    fmt.Printf("Name: %s, Age: %d\n", name, age)
}
```

In this example:

- %s is the placeholder for a string (name), and %d is the placeholder for an integer (age).
- fmt.Printf() gives you more control over the output format, making it ideal for printing structured data.

3. Writing to a File

Beyond the console, you may want to output data to a file. Go provides easy-to-use packages for handling file I/O, including os for opening files and fmt for writing formatted data.

Here's how you can write output to a file:

go

Copy

```
package main

import (

    "fmt"

    "os"

)

func main() {
    file, err := os.Create("output.txt") // Create a file
    if err != nil {
        fmt.Println("Error creating file:", err)
        return
```

```
    }

    defer file.Close() // Ensure the file is closed when done

    fmt.Fprintln(file, "This is a line written to a file.") // Write to the file

    fmt.Fprintln(file, "Go makes file handling simple!")

    fmt.Println("Data written to file.")

}
```

Explanation:

- os.Create() creates a new file (or overwrites an existing one). It returns a file object and an error (if any).
- fmt.Fprintln() writes formatted text to the file instead of the console.
- defer file.Close() ensures that the file is closed after the program finishes writing.

Input and output are essential for any program that interacts with users, files, or external systems. In Go, handling user input and output is straightforward, thanks to the powerful and easy-to-use fmt package.

- **Input** can be gathered from users using fmt.Scan(), fmt.Scanln(), or fmt.Scanf() for formatted input.
- **Output** can be displayed on the console using fmt.Println(), fmt.Print(), or fmt.Printf(), or written to files using fmt.Fprintln().

By mastering the basics of input and output in Go, you will be able to build interactive programs that can accept user data and display results dynamically. In the next section, we'll explore more advanced topics in Go programming, including how to work with variables, data types, and other building blocks.

Chapter 2: Getting Started with Go

2.1. Installing Go and Setting Up Your Development Environment

Before you can start writing Go programs, you need to set up the Go programming environment on your computer. This involves installing Go itself and configuring your system so that Go can compile and run your programs. In this section, we'll walk through the process of installing Go on various operating systems and setting up your development environment.

Installing Go on Different Operating Systems

Go is a cross-platform language, meaning it can be installed and run on various operating systems, including **Windows, macOS**, and **Linux**. The installation process is straightforward on all platforms, and we'll walk you through each one step-by-step.

1. Installing Go on Windows

To install Go on a Windows machine, follow these steps:

Step 1: Download Go

1. Visit the official Go website at https://golang.org/dl/.
2. Under the **Windows** section, click the link to download the **Windows 64-bit** installer (the file should have a .msi extension).

Step 2: Run the Installer

1. After the .msi file has finished downloading, double-click it to start the installation process.
2. The Go installer will guide you through the installation process. You can accept the default settings, which will install Go in the C:\Go directory, or choose a different directory if desired.
3. Follow the prompts to complete the installation.

Step 3: Verify the Installation

After the installation is complete, you can verify that Go is installed correctly by checking the version:

1. Open the **Command Prompt** (search for "cmd" in the Start menu).

Type the following command and press Enter:
bash
Copy
go version
If Go is installed correctly, you should see output that looks like this:
bash
Copy
go version go1.17.6 windows/amd64

2. This confirms that Go is installed and ready to use.

Step 4: Set Up Your Workspace

Go works best when you follow its workspace structure, which helps to keep your code organized. You need to set up the **GOPATH** and **GOBIN** environment variables, though Go has made this easier with the introduction of **modules** (which we'll discuss later). For now, the setup steps are as follows:

1. **Create a Workspace Directory**: Go traditionally uses a workspace directory (often ~/go), but now, with Go modules, you can work from any directory. For simplicity, create a folder like C:\GoWorkspace to store your Go code.

2. **Set the GOPATH**:
   - Right-click on **This PC** or **Computer** on your desktop or in File Explorer and select **Properties**.
   - Click on **Advanced system settings** and then click on **Environment Variables**.
   - Under **User variables**, click **New**, and add the following variable:
     - **Variable name**: GOPATH
     - **Variable value**: C:\GoWorkspace (or any directory you prefer)
   - Click **OK** to save the changes.

3. **Update the PATH**:
   - In the same **Environment Variables** window, find the **Path** variable under **System variables**, and click **Edit**.
   - Add the following paths to the **Path** variable:
     - C:\Go\bin
     - C:\GoWorkspace\bin

4. **Create Your First Go File**:
   ○ In C:\GoWorkspace, create a new folder called src (this is where your Go code will live).
   ○ Inside src, create a new file called hello.go and add the following Go code:

go
Copy
```
package main

import "fmt"

func main() {
    fmt.Println("Hello, World!")
}
```

5. **Run Your Go Program**:

Open **Command Prompt**, navigate to your src folder, and run the Go program:
bash
Copy
```
cd C:\GoWorkspace\src
go run hello.go
```

You should see the output Hello, World!.

---

2. Installing Go on macOS

The process of installing Go on macOS is equally simple, and macOS users can take advantage of Homebrew, a popular package manager for macOS.

Step 1: Download Go

1. Visit the official Go website at https://golang.org/dl/.
2. Under the **macOS** section, click the link to download the **macOS 64-bit** package (the file should have a .pkg extension).

Step 2: Run the Installer

1. After the .pkg file has finished downloading, double-click it to start the installation process.
2. Follow the on-screen instructions to complete the installation.

Step 3: Verify the Installation

Once Go is installed, verify the installation by opening a **Terminal** window (found in **Applications > Utilities**) and running the following command:

bash
Copy
```
go version
```

If Go is installed correctly, you should see output similar to:

bash
Copy
```
go version go1.17.6 darwin/amd64
```

Step 4: Set Up Your Workspace

Like Windows, macOS traditionally uses a workspace structure, but with Go modules, this is no longer strictly necessary. However, for compatibility, we'll follow the workspace setup:

Create a Workspace Directory: Create a folder in your home directory called go to store your Go code. You can use the following command in the terminal:
bash
Copy
```
mkdir ~/go
```

1. **Set the GOPATH**: Open your terminal and edit your profile file (.bash_profile, .zshrc, or .bashrc depending on your shell) to set the GOPATH environment variable. For example, for the zsh shell:

bash

Copy

nano ~/.zshrc

Add the following lines to the file:

bash

Copy

export GOPATH=$HOME/go

export PATH=$PATH:$GOPATH/bin

Save the file and close it. Then, run:

bash

Copy

source ~/.zshrc

2. **Run Your Go Program**:
   - Create a new Go file, say hello.go, in the ~/go/src folder.

Open the terminal and run:

bash

Copy

go run ~/go/src/hello.go

---

3. Installing Go on Linux

Installing Go on Linux is fairly straightforward. Most Linux distributions provide Go as a precompiled binary.

Step 1: Download Go

1. Visit the official Go website at https://golang.org/dl/.
2. Under the **Linux** section, choose the appropriate version (usually the **Linux 64-bit** version).

Alternatively, if you are using Ubuntu or a similar distribution, you can use apt to install Go directly.

Step 2: Extract the Archive

If you downloaded the binary archive, use the following commands to extract and install Go:

1. Open your terminal.
2. Navigate to the directory where you downloaded the .tar.gz file.

3. Run the following commands to extract and install Go:
bash
Copy
```
sudo tar -C /usr/local -xvzf go1.17.6.linux-amd64.tar.gz
```

This command extracts the Go files to the /usr/local/go directory.

Step 3: Set Up Your Workspace
Create the Go workspace directory:
bash
Copy
```
mkdir ~/go
```

Set the GOPATH and PATH environment variables by adding the following lines to your .bashrc (or .zshrc if you use zsh):
bash
Copy
```
export GOPATH=$HOME/go
export PATH=$PATH:/usr/local/go/bin:$GOPATH/bin
```
After editing the file, reload your shell configuration:
bash
Copy
```
source ~/.bashrc
```

Step 4: Verify the Installation

Verify the Go installation by running the following command:

bash
Copy
```
go version
```

You should see output like:

bash
Copy
```
go version go1.17.6 linux/amd64
```

Step 5: Run Your First Go Program

Create a Go file in your ~/go/src directory:
bash
Copy
```
mkdir -p ~/go/src/hello
cd ~/go/src/hello
nano hello.go
```

Add the following Go code to hello.go:
go
Copy
```
package main

import "fmt"

func main() {
    fmt.Println("Hello, World!")
}
```

Run your Go program:
bash
Copy
go run hello.go

Installing Go and setting up your development environment is a straightforward process, regardless of your operating system. Once you've installed Go and set up your workspace, you're ready to begin writing and running Go programs.

Setting Up an IDE or Text Editor

To write and edit Go code, you'll need a **text editor** or **Integrated Development Environment (IDE)**. An IDE provides tools to assist with writing code, debugging, and managing project files, while a text editor allows you to write code without the added complexity of integrated features. Choosing the right tool depends on your preferences and what works best for your development style.

Go works well with a variety of text editors and IDEs. In this section, we'll look at some popular options for Go development and how to set them up.

Popular Text Editors for Go

1. Visual Studio Code (VS Code)

Visual Studio Code (VS Code) is one of the most popular and powerful text editors for Go development. It's lightweight, fast, and highly customizable with extensions, which makes it an excellent choice for Go programmers.

Setting Up VS Code for Go

1. **Install VS Code**: Download and install Visual Studio Code from https://code.visualstudio.com/.
2. **Install the Go Extension**: Once you've installed VS Code, you need to install the Go extension. This extension provides syntax highlighting, autocompletion,

linting, debugging support, and many other features.

To install the Go extension:

- ○ Open VS Code.
- ○ Press Ctrl+P (Windows/Linux) or Cmd+P (macOS) to bring up the command palette.
- ○ Type ext install golang.Go and press Enter. This will install the Go extension.

3. **Install Go Tools**: When you first open a Go file in VS Code, you'll likely be prompted to install a set of recommended Go tools. These tools help with code formatting, error checking, and more. Click on the **Install** button when prompted, and the tools will be installed automatically.

4. **Configure Go in VS Code**: After installing the Go extension and the necessary tools, VS Code should be ready for Go development. You can start writing Go code, and VS Code will automatically detect your Go workspace and environment.

2. GoLand

GoLand is a powerful IDE specifically designed for Go development by JetBrains. It offers advanced features such as code analysis, debugging tools, and integrated testing frameworks, which can be very helpful for larger Go projects. It's a paid product, but you can try it for free with a 30-day trial.

Setting Up GoLand for Go

1. **Install GoLand**: Download and install GoLand from https://www.jetbrains.com/go/.

2. **Set Up Go SDK**: After installing GoLand, you'll need to configure the Go SDK. Go to **Preferences** (macOS) or **File** > **Settings** (Windows/Linux), then navigate to **Go** > **GOROOT** and set it to the Go installation directory (e.g., /usr/local/go on macOS or C:\Go on Windows).

3. **Start Writing Go Code**: Once GoLand is set up, you can start creating Go projects, and the IDE will provide you with intelligent code completion, refactoring, and integrated testing capabilities.

3. Sublime Text

Sublime Text is another lightweight, fast text editor that works well for Go development, especially when combined with the right plugins.

Setting Up Sublime Text for Go

1. **Install Sublime Text**: Download and install Sublime Text from https://www.sublimetext.com/.
2. **Install Package Control**: Package Control is a package manager for Sublime Text that allows you to easily install plugins. You can install it by following the instructions on the official website: https://packagecontrol.io/installation.
3. **Install Go Plugin**:
   - Press Ctrl+Shift+P (Windows/Linux) or Cmd+Shift+P (macOS) to open the Command Palette.
   - Type Install Package and select it.
   - Search for **GoSublime** and install it. This plugin provides Go-specific features like autocompletion and syntax highlighting.
4. **Configure Sublime Text**: After installing the plugin, you should be ready to start coding in Go. Sublime Text also supports Go modules, and you can configure your workspace with specific build systems to streamline development.

4. Vim

Vim is a powerful text editor known for its efficiency and versatility, favored by many developers who prefer to work in the terminal.

Setting Up Vim for Go

1. **Install Vim**:

On most Linux distributions, you can install Vim using a package manager:
bash
Copy

```
sudo apt-get install vim
```

On macOS, you can install Vim via Homebrew:
bash
Copy

```
brew install vim
```

1. **Install Go Plugin**: To enhance Vim for Go development, you'll need the **vim-go** plugin, which provides features like autocompletion, syntax highlighting, and error checking.
   To install vim-go, use **Vundle** or **Pathogen**, two popular plugin managers for Vim. For example, using Vundle:
   vim
   Copy
   ```
   Plugin 'fatih/vim-go'
   ```

After adding this line to your .vimrc file, run the following command to install the plugin:
vim
Copy
```
:PluginInstall
```

2. **Configure Vim**: After the plugin is installed, you'll have access to Go-specific features like linting, formatting, and quick fixes directly within Vim.

Running Your First Go Program

Now that you've chosen and set up an IDE or text editor, you're ready to write and run your first Go program. Let's walk through the steps.

Step 1: Create Your First Go Program

1. Open your chosen IDE or text editor.
2. Create a new Go file, for example, hello.go, and add the following code:

go

Copy

```
package main


import "fmt"
```

```
func main() {

    fmt.Println("Hello, World!")

}
```

Explanation:

- package main: Every Go program starts with a main package. This is where the execution of the program begins.
- import "fmt": This imports the fmt package, which is used for formatted input and output in Go.
- func main() {}: This is the main function, the entry point of the Go program.
- fmt.Println("Hello, World!"): This prints the string Hello, World! to the console.

Step 2: Running the Program

In VS Code or GoLand:

- Once your Go code is written, simply press the **Run** button (or use the integrated terminal to execute the go run command) to execute the program.

In Terminal or Command Line:

1. Open a terminal or command prompt and navigate to the directory where you saved the hello.go file.

2. Run the following command to execute the Go program:
bash
Copy
go run hello.go

This command will compile and run the hello.go file in one step. You should see the output:

Copy

Hello, World!

Step 3: Understanding the Output

- The go run command compiles the hello.go file into an executable program and runs it immediately. This eliminates the need to manually compile the code before running it.
- The output Hello, World! is printed to the terminal or console, showing that your Go program ran successfully.

Step 4: Compiling the Program (Optional)

If you want to compile the program into an executable file (for example, to run it later without needing Go installed on the machine), you can use the go build command.

1. Run the following command in the terminal:
   bash
   Copy
   ```
   go build hello.go
   ```

   This will create an executable file named hello (on Linux/macOS) or hello.exe (on Windows).

2. You can then run the executable directly:

On Linux/macOS:
bash
Copy
```
./hello
```

On Windows:
bash
Copy
hello.exe

You should see the same output: Hello, World!

Setting up your Go development environment is a simple yet important step in your Go programming journey. By choosing the right text editor or IDE and configuring it for Go, you've laid the foundation for writing and running Go programs efficiently.

In this section, you learned how to install Go on different operating systems, set up your development environment, and run your first Go program. This hands-on experience will help you get comfortable with the basics of Go development.

As we continue through this book, we'll dive deeper into Go's syntax, variables, and data types, and begin writing more complex programs. But first, let's ensure you're confident with Go's core tools, so you can continue building on this knowledge. Let's get started with more in-depth Go programming!

2.2. Writing and Running Your First Program

Now that you've set up your Go development environment, it's time to write and run your first Go program. In this section, we'll walk through creating a simple "Hello, World!" program, which is often the first program written in any programming language. This exercise will not only get you familiar with the syntax of Go but also help you understand how Go compiles and executes code.

"Hello World!" in Go

To start, we will write a very simple Go program that outputs the text "Hello, World!" to the console.

Step 1: Write the Code

1. Open your text editor or IDE (like Visual Studio Code, GoLand, or any editor you prefer).
2. Create a new file and name it hello.go. The .go extension indicates that this is a Go source file.
3. Inside the file, write the following code:

go

Copy

```go
package main

import "fmt"

func main() {
    fmt.Println("Hello, World!")
}
```

Step 2: Understanding the Code

Let's break down the code and explain each part.

1. package main:
   - Every Go program starts with a **package declaration**. The main package is special in Go because it is the entry point of the program. When you run a Go program, execution begins from the main package.
2. import "fmt":
   - The import statement is used to include external libraries or packages that provide additional functionality. In this case, the fmt package (short for **format**) is imported to handle input and output operations.

- The fmt package includes functions like Println to print text to the console.

3. **func main() {}:**
   - This is the **main function**, where the program starts executing. The main function is essential in every Go program. It doesn't take any arguments and doesn't return anything.
   - The code inside the curly braces {} defines what the program does when it runs.

4. **fmt.Println("Hello, World!"):**
   - This line uses the Println function from the fmt package to print the text Hello, World! to the console.
   - Println prints the string and moves to the next line, so when the program runs, the output will appear on a new line.

Step 3: Running the Program

After writing the code, you are ready to run it. Let's go through the steps for running the program on different systems.

In Visual Studio Code (VS Code) or GoLand:

Save the hello.go file.

Click the **Run** button (or use the integrated terminal to run the program using the go run command). You should see the output:
Copy
Hello, World!

In the Terminal (Command Line):

1. Open your terminal or command prompt.
2. Navigate to the directory where you saved the hello.go file.

Type the following command and press Enter:
bash
Copy
go run hello.go

The go run command compiles and runs your Go code in one step. You should see the following output in the terminal:

Copy

Hello, World!

Compiling the Program (Optional)

If you want to compile the program into an executable file and run it independently of the Go runtime, you can use the go build command.

1. Run the following command in your terminal to compile the Go program:
   bash
   Copy

   go build hello.go

   After this, an executable file named hello (or hello.exe on Windows) will be created in the current directory.
2. Run the executable by typing:

On **Linux/macOS**:
bash
Copy
./hello

On **Windows**:
bash
Copy
hello.exe

The output should be the same:
Copy
Hello, World!

Understanding the Output

When you run the program, you should see the text **"Hello, World!"** printed to the console. But what happens behind the scenes?

1. **Compilation**:
   o When you run go run hello.go, Go first compiles the hello.go source code into machine-readable code. This is done by the Go compiler. If there are any errors in your code (like a missing semicolon or incorrect syntax), Go will show you an error message before running the program.

2. **Execution**:
   o After compiling, Go executes the compiled code. Since there are no errors in this simple program, it runs successfully and executes the fmt.Println("Hello, World!") statement. This tells the computer to display the string "Hello, World!" on the screen.

3. **Output**:
   o The output "Hello, World!" is printed on your terminal or console. The Println function adds a new line at the end, so the output is displayed on a new line.

Key Takeaways:

- **Go Programs Start with the main Package**: Every executable Go program must contain a main package, and the entry point for execution is the main function.
- **Importing Packages**: The import statement is used to bring in external packages like fmt to handle specific tasks such as input/output.
- **Running Code**: You can run Go programs with go run, which compiles and runs the program in one step, or use go build to compile it into an executable and run it independently.
- **Output**: The fmt.Println() function is commonly used to display output to the terminal or console, making it easy to interact with users and present information.

Writing and running your first Go program is a great way to get started with programming in Go. The simple "Hello, World!" program introduces you to the Go syntax and structure, and it gives you the confidence to start building more complex applications. Understanding how to compile and run your Go programs, as well as the basic concepts of packages, functions, and output, will serve as the foundation for everything you build next.

2.3. Your First Go Program: Code Walkthrough

In this section, we'll take a deeper dive into the Go program you just wrote and run: the classic **"Hello, World!"** program. Understanding how each part of the code works and how to debug your code effectively will be crucial as you build more complex Go applications.

Let's break down the structure of the program, explain how it works step by step, and give you tips on running and debugging your code.

Breaking Down Your First Go Program

Here's the simple code we wrote earlier:

go

Copy

```go
package main

import "fmt"

func main() {
    fmt.Println("Hello, World!")
}
```

Let's go through this code in detail:

1. package main

Every Go program starts with a **package declaration**. In Go, a **package** is a collection of related Go files that work together. Packages allow Go to organize code logically, which is useful for large applications.

- main is the name of the package in this program. The main package is special in Go, because it contains the entry point for a Go program. When you run a Go program, execution always begins with the main function inside the main package.
- The main package is required for creating executable programs in Go. If you're writing a library, you wouldn't use main; instead, you'd create a package that can be imported into other programs.

2. import "fmt"

The import statement is used to bring in **external libraries** or **packages**. In this case, the program is importing the fmt package, which provides formatted I/O functions like Println.

- fmt stands for **format** and provides functions for formatting text, such as printing text to the screen or reading input.
- In Go, every time you want to use functions or data from a library, you must explicitly import that library. The import statement at the top of your program indicates which external libraries your code depends on.

3. func main()

This is the **main function**, and it's where the program begins execution. The main function is the entry point of any Go program, and every executable Go program must have a main function.

- func is a keyword in Go used to define a function.
- main() is the name of the function, and since it is the entry point, it has a special meaning in Go.

- Inside the curly braces {}, you write the code that you want the program to execute.

In our case, inside the main function, we have just one line of code, which prints the message "Hello, World!".

4. fmt.Println("Hello, World!")

- **fmt.Println** is a function from the fmt package. It prints the string you give it to the console, followed by a new line.
- "Hello, World!" is the string that will be printed on the screen. This is the output of the program.

This function is the most basic form of output in Go. The Println function ensures that the message is followed by a newline, so the next output (if any) will be printed on a new line.

Running and Debugging Your Code

Now that you've broken down your first Go program, it's time to look at how to **run** and **debug** it. Running a program is straightforward, but debugging is an essential skill to master as you start writing more complex applications.

---

1. Running Your Code

In Go, there are two primary ways to run your code: using go run for quick execution or go build to compile your program and execute it directly.

Using go run (Quick Execution)

1. After writing your Go program, open a terminal or command prompt.
2. Navigate to the folder where your hello.go file is located.

3.Run the program using the go run command:
bash
Copy
go run hello.go

This command compiles the hello.go file and immediately runs the program, outputting:
Copy
Hello, World!

The go run command is perfect for quickly testing and running small programs or scripts.

Using go build (Compile and Execute)

If you want to compile your code into an executable file, you can use the go build command.

1. In the terminal, run:
   bash
   Copy
   go build hello.go

   This creates an executable file named hello (or hello.exe on Windows).
2. Run the program directly by typing:

On Linux/macOS:
bash
Copy
./hello

   o

On Windows:
bash
Copy
hello.exe

   o

79

This method is useful when you want to create a stand-alone program that can be run independently of Go.

---

2. Debugging Your Code

Go provides various tools to help you debug your code. Although Go's error messages are generally helpful, you might still encounter situations where you need to troubleshoot your program. Debugging allows you to find and fix issues in your code quickly.

Common Errors and How to Fix Them

1. **Syntax Errors**:
   - These errors occur when you violate the rules of Go's syntax. For example, forgetting to close a curly brace or using an incorrect keyword will result in a syntax error.

Example:
go
Copy

```go
package main

import "fmt"


func main() {

    fmt.Println("Hello, World!"  // Missing closing parenthesis

}
```

The Go compiler will give you an error message, indicating where the mistake occurred:
bash
Copy

```
./hello.go:6: missing ')' in function call
```

- To fix this, simply add the missing parenthesis.

2. **Runtime Errors**:
   - These errors occur when the program runs but encounters an issue. For example, trying to divide by zero or accessing an index outside the bounds of a slice can result in a runtime error.

Example:
go
Copy

```go
package main

import "fmt"


func main() {

    numbers := []int{1, 2, 3}

    fmt.Println(numbers[5]) // Attempt to access an invalid index

}
```

The Go runtime will output an error message like this:
go
Copy

```
panic: runtime error: index out of range
```

3.
   - To resolve this, ensure that you are accessing a valid index within the slice.

4. **Debugging with Print Statements**:
   - One of the simplest debugging techniques is to add fmt.Println() statements throughout your code to display the values of variables and see where things go wrong.

Example:
go
Copy

```go
package main
```

```go
import "fmt"

func main() {
    num := 5
    fmt.Println("Before:", num) // Print before calculation
    num *= 2
    fmt.Println("After:", num)  // Print after calculation
}
```

Output:
makefile
Copy
Before: 5

After: 10

5.
   o By printing intermediate values, you can track the flow of your program and identify where things go wrong.
6. **Using the Go Debugger**:
   o For more advanced debugging, Go provides a **debugger** called **Delve**. Delve allows you to set breakpoints, step through code, and inspect variables during runtime.

To install Delve:
bash
Copy
go install github.com/go-delve/delve/cmd/dlv@latest

To run Delve and debug a Go program:
bash
Copy
dlv debug hello.go

7. Delve offers a full suite of debugging tools, which is helpful when dealing with larger programs or complex bugs.

Running and debugging your first Go program is an essential skill to master as you begin learning Go. By understanding how to execute your code and troubleshoot errors, you'll be able to work through challenges and develop more sophisticated Go applications.

To recap:

- **Running Your Code**: You can use go run for quick execution or go build to compile your code into an executable.
- **Debugging**: Common errors like syntax and runtime errors are inevitable, but Go provides helpful error messages to guide you. Using fmt.Println() for simple debugging or Delve for more advanced debugging allows you to track down issues efficiently.

Chapter 3: Variables and Data Types

3.1. Understanding Variables

In any programming language, **variables** are fundamental concepts. They are the building blocks that allow a program to store, manipulate, and retrieve data during execution. Understanding variables is crucial for writing effective Go code, as they hold the values that your program operates on.

In this section, we'll explore what variables are, how they are used in Go, and the different types of variables you can work with. We'll also cover the key principles behind variable scope, initialization, and assignment in Go.

What is a Variable?

In programming, a **variable** is a container that holds a value. A variable is associated with a unique name (identifier), and that name is used to refer to the value stored inside the container. This allows you to manipulate the data through its associated variable name throughout the course of your program.

To understand how variables work, let's break down the key aspects:

1. **Name:** Every variable has a name (like age, height, score, etc.), which serves as a reference to the value it holds. This name should follow the rules of Go identifiers (it must start with a letter or underscore, followed by letters, digits, or underscores).
2. **Type:** A variable also has a type, which defines what kind of data it can hold. For example, a variable can be of type int (for integers), float64 (for floating-point numbers), or string (for text).
3. **Value:** The value is the actual data stored in the variable. The type of the variable determines what kind of values it can hold. For instance, an int variable holds whole numbers, while a string variable holds a sequence of characters.
4. **Scope:** A variable's scope defines where in the program it can be accessed. In Go, the scope of a variable is typically defined by where it is declared. A variable declared inside a function can only be used within that function, while a variable declared outside a function is accessible globally.

Example of a Variable in Go

Let's take a look at an example of declaring and using variables in Go:

```go
Copy
package main

import "fmt"

func main() {
    var name string = "John"  // Declare a variable 'name' of type string
    var age int = 30          // Declare a variable 'age' of type int

    fmt.Println("Name:", name) // Access and print the value of 'name'
    fmt.Println("Age:", age)   // Access and print the value of 'age'
}
```

In this example:

- **var name string = "John"**: This declares a variable named name of type string and initializes it with the value "John".
- **var age int = 30**: This declares a variable named age of type int and initializes it with the value 30.

Here, name and age are variables that store data, and fmt.Println is used to print those values.

Declaring Variables in Go

There are a few ways to declare variables in Go, each with its specific syntax.

1. Explicit Declaration (Using var)

You can declare a variable by explicitly specifying its name and type. This is the most common and flexible way of declaring variables in Go.

```
go
Copy
var name string = "Alice"  // Declare 'name' as a string
```

In this case, var is used to declare a variable, name is the name of the variable, string is the type, and "Alice" is the value assigned to it.

2. Implicit Declaration (Using var Without Initializing)

You can also declare a variable without initializing it. If you don't provide an initial value, Go automatically assigns the zero value of the type (e.g., 0 for integers, "" for strings).

```
go
Copy
var age int  // 'age' is an integer, automatically initialized to 0
```

In this case, Go assigns 0 as the default value to the age variable because int has a zero value of 0.

3. Short Declaration (Using :=)

In Go, you can use the **short declaration operator** (:=) to declare and initialize variables in one step. This syntax is only allowed within functions and provides a concise way to write code.

```
go
Copy
name := "Bob"  // Declare and initialize 'name' in one step
age := 25      // Declare and initialize 'age' in one step
```

With the short declaration, Go automatically infers the type of the variable based on the value you assign to it. In this case, Go infers that name is a string and age is an int.

Types of Variables in Go

Go supports a variety of data types that determine what kind of data a variable can hold. Understanding the basic data types is essential, as it influences how your program handles and stores data.

1. Basic Types

- **Integer Types**:
  - int: A signed integer type that can hold either 32-bit or 64-bit values, depending on your platform.
  - int8, int16, int32, int64: These are the signed integer types with specific bit sizes.
  - uint, uint8, uint16, uint32, uint64: Unsigned integer types, which can only hold positive numbers and zero.
- **Floating-Point Types**:
  - float32, float64: These types are used for numbers that require decimals. float64 is the most commonly used type, offering higher precision.
- **Boolean Type**:
  - bool: A variable of type bool can hold one of two values: true or false.
- **String Type**:
  - string: This type holds a sequence of characters, such as "hello" or "Go programming".

2. Composite Types

- **Arrays**: A fixed-size collection of elements of the same type.
- **Slices**: A more flexible version of arrays that can grow and shrink in size.
- **Maps**: Key-value pairs, similar to dictionaries in Python or hash tables in other languages.
- **Structs**: A composite type that groups together variables (fields) of different types.

3. Zero Values

Every variable in Go has a **zero value** for its type. This is the default value assigned to a variable when it is declared without an explicit initialization.

- For **integers**, the zero value is 0.
- For **floating-point numbers**, the zero value is 0.0.
- For **strings**, the zero value is "" (an empty string).

- For **booleans**, the zero value is false.
- For **pointers**, the zero value is nil.

This is helpful because it ensures that every variable has a predictable default state.

Initializing and Assigning Values to Variables

In Go, variables can be **initialized** at the time of declaration or later in the code. Let's look at both scenarios.

1. Declaring and Initializing a Variable at the Same Time

As shown earlier, you can declare and initialize a variable at once by specifying its type and value:

```go
Copy
var name string = "Alice" // Declaring and initializing 'name' at the same time
```

Alternatively, using the short declaration:

```go
Copy
name := "Alice" // Short declaration of 'name'
```

2. Assigning a Value to an Already Declared Variable

You can assign a value to an already declared variable using the assignment operator =:

```go
Copy
var age int  // Declare 'age' without initializing it
age = 30     // Assign a value to 'age'
```

In this case, the variable age is declared first, and then the value 30 is assigned to it later in the code.

3. Multiple Variable Declaration

Go allows you to declare and initialize multiple variables at once, either of the same type or of different types:

go
Copy
```
var name, city string = "Alice", "New York"
```

Here, two variables, name and city, are declared and initialized in one line. This is a more concise way to handle related variables.

Variable Scope

The **scope** of a variable determines where in your code the variable can be accessed. Go has **block-level scope**, meaning variables are accessible only within the block (enclosed by {}) in which they are declared.

- **Local Variables**: Variables declared within a function or block are only accessible within that function or block.
- **Global Variables**: Variables declared outside of any functions are global and can be accessed by all functions within the package.

Example of local scope:

go
Copy
```
package main

import "fmt"

func main() {
    var name string = "Bob"
    fmt.Println(name) // Accesses 'name' inside main()
}
// fmt.Println(name) // Error: 'name' is not accessible here (out of scope)
```

In this example, the variable name is only accessible inside the main function. Trying to access it outside of main() will result in an error.

Variables are one of the most fundamental aspects of programming. They are essential for storing and manipulating data throughout the course of a program. In Go, variables can be declared explicitly or implicitly, and they must always have a type. Understanding how to declare, assign, and use variables in Go will be critical as you write more complex programs.

To recap:

- **Variables** hold data and have a name, type, and value.
- **Go provides several types** for variables, including integers, strings, booleans, and more.
- You can declare variables explicitly or use shorthand (:=) for implicit declaration and initialization.
- **Scope** dictates where a variable can be accessed within your program.

With a strong grasp of variables and how to use them, you're now ready to move on to learning about **data types** and how to work with more complex data in Go. In the next section, we'll explore Go's data types in more detail, including numeric types, strings, and more.

Declaring and Initializing Variables in Go

In Go, variables are used to store data that can be modified and referenced throughout the execution of a program. Understanding how to declare and initialize variables correctly is key to writing clean, functional Go code.

Go provides a few different ways to declare and initialize variables, depending on the level of flexibility you need. Let's break down how to declare and initialize variables in Go and how Go's flexibility in variable initialization works.

1. Explicit Variable Declaration

To declare a variable explicitly in Go, you use the var keyword followed by the variable name, the type, and, optionally, an initial value. Here's the syntax:

go

Copy

```
var variableName type
```

For example, if you want to declare a variable named age that will hold an integer, you would write:

go

Copy

```
var age int
```

This declares age as a variable of type int, but it doesn't assign a value yet. The zero value of the int type (which is 0) is automatically assigned to age.

You can also declare and initialize a variable in one step by providing an initial value:

go

Copy

```
var name string = "Alice"
```

This declares a variable name of type string and assigns it the value "Alice".

2. Implicit Variable Declaration with Short Declaration (:=)

The most common way to declare and initialize variables in Go, especially within functions, is using the **short declaration operator** (:=). This allows Go to infer the type of the variable based on the assigned value. The syntax is:

go

Copy

```
variableName := value
```

For example:

go

Copy

```
name := "Alice"  // The type of 'name' is inferred as string

age := 30       // The type of 'age' is inferred as int
```

Here, name is automatically inferred to be a string, and age is inferred to be an int. You don't need to explicitly declare the type, making this shorthand very convenient for most situations.

3. Multiple Variable Declarations

You can also declare and initialize multiple variables in one line, either of the same type or of different types.

- **Same Type:**

go

Copy

```
var name, city string = "Alice", "New York"
```

- **Different Types with Short Declaration:**

go

Copy

```
name, age := "Alice", 30
```

In this case, Go infers that name is a string and age is an int.

4. Declaring Multiple Variables Without Initialization

You can also declare multiple variables without initializing them immediately. This is useful when you want to declare variables and assign values to them later in the program.

go

Copy

```
var name string

var age int
```

In this case, name is initialized with the zero value for strings (""), and age is initialized with the zero value for integers (0).

If you want to initialize variables later with specific values, you can use the assignment operator:

go

Copy

```
name = "Alice"

age = 30
```

5. Constants in Go

In addition to variables, Go also allows you to declare **constants** using the const keyword. Constants are similar to variables, but their values cannot be changed once set.

go

Copy

```
const Pi = 3.14
```

Here, Pi is a constant of type float64 with a value of 3.14.

Variable Scope and Lifetime

The **scope** and **lifetime** of a variable are key concepts in programming. These concepts determine where a variable can be accessed in your program (scope) and how long it lasts during the execution of your program (lifetime).

1. Variable Scope

Scope refers to the part of the program where a variable is accessible. In Go, there are two main types of variable scope:

- **Local Scope**: Variables declared inside a function or block are only accessible within that function or block. Once the function finishes executing, the variable is destroyed, and it cannot be accessed outside of that function.
- **Global Scope**: Variables declared outside of any function (usually at the top of the file) are accessible to all functions within the same package. These are known as **global variables**.

Let's look at both types of scope in action:

Local Variables

Local variables are only accessible within the function where they are declared. Here's an example:

go

Copy

```go
package main

import "fmt"

func main() {
    var name string = "Alice"  // Local variable to 'main'
    fmt.Println(name)
}


func anotherFunction() {
    // This will result in an error: 'name' is not defined in this function
    // fmt.Println(name)
}
```

In this case, the name variable is declared inside the main() function, so it can only be accessed within main(). Trying to access it inside anotherFunction() would result in an error.

95

Global Variables

Global variables are declared outside of any function and can be accessed from anywhere in the program within the same package.

go

Copy

```go
package main

import "fmt"

var globalName string = "Global Alice" // Global variable

func main() {
    fmt.Println(globalName) // Can access 'globalName' in 'main'
}

func anotherFunction() {
    fmt.Println(globalName) // Can also access 'globalName' in anotherFunction
}
```

In this case, globalName is accessible from both main() and anotherFunction(), as it has global scope within the package.

2. Variable Lifetime

Lifetime refers to how long a variable exists in memory while the program is running. In Go, the lifetime of a variable is closely tied to its **scope**:

- **Local Variables**: Local variables only exist while the function or block they are declared in is running. Once the function or block finishes executing, the variable is destroyed and its memory is freed.

For example:

go

Copy

```
package main

import "fmt"

func main() {
    var temp int = 10
    fmt.Println(temp) // temp exists here
}
// temp is destroyed after main finishes executing
```

In this case, the variable temp is created when the main() function starts, and it is destroyed as soon as main() finishes executing.

- **Global Variables**: Global variables exist for the entire duration of the program's execution, from when the program starts until it terminates. As a result, they persist across function calls.

97

Example of a global variable with a long lifetime:

go

Copy

```go
package main

import "fmt"

var globalCounter int = 0  // Global variable

func main() {
    globalCounter++
    fmt.Println(globalCounter)
    anotherFunction()
}

func anotherFunction() {
    globalCounter++
    fmt.Println(globalCounter)
}
```

Here, globalCounter is accessible and persists between both main() and anotherFunction() function calls, and it continues to exist for the lifetime of the program.

3. Stack vs Heap Memory

Understanding where variables are stored is also important in understanding their lifetime. In Go:

- **Local variables** are usually stored on the **stack**, which is a region of memory that is automatically managed. When a function returns, any local variables stored on the stack are automatically destroyed.
- **Global variables** (and variables created using new() or make()) are stored in the **heap**, a memory area that is managed by the Go runtime and persists until the program terminates.

To summarize:

- **Variables** in Go hold data and are declared with the var keyword or the shorthand := operator. They are named, typed, and hold values.
- **Variable Scope** refers to where a variable can be accessed within the program. Local variables are only accessible within the function they are declared in, while global variables can be accessed by any function within the package.
- **Variable Lifetime** defines how long a variable remains in memory. Local variables are typically destroyed once the function or block finishes executing, whereas global variables persist for the entire duration of the program.

Understanding these core principles of variables, scope, and lifetime will help you write more efficient and readable Go code. In the next section, we'll dive deeper into Go's data types, including numeric types, strings, and more, which will allow you to better manage the data in your program.

3.2. Go's Data Types

In Go, **data types** define the kind of data that a variable can store and the operations that can be performed on that data. Understanding the different types of data you can work with in Go is essential for writing effective and efficient programs. In this section, we will explore the various **primitive data types** (such as integers, floats, strings, and booleans) as well as **complex data types** (like arrays, slices, and maps) that Go provides.

Primitive Data Types

Primitive data types are the most basic types in Go. They represent the raw data that can be used for simple operations. Go provides several primitive data types that you can use to store numbers, text, and truth values.

1. Integers

Integers are used to store whole numbers, both positive and negative. Go has several different integer types based on the number of bits used to represent the integer, each with its own range of values.

- int: A signed integer type that can hold either 32-bit or 64-bit values depending on the platform (i.e., 32-bit on a 32-bit machine and 64-bit on a 64-bit machine).
- int8, int16, int32, int64: Signed integers with specific bit sizes.
- uint: Unsigned integer type, which can only hold non-negative values.
- uint8, uint16, uint32, uint64: Unsigned integers with specific bit sizes.

Here's an example using an int:

go

Copy

```
package main

import "fmt"

func main() {
    var age int = 30      // 'age' is an integer
    var height int16 = 175 // 'height' is a 16-bit integer
    fmt.Println("Age:", age)
    fmt.Println("Height:", height)
}
```

100

- **Zero Value**: When you declare an integer without initializing it, it takes the default value, which is 0.

2. Floats

Go has two floating-point types: float32 and float64. These types are used to store numbers with decimal points.

- **float32**: A 32-bit floating-point number.
- **float64**: A 64-bit floating-point number, with greater precision than float32.

Here's an example using a float64:

go

Copy

```go
package main

import "fmt"

func main() {
    var price float64 = 12.99  // 'price' is a floating-point number
    fmt.Println("Price:", price)
}
```

- **Zero Value**: For floats, the default value is 0.0.

3. Strings

Strings are used to represent sequences of characters (text). In Go, strings are immutable, meaning that once a string is created, it cannot be changed. However, you can create new strings by concatenating or manipulating existing ones.

Here's an example using a string:

go

Copy

```go
package main

import "fmt"

func main() {
    var name string = "Alice"  // 'name' is a string
    fmt.Println("Hello,", name)
}
```

- **Zero Value**: The default value for strings is an empty string ("").

You can also use string concatenation with the + operator:

go

Copy

```go
greeting := "Hello, " + "World!"  // Concatenate strings
fmt.Println(greeting)
```

4. Booleans

Booleans are used to store true/false values. They are often used in conditional statements and loops.

- **bool**: A variable of type bool can hold either true or false.

Here's an example using a bool:

go

Copy

```go
package main

import "fmt"

func main() {
    var isAdult bool = true  // 'isAdult' is a boolean
    fmt.Println("Is Adult:", isAdult)
}
```

- **Zero Value**: The default value for booleans is false.

Complex Data Types

In addition to the primitive types, Go also supports more complex data types that allow you to organize and manipulate collections of data. These include **arrays**, **slices**, and **maps**.

103

1. Arrays

An **array** is a fixed-size collection of elements of the same type. Once an array is created, its size cannot be changed.

Here's an example of an array:

go

Copy

```go
package main

import "fmt"

func main() {
    var numbers [3]int // Array of 3 integers
    numbers[0] = 10
    numbers[1] = 20
    numbers[2] = 30


    fmt.Println(numbers) // Output: [10 20 30]
}
```

- **Zero Value**: The default value for arrays is an array filled with the zero value of the element type (e.g., 0 for int, false for bool, "" for string).

Arrays in Go are **fixed in size**, which makes them less flexible for certain applications. In many cases, **slices** (a more flexible data structure) are used instead.

2. Slices

A **slice** is a dynamically-sized, flexible view into an array. Slices are more commonly used than arrays in Go because they provide more functionality and can grow and shrink in size.

Slices can be created from arrays or other slices, and their size can change as you add or remove elements. Here's how you can create and use slices:

go

Copy

```go
package main

import "fmt"

func main() {
    var fruits []string = []string{"apple", "banana", "cherry"} // Create a slice
    fruits = append(fruits, "date") // Add an element to the slice


    fmt.Println(fruits) // Output: [apple banana cherry date]
}
```

- **Zero Value**: The zero value for a slice is nil, which means it's not initialized. When declared but not initialized, slices have no underlying array, and their length is zero.

Slices are more flexible than arrays because they can dynamically resize as you add or remove elements.

3. Maps

A **map** is a built-in data type in Go that associates keys with values. Maps are like dictionaries in Python or hash tables in other languages. They allow you to store key-value pairs and efficiently retrieve, update, or delete values based on their keys.

Here's an example of a map:

go

Copy

```go
package main

import "fmt"

func main() {
    var ages = map[string]int{
        "Alice": 25,
        "Bob":   30,
        "Charlie": 35,
    }

    fmt.Println(ages) // Output: map[Alice:25 Bob:30 Charlie:35]
    fmt.Println(ages["Bob"]) // Output: 30
}
```

In this example:

- The **keys** are of type string (the names of the people), and the **values** are of type int (their ages).

106

- You can retrieve the value associated with a key by accessing the map using the key (e.g., ages["Bob"]).
- **Zero Value**: The zero value for a map is nil. A nil map behaves like an empty map when reading, but you cannot add new elements to it unless you initialize it first.

Maps provide a way to associate arbitrary data in an easy-to-use key-value structure.

Summary of Go's Data Types

Here's a quick recap of the primary data types in Go:

- **Primitive Data Types**:
  - **Integers**: int, int8, int16, int32, int64, uint, uint8, uint16, uint32, uint64
  - **Floating-point numbers**: float32, float64
  - **Strings**: string
  - **Booleans**: bool
- **Complex Data Types**:
  - **Arrays**: Fixed-size collections of elements of the same type.
  - **Slices**: Flexible, dynamically-sized arrays.
  - **Maps**: Collections of key-value pairs.

Each data type in Go serves a specific purpose and is optimized for different types of operations. Choosing the right data type is essential for ensuring your programs are both efficient and easy to maintain.

Understanding the various data types available in Go is essential for writing efficient and functional programs. Go's primitive data types, such as integers, floats, strings, and booleans, are simple but powerful building blocks for storing and manipulating data. On the other hand, complex types like arrays, slices, and maps offer more flexibility and are used for handling collections of data.

3.3. Type Conversion and Type Inference

In Go, **type conversion** and **type inference** are important concepts that help you work with different data types and assign values to variables efficiently. Understanding how Go handles type conversion and type inference allows you to write more flexible and readable code. In this section, we will cover the basics of **converting between data types** and **type inference** using the shorthand := operator in Go.

Converting Between Data Types

Go is a statically typed language, meaning that you must specify the type of a variable when you declare it. While this gives Go programs clarity and type safety, it also means that you may occasionally need to convert between different data types, especially when working with functions that expect a particular type.

1. Explicit Type Conversion

Go does not perform implicit type conversions (also known as type coercion) automatically. Instead, you must explicitly convert one type to another when necessary. This explicit conversion is done using the **type conversion syntax**, which is as follows:

go

Copy

```
type(variable)
```

Where type is the target type to which you want to convert, and variable is the variable you want to convert.

Example: Converting from float64 to int

If you want to convert a float64 value to an int, you use the type conversion syntax to discard the decimal part:

go

Copy

```
package main
```

```go
import "fmt"

func main() {
    var pi float64 = 3.14159
    var integerValue int = int(pi)  // Convert float64 to int

    fmt.Println("Pi as float64:", pi)  // Output: 3.14159
    fmt.Println("Pi as int:", integerValue)  // Output: 3
}
```

- In this example, pi is a float64 with a value of 3.14159, and we convert it to an int using the int(pi) syntax. The fractional part .14159 is discarded in the conversion.

Example: Converting from int to string

You can also convert from an integer to a string, which can be useful when you need to concatenate numbers with text or perform string-related operations:

go

Copy

```go
package main

import "fmt"

func main() {
```

```go
    var age int = 25

    var ageString string = string(age)  // Incorrect: this converts the int to a character, not
a string


    fmt.Println(ageString)  // Output is not the expected string
}
```

However, to correctly convert an integer to its string representation, you should use the strconv **package:**

go

Copy

```go
package main


import (
    "fmt"
    "strconv"
)


func main() {
    var age int = 25
    var ageString string = strconv.Itoa(age)  // Correct conversion using strconv.Itoa


    fmt.Println("Age as string:", ageString)  // Output: "25"
}
```

In this case, strconv.Itoa() converts the integer value 25 into the string "25".

2. Type Conversion Between Numeric Types

When converting between numeric types (such as int, float64, and uint), Go requires explicit type conversion. For example:

go

Copy

```go
package main

import "fmt"

func main() {
    var i int = 42
    var f float64 = float64(i)  // Convert int to float64

    fmt.Println("Integer:", i)
    fmt.Println("Float:", f)
}
```

- Here, we convert an int (i) to a float64 (f). Type conversion ensures that the data is represented with the proper type and precision.

3. Handling Invalid Conversions

Go will not allow invalid conversions, and attempting to convert incompatible types will result in a compilation error. For instance, you cannot convert a string directly to an int:

go

Copy

```
package main

import "fmt"

func main() {
    var str string = "123"
    // Invalid conversion: cannot convert a string to an integer without using strconv
    var num int = int(str)  // This line will cause a compile-time error

    fmt.Println(num)
}
```

To handle this, you must use a function like strconv.Atoi() from the strconv package to convert a string to an integer:

go

Copy

```
package main
```

```go
import (

    "fmt"

    "strconv"

)


func main() {

    str := "123"

    num, err := strconv.Atoi(str) // Correct conversion


    if err != nil {

        fmt.Println("Error converting string to int:", err)

    } else {

        fmt.Println("Converted number:", num)

    }

}
```

This will correctly convert the string "123" to the integer 123.

Type Inference in Go (Using :=)

In Go, type inference allows you to declare variables without explicitly specifying their types, provided the compiler can deduce the type from the value assigned to the variable. This is done using the **short declaration operator** :=.

The := operator automatically infers the type of a variable based on the value assigned to it. This is very convenient for quick variable initialization and makes the code shorter and more readable.

1. How Type Inference Works

When you use := to declare a variable, Go automatically figures out the type based on the value provided. For example:

go

Copy

```go
package main

import "fmt"

func main() {
    // Type inferred as string
    name := "Alice"

    // Type inferred as int
    age := 30

    // Type inferred as bool
    isAdult := true

    fmt.Println("Name:", name)
    fmt.Println("Age:", age)
```

114

```
fmt.Println("Is adult:", isAdult)
}
```

In this example:

- Go infers that name is a string because "Alice" is a string.
- Go infers that age is an int because 30 is an integer.
- Go infers that isAdult is a bool because true is a boolean.

2. Inferred Types with Expressions

Type inference also works with expressions, not just simple values. For example:

go

Copy

```
package main

import "fmt"

func main() {
    x := 10   // Type inferred as int
    y := 3.14 // Type inferred as float64


    sum := x + int(y) // Type inference: 'sum' will be of type int after explicit conversion
    fmt.Println("Sum:", sum)
}
```

- In this case, x is inferred to be an int, and y is inferred to be a float64.
- We explicitly convert y to int in the expression int(y) before performing the addition.

3. Using := for Multiple Variable Declarations

You can also use := to declare and initialize multiple variables in a single line. Go will infer the type of each variable individually:

go

Copy

```
package main

import "fmt"

func main() {
    a, b := 5, 10  // a is inferred as int, b is inferred as int
    x, y := 3.14, "hello"  // x is inferred as float64, y is inferred as string

    fmt.Println("a:", a)
    fmt.Println("b:", b)
    fmt.Println("x:", x)
    fmt.Println("y:", y)
}
```

Here, Go infers the types for each variable in the declaration:

- a and b are both inferred to be of type int.

116

- x is inferred to be a float64 and y is inferred to be a string.

In Go, understanding **type conversion** and **type inference** is essential for working with variables efficiently. Type conversion allows you to convert between different data types explicitly, while Go's type inference system helps you write cleaner, more concise code by automatically determining the type of variables when using :=.

To recap:

- **Type Conversion**: You must use explicit type conversion to change the type of a variable, like converting from float64 to int or using strconv functions to convert strings to integers.
- **Type Inference**: Go infers the type of a variable when using := based on the value assigned to it, eliminating the need for explicit type declarations in many cases.
- **Short Declaration**: The := operator is convenient for initializing variables with inferred types, especially in functions.

By mastering type conversion and type inference, you'll be able to write more efficient and flexible Go code that can handle different data types seamlessly. In the next section, we'll explore more advanced features of Go, such as constants and pointers, which will further enhance your ability to work with data in Go.

3.4. Practical Exercises with Variables and Types

In this section, we will put the concepts of **variables** and **data types** into practice by walking through several hands-on exercises. These exercises will help solidify your understanding of how variables are declared, initialized, and manipulated in Go. By the end of this section, you will have a strong foundation to tackle more complex Go programming challenges.

Exercise 1: Declaring and Initializing Variables

In this exercise, you will declare and initialize variables of different types. After that, you'll print their values to the console.

Task:

1. Declare a variable age of type int and assign it a value of 25.
2. Declare a variable name of type string and assign it the value "John".
3. Declare a variable height of type float64 and assign it the value 5.9.
4. Declare a variable isStudent of type bool and assign it the value false.
5. Print all the variables to the console using fmt.Println().

Solution:

go

Copy

```go
package main

import "fmt"

func main() {
    var age int = 25
    var name string = "John"
    var height float64 = 5.9
    var isStudent bool = false

    fmt.Println("Age:", age)
    fmt.Println("Name:", name)
    fmt.Println("Height:", height)
    fmt.Println("Is Student:", isStudent)
}
```

Expected Output:

vbnet

Copy

Age: 25

Name: John

Height: 5.9

Is Student: false

Exercise 2: Type Conversion

This exercise involves converting between different data types. You'll convert a float64 to an int and a string to an int.

Task:

1. Declare a float64 variable temperature and assign it a value of 98.6.
2. Convert the temperature value to an integer and assign it to a new variable tempInt.
3. Declare a string variable ageString and assign it the value "30".
4. Convert ageString to an integer and assign it to a new variable ageInt.
5. Print both tempInt and ageInt to the console.

Solution:

go

Copy

package main

```go
import (

    "fmt"

    "strconv"

)


func main() {

    var temperature float64 = 98.6

    tempInt := int(temperature)  // Convert float64 to int


    var ageString string = "30"

    ageInt, err := strconv.Atoi(ageString)  // Convert string to int


    if err != nil {

        fmt.Println("Error converting string to int:", err)

        return

    }


    fmt.Println("Temperature as integer:", tempInt)

    fmt.Println("Age as integer:", ageInt)

}
```

Expected Output:

php

Copy

Temperature as integer: 98

Age as integer: 30

Exercise 3: Working with Arrays and Slices

In this exercise, you will practice working with arrays and slices. You'll declare an array and a slice, manipulate them, and print their contents.

Task:

1. Declare an array numbers of type int with 5 elements: [1, 2, 3, 4, 5].
2. Declare a slice newNumbers and initialize it with elements [6, 7, 8].
3. Append a new number 9 to the newNumbers slice.
4. Print the contents of the numbers array and the newNumbers slice.

Solution:

go

Copy

```go
package main


import "fmt"


func main() {
    var numbers [5]int = [5]int{1, 2, 3, 4, 5}  // Declare an array
```

```go
newNumbers := []int{6, 7, 8}          // Declare a slice

newNumbers = append(newNumbers, 9)    // Append an element to the slice

fmt.Println("Array:", numbers)        // Print array
fmt.Println("Slice:", newNumbers)     // Print slice
}
```

Expected Output:

makefile

Copy

Array: [1 2 3 4 5]
Slice: [6 7 8 9]

Exercise 4: Map Operations

In this exercise, you will practice using Go's map data type. You'll create a map to store key-value pairs, access values, and update entries in the map.

Task:

1. Create a map personAge where the keys are string (names of people) and the values are int (their ages).
2. Add three key-value pairs to the map: Alice: 25, Bob: 30, and Charlie: 35.
3. Access and print the age of Bob.
4. Update Alice's age to 26 and print the updated map.

Solution:

go

Copy

```go
package main

import "fmt"

func main() {
    personAge := make(map[string]int) // Create an empty map

    personAge["Alice"] = 25  // Add key-value pairs
    personAge["Bob"] = 30
    personAge["Charlie"] = 35

    fmt.Println("Bob's Age:", personAge["Bob"]) // Access value by key

    personAge["Alice"] = 26  // Update Alice's age
    fmt.Println("Updated Age of Alice:", personAge["Alice"])

    fmt.Println("All Ages:", personAge) // Print the entire map
}
```

Expected Output:

yaml

Copy

Bob's Age: 30

Updated Age of Alice: 26

All Ages: map[Alice:26 Bob:30 Charlie:35]

Exercise 5: Type Inference with := Operator

In this exercise, you'll practice using Go's **type inference** with the := shorthand. You'll declare variables and allow Go to automatically determine their types based on the values assigned to them.

Task:

1. Declare a variable score and assign it the value 95.5.
2. Declare a variable isPassed and assign it the value true.
3. Declare a variable subject and assign it the value "Math".
4. Print all the variables, showing their values and inferred types.

Solution:

go

Copy

```
package main


import "fmt"
```

124

```
func main() {

    score := 95.5        // type inferred as float64

    isPassed := true     // type inferred as bool

    subject := "Math"    // type inferred as string


    fmt.Println("Score:", score)

    fmt.Println("Is Passed:", isPassed)

    fmt.Println("Subject:", subject)

}
```

Expected Output:

vbnet

Copy

Score: 95.5

Is Passed: true

Subject: Math

In this example:

- score is inferred to be a float64 because 95.5 is a floating-point number.
- isPassed is inferred to be a bool because true is a boolean value.
- subject is inferred to be a string because "Math" is a string.

These practical exercises have allowed you to explore and practice working with variables, data types, type conversions, and Go's shorthand declaration syntax. By completing these exercises, you now have a deeper understanding of how to:

1. Declare and initialize variables of different types.
2. Convert between types when necessary.
3. Work with collections like arrays, slices, and maps.
4. Use type inference with the := shorthand to simplify your code.

As you continue to practice and experiment with Go's types and variables, you'll develop the skills necessary to write more complex and efficient programs. In the next chapter, we will dive into **control flow** in Go, including **conditionals** and **loops**, which are essential for creating dynamic and interactive programs.

Chapter 4: Control Flow (Conditionals & Loops)

4.1. Conditional Statements: if and else

Control flow is an essential concept in programming that allows you to make decisions based on certain conditions. **Conditional statements** enable you to control the flow of your program by choosing which block of code to execute depending on whether a specified condition evaluates to true or false. In Go, the most commonly used conditional statements are if and else.

In this section, we will explore how conditional statements work in Go, with a focus on the if and else statements. We'll also walk through some practical examples to help you understand how and when to use them effectively in your programs.

Writing Simple Conditionals

1. The if Statement

The if statement allows you to execute a block of code only if a specified condition evaluates to **true**. If the condition is false, the code inside the if block is skipped.

Syntax of if:

go
Copy
```go
if condition {
    // Code to be executed if the condition is true
}
```

Here's a simple example that checks whether a number is greater than 10 and prints a message accordingly:

go
Copy
```go
package main
```

```go
import "fmt"

func main() {
    var number int = 15

    if number > 10 {
        fmt.Println("The number is greater than 10.")
    }
}
```

In this example:

- The condition number > 10 is **true** because 15 is greater than 10, so the code inside the if block is executed, and the message "The number is greater than 10." is printed to the console.

2. The else Statement

The else statement provides an alternative block of code to execute when the if condition is **false**. The code inside the else block will run if the if condition evaluates to false.

Syntax of if and else:

go
Copy
```go
if condition {
    // Code to execute if condition is true
} else {
    // Code to execute if condition is false
}
```

Here's an example that checks if a number is positive or negative:

go
Copy
```go
package main

import "fmt"
```

```
func main() {
    var number int = -5

    if number > 0 {
        fmt.Println("The number is positive.")
    } else {
        fmt.Println("The number is negative or zero.")
    }
}
```

In this example:

- The condition number > 0 is **false** because -5 is not greater than 0.
- The code inside the else block is executed, and the message "The number is negative or zero." is printed to the console.

3. The else if Statement

In some cases, you may need to check multiple conditions. You can use else if to check for additional conditions after the if statement. The else if statement allows you to specify multiple conditions and execute different blocks of code based on which condition is true.

Syntax of if, else if, and else:

go
Copy
```
if condition1 {
    // Code to execute if condition1 is true
} else if condition2 {
    // Code to execute if condition1 is false and condition2 is true
} else {
    // Code to execute if both condition1 and condition2 are false
}
```

Let's look at an example where we check if a number is positive, negative, or zero:

go
Copy
```go
package main

import "fmt"

func main() {
    var number int = 0

    if number > 0 {
        fmt.Println("The number is positive.")
    } else if number < 0 {
        fmt.Println("The number is negative.")
    } else {
        fmt.Println("The number is zero.")
    }
}
```

In this example:

- The condition number > 0 is **false**, so the program checks the else if condition number < 0, which is also false.
- Since neither condition is true, the code in the else block is executed, and "The number is zero." is printed to the console.

4. Logical Operators in Conditionals

You can combine multiple conditions using **logical operators** to create more complex decision-making logic. The most commonly used logical operators in Go are:

- && (AND): Returns true if both conditions are true.
- || (OR): Returns true if at least one of the conditions is true.
- ! (NOT): Reverses the condition (true becomes false and false becomes true).

Here's an example using the && operator to check if a number is between two values:

go
Copy
```go
package main

import "fmt"

func main() {
    var number int = 25

    if number > 10 && number < 30 {
        fmt.Println("The number is between 10 and 30.")
    } else {
        fmt.Println("The number is not between 10 and 30.")
    }
}
```

In this example:

- The condition number > 10 && number < 30 evaluates to **true** because 25 is greater than 10 and less than 30.
- The message "The number is between 10 and 30." is printed to the console.

Let's look at an example using the || operator (OR):

go
Copy
```go
package main

import "fmt"

func main() {
    var number int = 5

    if number < 10 || number > 20 {
        fmt.Println("The number is either less than 10 or greater than 20.")
    } else {
        fmt.Println("The number is between 10 and 20.")
```

```
    }
}
```

Here:

- The condition number < 10 || number > 20 is **true** because 5 is less than 10.
- The message "The number is either less than 10 or greater than 20." is printed to the console.

5. Nested if Statements

In Go, you can nest if statements inside each other. This is useful when you need to check multiple conditions at different levels.

Here's an example that checks multiple conditions to determine whether a number is positive, negative, or zero, and also whether it is even or odd:

go
Copy
```
package main

import "fmt"

func main() {
    var number int = -6

    if number != 0 {
        if number > 0 {
            fmt.Println("The number is positive.")
        } else {
            fmt.Println("The number is negative.")
        }

        if number%2 == 0 {
            fmt.Println("The number is even.")
        } else {
            fmt.Println("The number is odd.")
        }
    } else {
```

```
    fmt.Println("The number is zero.")
  }
}
```

In this case:

- The program first checks if the number is **non-zero**.
- Then, it checks whether the number is positive or negative.
- It further checks whether the number is even or odd using the modulus operator (%), which calculates the remainder of the division.

The if and else statements are the building blocks of conditional logic in Go. They allow your programs to make decisions based on specific conditions, enabling you to implement complex behaviors. In this section, you've learned how to:

- Use the if statement to execute code when a condition is true.
- Use else and else if to handle alternative conditions.
- Combine multiple conditions with logical operators (&&, ||, !).
- Nest if statements to create more complex decision-making logic.

Conditional statements are fundamental for writing interactive programs and handling different scenarios based on the input or state of the program. In the next section, we will dive into **loops** and how to repeat code efficiently in Go, further enhancing your control flow skills.

Using else and else if

The else and else if statements are essential tools in Go for expanding conditional logic beyond simple checks. By allowing your program to choose from multiple paths based on different conditions, they make your code more flexible and capable of handling a variety of situations. Let's dive into the use of else and else if in Go and explore how they can help you write more advanced decision-making code.

The else Statement

The else statement provides an alternative block of code that gets executed when the if condition evaluates to false. It allows you to write more comprehensive logic by ensuring that a block of code is executed if none of the if or else if conditions are met.

Syntax of else:

go

Copy

```go
if condition {
    // Code to be executed if condition is true
} else {
    // Code to be executed if condition is false
}
```

Let's look at an example where we check whether a number is positive or negative, and use else to handle the case where the number is not positive:

go

Copy

```go
package main

import "fmt"

func main() {
    var number int = -5
```

```go
if number > 0 {

    fmt.Println("The number is positive.")

} else {

    fmt.Println("The number is negative or zero.")

}

}
```

- In this example, the condition number > 0 is **false** (because -5 is not greater than 0), so the else block is executed, and the message "The number is negative or zero." is printed.
- If the number had been positive (for example, 10), the code inside the if block would have executed instead.

The else if Statement

The else if statement allows you to check multiple conditions sequentially. If the first if condition is false, Go checks the next else if condition. You can have as many else if conditions as you need.

Syntax of else if:

go

Copy

```go
if condition1 {

    // Code to execute if condition1 is true

} else if condition2 {

    // Code to execute if condition1 is false and condition2 is true

} else {
```

```go
    // Code to execute if both condition1 and condition2 are false
}
```

The else if statement is ideal when you have multiple potential conditions that are mutually exclusive and you want to handle them separately.

Let's consider an example where we check if a number is positive, negative, or zero:

go

Copy

```go
package main

import "fmt"

func main() {
    var number int = 0

    if number > 0 {
        fmt.Println("The number is positive.")
    } else if number < 0 {
        fmt.Println("The number is negative.")
    } else {
        fmt.Println("The number is zero.")
    }
}
```

136

In this example:

- The first condition number > 0 is **false**, so Go moves to the else if statement.
- The condition number < 0 is also **false** (because 0 is neither positive nor negative).
- Finally, the else block executes because neither of the previous conditions were true, printing "The number is zero."

Combining else, else if, and Multiple Conditions

You can combine else, else if, and logical operators to create more complex conditional checks. For instance, you might want to check if a number is within a certain range, or if it satisfies multiple conditions at once.

Let's look at an example where we check if a number is in one of several ranges:

go

Copy

```go
package main

import "fmt"

func main() {
    var number int = 15

    if number < 0 {
        fmt.Println("The number is negative.")
    } else if number >= 0 && number <= 10 {
```

```
    fmt.Println("The number is between 0 and 10.")

  } else if number > 10 && number <= 20 {

    fmt.Println("The number is between 11 and 20.")

  } else {

    fmt.Println("The number is greater than 20.")

  }

}
```

- The condition number < 0 is **false** (because 15 is not negative).
- The condition number >= 0 && number <= 10 is also **false** (because 15 is not between 0 and 10).
- The condition number > 10 && number <= 20 is **true** (because 15 is between 11 and 20), so the message "The number is between 11 and 20." is printed.
- If the number had been greater than 20, the else block would have executed.

Using else and else if for Validating Inputs

A common use case for else and else if is validating user input. For instance, you might want to check if a user's input meets certain criteria, such as whether a number is valid or whether a string is not empty.

Let's consider an example where we validate if a user's input is within a specified range:

go

Copy

package main

import "fmt"

```go
func main() {

    var age int

    fmt.Print("Enter your age: ")

    fmt.Scanln(&age)


    if age < 0 {

        fmt.Println("Invalid input. Age cannot be negative.")

    } else if age < 18 {

        fmt.Println("You are a minor.")

    } else if age >= 18 && age <= 65 {

        fmt.Println("You are an adult.")

    } else {

        fmt.Println("You are a senior citizen.")

    }

}
```

- If the user enters a negative number, the program will print "Invalid input. Age cannot be negative."
- If the user enters an age less than 18, it will print "You are a minor."
- If the user enters an age between 18 and 65, it will print "You are an adult."
- If the user enters an age greater than 65, it will print "You are a senior citizen."

This pattern of using else if and else allows you to make decisions based on multiple conditions in a clear and organized way.

Using Logical Operators with else if and else

As we've seen in the examples above, you can combine if, else if, and else with logical operators (&&, ||, and !) to check multiple conditions at once. This is particularly useful when your conditions are more complex.

Here's an example where we use both && (AND) and || (OR) operators with else if to check different ranges of numbers:

go

Copy

```go
package main

import "fmt"

func main() {
    var number int = 45

    if number < 0 {
        fmt.Println("Negative number")
    } else if number >= 0 && number <= 10 {
        fmt.Println("Number is between 0 and 10")
    } else if (number >= 11 && number <= 20) || (number >= 30 && number <= 40) {
        fmt.Println("Number is between 11-20 or 30-40")
    } else {
        fmt.Println("Number is outside the specified ranges")
```

```
        }

}
```

In this example:

- We use the $\&\&$ operator to check if the number is within the ranges of 0-10 and 11-20.
- We use the $\|$ operator to check if the number is in the ranges of 11-20 or 30-40.

If the number is 45, the program will print "Number is outside the specified ranges" because it does not meet any of the conditions.

The if, else if, and else statements form the backbone of conditional logic in Go, allowing you to make decisions based on specific conditions. Understanding how to use these control flow structures enables you to write programs that can handle a variety of scenarios, whether you're checking user input, validating data, or controlling program execution based on specific conditions.

In this section, you have learned how to:

- Use the if statement to execute code based on a condition.
- Use else to provide an alternative block of code when the if condition is false.
- Use else if to check multiple conditions in sequence.
- Combine conditions using logical operators ($\&\&$, $\|$, and !) for more complex decision-making.

In the next section, we'll dive into **loops**, which are another essential tool for controlling the flow of your program, allowing you to repeat blocks of code based on conditions. Let's take the next step in mastering Go's control flow!

4.2. Switch Statements

In Go, the switch statement provides a more concise and flexible way to evaluate multiple conditions compared to using a series of if-else statements. It's particularly useful when you have several possible values for a variable and want to execute different blocks of code based on which value is matched.

In this section, we will explore how to implement switch statements in Go, when to use switch instead of if-else, and how switch can simplify your code.

Implementing switch for Multiple Conditions

A switch statement in Go evaluates an expression and executes the corresponding block of code based on the result of the expression. It allows you to handle multiple possible conditions more cleanly than using multiple if-else statements.

Basic Syntax of switch:

go

Copy

```
switch expression {
case value1:
    // Code to execute if expression == value1
case value2:
    // Code to execute if expression == value2
default:
    // Code to execute if expression doesn't match any case
}
```

- expression: The value or variable being evaluated.

142

- **case value**: A condition that is compared against the expression. If the expression matches the value, the corresponding code block will be executed.
- **default**: This is an optional block that runs if no case values match the expression.

Example: Simple switch Statement

Let's look at a simple example that checks the value of a variable and executes a block of code based on the value:

go

Copy

```go
package main

import "fmt"

func main() {
    var day int = 3

    switch day {
    case 1:
        fmt.Println("Monday")
    case 2:
        fmt.Println("Tuesday")
    case 3:
        fmt.Println("Wednesday")
    case 4:
```

```go
        fmt.Println("Thursday")
    case 5:
        fmt.Println("Friday")
    case 6:
        fmt.Println("Saturday")
    case 7:
        fmt.Println("Sunday")
    default:
        fmt.Println("Invalid day")
    }
}
```

In this example:

- The switch expression evaluates the value of day.
- It checks each case to see if day matches the corresponding number.
- When the case 3 is matched, the output will be "Wednesday".
- If none of the case values match, the default case will be executed, printing "Invalid day".

Multiple Values in a case

In Go, you can list multiple values in a single case, which allows you to match more than one condition without writing separate case statements for each value. You simply separate the values by commas.

go

Copy

```go
package main
```

144

```go
import "fmt"

func main() {
    var number int = 2

    switch number {
    case 1, 3, 5:
        fmt.Println("Odd number")
    case 2, 4, 6:
        fmt.Println("Even number")
    default:
        fmt.Println("Unknown number")
    }
}
```

In this case:

- The switch checks if the number is one of 1, 3, 5 (odd) or 2, 4, 6 (even).
- Since number is 2, it matches the second case, and the output will be "Even number".

When to Use switch Instead of if-else

While both switch and if-else can be used to implement conditional logic, there are specific situations where switch is a better choice:

1. When You Have Multiple Conditions for One Variable

If you need to evaluate the same variable or expression against several possible values, a switch statement is a cleaner and more readable option than using multiple if-else statements.

Example: Using if-else

go

Copy

```go
var score int = 85


if score >= 90 {

    fmt.Println("Grade A")

} else if score >= 80 {

    fmt.Println("Grade B")

} else if score >= 70 {

    fmt.Println("Grade C")

} else if score >= 60 {

    fmt.Println("Grade D")

} else {

    fmt.Println("Grade F")

}
```

146

Example: Using switch

go

Copy

```go
var score int = 85

switch {
case score >= 90:
    fmt.Println("Grade A")
case score >= 80:
    fmt.Println("Grade B")
case score >= 70:
    fmt.Println("Grade C")
case score >= 60:
    fmt.Println("Grade D")
default:
    fmt.Println("Grade F")
}
```

In this case, the switch statement is more compact and easier to follow. The conditions are evaluated sequentially, and the code block corresponding to the first true condition is executed.

2. When You Have a Range of Values to Check

If you need to compare the value of an expression against different ranges or sets of values, using switch can simplify your code. In Go, you can use **fallthrough** to make a switch statement behave like an if-else chain, or simply use a switch with case statements.

For example:

go

Copy

```go
package main

import "fmt"

func main() {
    var age int = 25

    switch {
    case age < 18:
        fmt.Println("Minor")
    case age >= 18 && age < 30:
        fmt.Println("Young Adult")
    case age >= 30 && age < 50:
        fmt.Println("Middle-aged")
    default:
        fmt.Println("Senior")
    }
}
```

148

In this example:

- We use switch to check ranges of values for age.
- Since age is 25, it matches the condition age >= 18 && age < 30 and prints "Young Adult".

3. When Checking Against Multiple Values

If you need to check a single expression against multiple values, switch allows you to list the possible values for that expression, which makes your code more concise and readable.

go

Copy

```go
var color string = "green"


switch color {
case "red":
    fmt.Println("Color is red")
case "green":
    fmt.Println("Color is green")
case "blue":
    fmt.Println("Color is blue")
default:
    fmt.Println("Unknown color")
}
```

In this case:

- The color variable is checked against "red", "green", and "blue".
- Since color is "green", it prints "Color is green".

4. When You Need a Default Case

Just like if-else statements, switch statements have the default case, which is executed if none of the conditions match. This makes switch a great choice when you want to handle unexpected or unhandled values in a clean way.

The fallthrough Statement

In Go, the switch statement does not automatically "fall through" from one case to the next like in some other languages (such as C or Java). In Go, you need to explicitly use the fallthrough keyword if you want to execute the code in the next case block, even if the condition for that case isn't met.

Here's an example of fallthrough in action:

go

Copy

```
package main

import "fmt"

func main() {
    var number int = 1

    switch number {
```

```go
        case 1:
            fmt.Println("Number is 1")
            fallthrough
        case 2:
            fmt.Println("Number is 2")
            fallthrough
        case 3:
            fmt.Println("Number is 3")
        default:
            fmt.Println("Unknown number")
        }
    }
```

Expected Output:

csharp

Copy

Number is 1

Number is 2

Number is 3

- In this example, when the number is 1, it matches the first case, but the fallthrough statement causes Go to execute the code in the subsequent case blocks, even though the conditions don't match.

151

- **Note**: The fallthrough statement does not check the condition of the next case; it simply executes the code in that case.

The switch statement in Go is a powerful tool for handling multiple conditions in a more readable and concise way compared to a series of if-else statements. You should consider using switch when you need to:

- Evaluate the same variable or expression against multiple values.
- Check ranges of values with greater clarity.
- Handle default or unexpected cases in a simple and structured way.

By mastering switch statements, you will be able to simplify your control flow logic and make your programs easier to read and maintain. In the next section, we will explore **loops**, which allow you to repeat blocks of code and further enhance the control flow in your Go programs.

4.3. Loops in Go

Loops are essential for performing repetitive tasks in a program. In Go, the primary loop construct is the **for loop**, which allows you to repeatedly execute a block of code as long as a specified condition is true. Go does not have a while loop or do-while loop, but the for loop can be used in various ways to achieve the same result.

In this section, we will explore how to use for loops, including how to create **infinite loops** and **range-based loops** to iterate over collections such as arrays, slices, and maps.

Using for Loops

The for loop in Go is versatile and can be used in different forms to suit various needs. The basic structure of a for loop includes three parts:

- **Initialization**: A statement that runs once before the loop starts.
- **Condition**: A boolean expression that determines whether the loop continues.

- **Post**: A statement that runs after each iteration (usually used to update loop variables).

Syntax of a for loop:

go

Copy

```
for initialization; condition; post {

    // Code to be executed in each iteration

}
```

Example: Simple for Loop

Let's start with a simple example that prints numbers from 1 to 5:

go

Copy

```
package main

import "fmt"

func main() {
    for i := 1; i <= 5; i++ {
        fmt.Println(i)
    }
}
```

153

In this example:

- **Initialization**: i := 1 starts the loop with i set to 1.
- **Condition**: i <= 5 ensures the loop runs as long as i is less than or equal to 5.
- **Post**: i++ increments i by 1 after each iteration.

The output will be:

Copy

1

2

3

4

5

Example: Decrementing Loop

The for loop can also be used to decrement a variable. For example, let's print numbers from 5 down to 1:

go

Copy

```go
package main

import "fmt"

func main() {
    for i := 5; i > 0; i-- {
        fmt.Println(i)
```

```
    }

}
```

This loop:

- Starts with i equal to 5.
- Continues as long as i is greater than 0.
- Decrements i by 1 on each iteration.

The output will be:

Copy

5

4

3

2

1

Infinite Loops

An **infinite loop** is a loop that runs indefinitely unless it is explicitly broken out of. In Go, you can create an infinite loop using a for loop with no condition. This results in the loop always evaluating to true, and it will run forever unless interrupted by a break or a return statement.

Syntax of an Infinite Loop:

go

Copy

```
for {
```

```
// Code to execute infinitely

}
```

Example: Infinite Loop

Let's write a simple program that runs indefinitely:

go

Copy

```
package main

import "fmt"

func main() {
    for {
        fmt.Println("This is an infinite loop!")
    }
}
```

This program will print "This is an infinite loop!" repeatedly until it is manually stopped (for example, by pressing Ctrl+C in the terminal).

Breaking Out of an Infinite Loop

You can use the break statement to exit an infinite loop based on a certain condition.

Here's an example where we break out of an infinite loop when a specific condition is met:

go

Copy

```go
package main

import "fmt"

func main() {
    count := 0
    for {
        count++
        fmt.Println("Loop count:", count)
        if count == 5 {
            break // Exit the loop when count reaches 5
        }
    }
}
```

In this example:

- The for loop runs indefinitely.
- We increment count in each iteration and print its value.
- Once count reaches 5, the break statement terminates the loop.

The output will be:

vbnet

Copy

Loop count: 1

Loop count: 2

Loop count: 3

Loop count: 4

Loop count: 5

After this, the program exits the loop.

Range Loops (Iterating Over Collections)

Go provides the range keyword to simplify iteration over collections such as arrays, slices, maps, and channels. The range loop automatically handles the iteration and provides the index (or key) and value for each element.

Syntax of a range Loop:

go

Copy

```
for index, value := range collection {

    // Code to be executed on each element

}
```

- index: The index or key of the current element (if applicable).
- value: The value of the current element.
- collection: The array, slice, or map you are iterating over.

158

Example: Iterating Over an Array

Here's an example that iterates over an array of integers and prints each element:

go

Copy

```go
package main

import "fmt"

func main() {
    numbers := [5]int{10, 20, 30, 40, 50}

    for index, value := range numbers {
        fmt.Printf("Index: %d, Value: %d\n", index, value)
    }
}
```

In this example:

- numbers is an array of integers.
- The range loop iterates over each element in the array.
- On each iteration, index contains the index of the current element, and value contains the value.

The output will be:

yaml

Copy

Index: 0, Value: 10

Index: 1, Value: 20

Index: 2, Value: 30

Index: 3, Value: 40

Index: 4, Value: 50

Example: Iterating Over a Slice

Slicing allows for more flexible and dynamic data handling. A range loop can also iterate over slices:

go

Copy

```
package main

import "fmt"

func main() {
    fruits := []string{"apple", "banana", "cherry"}

    for index, fruit := range fruits {
        fmt.Printf("Index: %d, Fruit: %s\n", index, fruit)
```

```
    }

}
```

Here:

- fruits is a slice of strings.
- The range loop iterates over each element in the slice.

The output will be:

yaml

Copy

```
Index: 0, Fruit: apple

Index: 1, Fruit: banana

Index: 2, Fruit: cherry
```

Example: Iterating Over a Map

You can also use the range loop to iterate over a **map**. In a map, the key-value pairs are iterated over in an unspecified order:

go

Copy

```
package main


import "fmt"


func main() {
```

```go
personAge := map[string]int{
    "Alice": 25,
    "Bob":   30,
    "Charlie": 35,
}

for name, age := range personAge {
    fmt.Printf("Name: %s, Age: %d\n", name, age)
}
}
```

In this example:

- personAge is a map with string keys and integer values.
- The range loop iterates over each key-value pair in the map.

The output will be:

yaml

Copy

```
Name: Alice, Age: 25

Name: Bob, Age: 30

Name: Charlie, Age: 35
```

Note that the order of iteration through the map is not guaranteed and may vary each time you run the program.

Loops in Go provide a powerful way to repeat code based on conditions, making your programs more efficient and capable of handling repetitive tasks. In this section, you've learned how to use for loops, including infinite loops and range-based loops, to iterate over arrays, slices, and maps.

To recap:

- **for loops** are the main looping mechanism in Go and can be used for iteration, counting, and performing repetitive tasks.
- **Infinite loops** are created with for {} and can be controlled with break or return.
- **range loops** provide a concise and effective way to iterate over collections like arrays, slices, and maps.
- **fallthrough** in switch statements allows the flow to continue to the next case if desired.

With a solid understanding of loops, you are now ready to explore more advanced concepts such as **concurrency** and **goroutines** in Go, where you can apply these looping techniques in multi-threaded environments. In the next section, we'll dive deeper into more advanced control flow topics and how to handle errors and exceptions in Go.

4.4. Control Flow Examples and Challenges

In this section, we will explore a series of examples and challenges that involve **conditionals** and **loops** to build more complex, interactive programs. These exercises will help you practice using if, else, else if, switch, for, and range loops in real-world scenarios. By solving these challenges, you will get a deeper understanding of how to control the flow of your programs.

Writing Interactive Programs with Conditionals and Loops

Example 1: Number Guessing Game

In this example, we will write a simple number guessing game where the user has to guess a number between 1 and 10. The program will give the user feedback on whether their guess is too high, too low, or correct. The game will continue until the user guesses the correct number.

Task:

1. Generate a random number between 1 and 10.
2. Prompt the user to enter a guess.
3. Use if statements to check if the guess is too high, too low, or correct.
4. Keep prompting the user until they guess correctly.

Solution:

go

Copy

```go
package main

import (
    "fmt"
    "math/rand"
    "time"
)

func main() {
    // Seed the random number generator
    rand.Seed(time.Now().UnixNano())

    // Generate a random number between 1 and 10
    target := rand.Intn(10) + 1
    var guess int
```

```go
fmt.Println("Welcome to the Number Guessing Game!")
fmt.Println("Guess a number between 1 and 10:")


// Loop until the user guesses the correct number
for {
        fmt.Print("Enter your guess: ")
        fmt.Scan(&guess)

        if guess < target {
                fmt.Println("Your guess is too low! Try again.")
        } else if guess > target {
                fmt.Println("Your guess is too high! Try again.")
        } else {
                fmt.Println("Congratulations!  You've  guessed  the  correct
number.")

                break // Exit the loop once the user guesses correctly

        }

    }

}
```

Explanation:

- We use rand.Seed(time.Now().UnixNano()) to generate a random number using the current time as a seed.
- rand.Intn(10) + 1 generates a random number between 1 and 10.
- The for loop keeps asking the user for a guess until they enter the correct number.
- We use if and else if statements to check whether the guess is too low, too high, or correct.

Example Output:

vbnet

Copy

Welcome to the Number Guessing Game!

Guess a number between 1 and 10:

Enter your guess: 5

Your guess is too low! Try again.

Enter your guess: 7

Your guess is too high! Try again.

Enter your guess: 6

Congratulations! You've guessed the correct number.

Example 2: ATM Withdrawal Program

Let's write an interactive ATM withdrawal program. The user will be asked to input their PIN, and once authenticated, they can check their balance, make a withdrawal, or exit the program. The program will use conditionals and loops to handle the user's input and perform the necessary actions.

Task:

1. Prompt the user for their PIN and check if it's correct.
2. Display a menu with options to check balance, make a withdrawal, or exit.
3. Use switch statements to handle the menu choices and implement appropriate actions.

Solution:

go

Copy

```go
package main

import "fmt"

func main() {
    // Set the correct PIN and initial balance
    const correctPIN = 1234
    var balance float64 = 1000.00
    var enteredPIN int

    // Ask the user for their PIN
    fmt.Print("Enter your PIN: ")
    fmt.Scan(&enteredPIN)

    // Check if the entered PIN is correct
    if enteredPIN != correctPIN {
```

```go
        fmt.Println("Incorrect PIN. Access denied.")

        return

}


// If the PIN is correct, show the menu

for {

        fmt.Println("\nATM Menu:")

        fmt.Println("1. Check balance")

        fmt.Println("2. Withdraw")

        fmt.Println("3. Exit")

        fmt.Print("Choose an option (1-3): ")


        var choice int

        fmt.Scan(&choice)


        switch choice {

        case 1:

                // Display current balance

                fmt.Printf("Your current balance is: $%.2f\n", balance)

        case 2:

                // Withdraw money

                var amount float64
```

```
                fmt.Print("Enter amount to withdraw: $")

                fmt.Scan(&amount)


                if amount > balance {

                        fmt.Println("Insufficient funds!")

                } else {

                        balance -= amount

                        fmt.Printf("You have withdrawn $%.2f. New balance:
$%.2f\n", amount, balance)

                }

        case 3:

                // Exit the program

                fmt.Println("Thank you for using our ATM. Goodbye!")

                return

        default:

                fmt.Println("Invalid choice. Please select a valid option.")

        }

    }

}
```

Explanation:

- The program first checks the user's PIN using an if statement.
- Once the correct PIN is entered, the program displays a menu using a switch statement.

- The user can choose to check their balance, make a withdrawal, or exit the program.
- If the withdrawal amount exceeds the balance, the program displays an error message.

Example Output:

mathematica

Copy

Enter your PIN: 1234

ATM Menu:

1. Check balance

2. Withdraw

3. Exit

Choose an option (1-3): 1

Your current balance is: $1000.00

ATM Menu:

1. Check balance

2. Withdraw

3. Exit

Choose an option (1-3): 2

Enter amount to withdraw: $500

You have withdrawn $500.00. New balance: $500.00

ATM Menu:

1. Check balance

2. Withdraw

3. Exit

Choose an option (1-3): 3

Thank you for using our ATM. Goodbye!

Example 3: FizzBuzz Program

The **FizzBuzz** problem is a classic programming challenge where you print the numbers from 1 to 100, but for multiples of 3, print "Fizz" instead of the number, and for multiples of 5, print "Buzz". For numbers that are multiples of both 3 and 5, print "FizzBuzz".

Task:

1. Loop through numbers from 1 to 100.
2. Use if-else or switch to check if the number is divisible by 3, 5, or both, and print the appropriate output.

Solution:

go

Copy

```
package main


import "fmt"
```

```go
func main() {

    for i := 1; i <= 100; i++ {

        switch {

        case i%3 == 0 && i%5 == 0:

            fmt.Println("FizzBuzz")

        case i%3 == 0:

            fmt.Println("Fizz")

        case i%5 == 0:

            fmt.Println("Buzz")

        default:

            fmt.Println(i)

        }

    }

}
```

Explanation:

- The program uses a for loop to iterate through numbers from 1 to 100.
- The switch statement checks the divisibility of the current number:
  - If the number is divisible by both 3 and 5, it prints "FizzBuzz".
  - If the number is divisible by only 3, it prints "Fizz".
  - If the number is divisible by only 5, it prints "Buzz".
  - If none of these conditions are true, it prints the number itself.

Example Output (first few numbers):

python-repl

Copy

```
1
2
Fizz
4
Buzz
Fizz
7
8
Fizz
Buzz
Fizz
11
Fizz
13
14
FizzBuzz
...
```

In this section, we've walked through several **interactive programs** using **conditionals** and **loops,** allowing you to apply these control flow concepts in practical ways. These examples demonstrate how to:

- Write **interactive programs** using if-else, else if, and switch to handle user input and decisions.
- Implement loops, such as the for loop, to repeat actions in programs like the **number guessing game** or the **ATM withdrawal program.**
- Use **range-based loops** to iterate over collections, such as slices or maps.

Through these examples, you should now have a solid understanding of how to use control flow effectively in Go. These tools will allow you to handle a wide variety of programming scenarios and create dynamic, interactive applications.

Chapter 5: Functions

5.1. Understanding Functions in Go

Functions are one of the core building blocks of Go programming, allowing you to organize your code into modular, reusable pieces. A **function** is essentially a named block of code that can be executed when called, performing specific tasks or computations and potentially returning values.

In this section, we will explore what a function is, how to declare and use functions in Go, and the key concepts surrounding functions. Whether you're new to programming or coming from another language, understanding how to use functions effectively will significantly improve the readability, reusability, and maintainability of your code.

What is a Function?

A **function** is a named block of code that performs a specific task or calculation. Functions in Go, as in most programming languages, help break down complex tasks into simpler, manageable pieces. Functions allow you to encapsulate logic, making your code easier to maintain and test.

Functions can take **inputs**, called **parameters**, and can **return** outputs, known as **return values**. Functions can be used to perform operations like performing calculations, processing data, or handling user input and output.

The primary benefits of using functions include:

- **Code Reusability**: Functions allow you to write a block of code once and reuse it in multiple places, reducing code duplication.
- **Code Modularity**: By dividing your program into smaller functions, your code becomes more organized, easier to understand, and easier to debug.
- **Abstraction**: Functions help abstract complex operations, making your code more readable by hiding unnecessary implementation details.

Syntax of a Function in Go

In Go, the syntax for defining a function is as follows:

go
Copy
```
func functionName(parameter1 type, parameter2 type) returnType {
    // Code to execute
    return result // Return a result of type 'returnType'
}
```

Let's break down the syntax:

- **func**: This keyword is used to declare a function.
- **functionName**: This is the name you assign to the function. It must start with a letter and follow Go's identifier rules (e.g., no spaces or special characters).
- **parameter1, parameter2, ...**: These are the inputs to the function, also known as parameters. You define the type of each parameter after its name.
- **returnType**: This is the type of the value the function will return. If the function doesn't return a value, the return type is omitted.
- **return result**: This is the value that the function returns. If the function doesn't return anything, the return statement is omitted.

Defining and Calling Functions

Let's see an example of defining and calling a simple function in Go.

Example 1: A Simple Function Without Parameters and Return Value

Here's a simple function that prints a greeting message:

go
Copy
```
package main

import "fmt"

// Function declaration
```

176

```go
func greet() {
    fmt.Println("Hello, welcome to Go programming!")
}

func main() {
    // Calling the function
    greet() // Output: Hello, welcome to Go programming!
}
```

In this example:

- greet() is a function that doesn't take any parameters and doesn't return any value.
- Inside the main function, we **call** the greet() function to print the greeting.

Example 2: A Function with Parameters and a Return Value

Let's now create a function that takes parameters and returns a result. In this case, we'll create a function that adds two numbers and returns the sum.

go
Copy
```go
package main

import "fmt"

// Function with parameters and a return value
func add(a int, b int) int {
    return a + b
}

func main() {
    sum := add(5, 7) // Call the function and store the result
    fmt.Println("The sum is:", sum) // Output: The sum is: 12
}
```

In this example:

- **add(a int, b int)** is a function that takes two integers as parameters and returns an integer.
- Inside the main function, we call the add() function with 5 and 7 as arguments and store the returned value in the variable sum.

Example 3: A Function with Multiple Return Values

Go allows functions to return multiple values. This feature is particularly useful when you need to return more than one piece of related data. Here's an example of a function that returns both the sum and the difference of two numbers:

go
Copy

```go
package main

import "fmt"

// Function with multiple return values
func sumAndDifference(a int, b int) (int, int) {
    sum := a + b
    diff := a - b
    return sum, diff
}

func main() {
    sum, diff := sumAndDifference(10, 3) // Call function and store multiple return values
    fmt.Println("Sum:", sum) // Output: Sum: 13
    fmt.Println("Difference:", diff) // Output: Difference: 7
}
```

In this example:

- **sumAndDifference(a int, b int) (int, int)** is a function that returns two integers, the sum and the difference of a and b.
- Inside the main function, we use **multiple assignment** to capture both return values and print them.

178

Function Parameters and Return Types

1. Parameter Types

In Go, each parameter must be given a type when you declare a function. The type comes immediately after the parameter name, as shown in the earlier examples.

Go also allows **multiple parameters of the same type** to be declared together. Here's an example:

go
Copy
```go
package main

import "fmt"

// Function with multiple parameters of the same type
func multiply(a, b, c int) int {
    return a * b * c
}

func main() {
    result := multiply(2, 3, 4)
    fmt.Println("The result is:", result) // Output: The result is: 24
}
```

In this example, a, b, and c are all declared as int parameters, and you can pass multiple arguments of the same type to the function.

2. Named Return Values

In Go, you can also **name the return values** of a function. This is an optional feature, but it can improve code clarity, especially when a function returns multiple values. Named return values allow you to directly assign values to the return variables.

go
Copy
```go
package main

import "fmt"
```

```go
// Function with named return values
func divide(a, b int) (quotient int, remainder int) {
    quotient = a / b
    remainder = a % b
    return // Return the named variables
}

func main() {
    q, r := divide(10, 3)
    fmt.Println("Quotient:", q)   // Output: Quotient: 3
    fmt.Println("Remainder:", r)  // Output: Remainder: 1
}
```

In this example:

- The divide() function has two **named return values**: quotient and remainder.
- You can simply use return without explicitly specifying the return values because the variables are already named in the function signature.

3. Returning Multiple Values

As shown in the earlier examples, Go allows you to return multiple values from a function. This feature makes Go functions powerful for cases where you need to return related data together, such as errors along with results.

go
Copy
```go
package main

import "fmt"

// Function that returns multiple values including an error
func calculate(a, b int) (int, error) {
    if b == 0 {
        return 0, fmt.Errorf("division by zero is not allowed")
    }
    return a / b, nil
}
```

180

```go
func main() {
  result, err := calculate(10, 0)
  if err != nil {
    fmt.Println("Error:", err)
  } else {
    fmt.Println("Result:", result)
  }
}
```

In this example:

- The calculate() function returns two values: the result of the division and an error type.
- If an error occurs (like division by zero), the function returns an error value, and we handle it in the main function.

Functions are a critical part of Go programming, allowing you to write modular, reusable, and organized code. In this section, we covered:

- The basic syntax for defining and calling functions.
- How to define functions with parameters and return values.
- The ability to return multiple values and use named return values.
- The flexibility of Go functions to handle multiple return types, including error handling.

Mastering functions will help you write more efficient and maintainable Go programs, enabling you to break down complex problems into simpler, manageable pieces. In the next section, we will dive deeper into advanced function topics, including **variadic functions, closures,** and **deferred function calls**.

Declaring and Calling Functions

Functions are a fundamental part of Go programming, as they allow you to break down complex operations into smaller, more manageable pieces. Let's review how to declare and call functions in Go, as well as how to handle **parameters** and **return values**.

Declaring Functions in Go

In Go, functions are declared using the func keyword, followed by the function name, parameters, and return types. The general syntax for declaring a function is as follows:

go

Copy

```
func functionName(parameter1 type, parameter2 type) returnType {

    // Code to execute

    return result // Return a result of type 'returnType'

}
```

Here's the breakdown:

- func: This keyword is used to declare a function.
- functionName: This is the name of the function. The function name must start with a letter and follow Go's naming rules.
- parameter1, parameter2, ...: These are the input values, also known as parameters. You define the type of each parameter after its name.
- returnType: This is the type of the value that the function will return. If the function does not return a value, this can be omitted.
- return result: This is the value the function will return. If the function doesn't return anything, this line is omitted.

Example 1: A Simple Function

Let's start with a simple example. The function will print a greeting message to the console.

go

Copy

```go
package main

import "fmt"

// Function declaration
func greet() {
    fmt.Println("Hello, welcome to Go programming!")
}

func main() {
    // Calling the function
    greet() // Output: Hello, welcome to Go programming!
}
```

In this example:

- greet() is a function that doesn't take any parameters or return any values.
- We call the function using greet() inside the main() function, which results in the greeting message being printed.

Calling Functions in Go

To call a function, simply use its name followed by parentheses. If the function requires parameters, pass the appropriate values inside the parentheses.

Example 2: Calling a Function with Parameters

In this example, we will write a function that takes two integers as parameters and returns their sum:

go

Copy

```go
package main

import "fmt"

// Function with parameters and a return value
func add(a int, b int) int {
    return a + b
}


func main() {
    // Calling the function with arguments and storing the return value
    result := add(5, 7)
    fmt.Println("The sum is:", result) // Output: The sum is: 12
}
```

In this example:

- The function **add(a int, b int)** takes two integers as input parameters and returns an integer.
- In the main() function, we call add(5, 7), which computes the sum of 5 and 7, and stores the result in the result variable.

Example 3: Calling a Function with Multiple Return Values

Go allows functions to return multiple values. Here's how we can call a function that returns multiple values:

go

Copy

```go
package main


import "fmt"


// Function with multiple return values
func sumAndDifference(a int, b int) (int, int) {

    sum := a + b

    diff := a - b

    return sum, diff

}


func main() {

    // Calling the function and handling multiple return values

    sum, diff := sumAndDifference(10, 5)
```

```go
    fmt.Println("Sum:", sum)      // Output: Sum: 15

    fmt.Println("Difference:", diff) // Output: Difference: 5

}
```

In this example:

- The function **sumAndDifference(a int, b int)** returns two values: the sum and the difference of a and b.
- In the main() function, we use multiple assignment to capture the two return values from the function call sumAndDifference(10, 5).

Parameters and Return Values

In Go, **parameters** are the input values that a function receives, and **return values** are the values that a function sends back after performing its task.

1. Parameters

Parameters are defined inside the parentheses when declaring a function. The parameters have a name and a type, and these values are passed into the function when it is called.

Example 4: Function with Parameters

Here's a simple example where we define a function that takes parameters and returns a result:

go

Copy

```go
package main


import "fmt"
```

```go
// Function with parameters

func multiply(a int, b int) int {

    return a * b

}


func main() {

    result := multiply(3, 4) // Calling the function with arguments

        fmt.Println("The result of multiplication is:", result) // Output: The result of
multiplication is: 12

}
```

In this example:

- The **parameters** a and b represent the two numbers that we multiply.
- The function returns the product of a and b, and the result is printed in the main()
  function.

2. Return Values

In Go, a function can return one or more values. If a function has multiple return values,
they must be declared in the function signature, separated by commas.

Example 5: Function Returning Multiple Values

Here's an example where a function returns both a sum and a product:

go

Copy

package main

```go
import "fmt"

// Function that returns multiple values
func calculate(a int, b int) (int, int) {
    sum := a + b
    product := a * b
    return sum, product
}

func main() {
    sum, product := calculate(5, 3)
    fmt.Println("Sum:", sum)          // Output: Sum: 8
    fmt.Println("Product:", product)  // Output: Product: 15
}
```

In this example:

- **calculate(a int, b int)** returns both the sum and the product of the numbers a and b.
- The main() function captures both return values and prints them.

3. Named Return Values

In Go, you can give names to the return values in the function signature. This is optional but can make your code more readable and clearer, especially when you are returning multiple values. When you use named return values, you don't need to explicitly specify return values in the function body, as they will automatically be returned.

Example 6: Named Return Values

go

Copy

```go
package main

import "fmt"

// Function with named return values
func divide(a, b int) (quotient int, remainder int) {
    quotient = a / b
    remainder = a % b
    return // Named return values are automatically returned
}

func main() {
    q, r := divide(10, 3)
    fmt.Println("Quotient:", q)   // Output: Quotient: 3
    fmt.Println("Remainder:", r) // Output: Remainder: 1
}
```

189

In this example:

- **quotient int, remainder int** are the named return values.
- The return statement in the function automatically returns the values of quotient and remainder without needing to explicitly reference them.

4. Parameter Types and Multiple Parameters of the Same Type

Go allows you to pass multiple parameters of the same type in one declaration. Instead of repeating the type for each parameter, you can group them together.

Example 7: Multiple Parameters of the Same Type

go

Copy

```go
package main

import "fmt"

// Function with multiple parameters of the same type
func addAndMultiply(a, b int) (int, int) {
    sum := a + b
    product := a * b
    return sum, product
}

func main() {
    sum, product := addAndMultiply(4, 5)
    fmt.Println("Sum:", sum)        // Output: Sum: 9
```

190

```
fmt.Println("Product:", product) // Output: Product: 20

}
```

Here, the parameters a and b are both of type int, and their type is declared only once in the function signature.

Functions are a cornerstone of Go programming, allowing you to break down complex problems into smaller, reusable units. In this section, we covered:

- **Declaring functions** with parameters and return values.
- **Calling functions** and passing arguments.
- Using **multiple return values** to return multiple results from a function.
- **Named return values** to simplify code when returning multiple values.
- **Grouping parameters of the same type** together for cleaner and more concise function signatures.

By mastering functions, you can structure your programs more effectively, promote code reuse, and make your codebase easier to maintain and debug. Functions are also crucial for implementing more advanced features, such as **variadic functions** and **closures**, which we will explore in future chapters.

5.2. Variadic Functions and Returning Multiple Values

In Go, functions can be more flexible and powerful by allowing variable numbers of arguments (also known as **variadic functions**) and the ability to return multiple values. These features make Go a highly expressive language when dealing with functions that need to handle a variety of inputs or produce several results simultaneously.

In this section, we will dive into **variadic functions**—functions that accept a variable number of arguments—and **functions that return multiple values**. We will explore their syntax, practical use cases, and how they can enhance the flexibility of your programs.

Functions with Variable Arguments (Variadic Functions)

A **variadic function** is a function that accepts a variable number of arguments. Instead of specifying a fixed number of parameters in the function signature, Go allows you to define a function that can accept any number of arguments for a given parameter, all of which must be of the same type. This is particularly useful when you don't know in advance how many arguments will be passed to the function.

Syntax of Variadic Functions

In Go, a function is defined as variadic by appending an ellipsis (...) before the type of the parameter that accepts the variable arguments. This ellipsis allows the function to accept a slice of values for that parameter.

go

Copy

```go
func functionName(parameterName ...type) returnType {

    // Code to process the variable arguments

}
```

- **parameterName ...type**: This declares that the function accepts an arbitrary number of parameters of the specified type, and these parameters are treated as a slice inside the function.

Example 1: Variadic Function to Calculate the Sum of Numbers

Let's write a function that accepts a variable number of integer arguments and calculates their sum:

go

Copy

```go
package main
```

```go
import "fmt"

// Variadic function to calculate sum of numbers
func sum(numbers ...int) int {
    total := 0
    for _, number := range numbers {
        total += number
    }
    return total
}

func main() {
    result := sum(1, 2, 3, 4, 5)
    fmt.Println("The sum is:", result) // Output: The sum is: 15
}
```

In this example:

- The function **sum(numbers ...int)** takes a variadic parameter numbers of type int. Inside the function, numbers behaves like a slice of integers.
- The function iterates over the numbers slice and adds each number to the total.
- When calling the sum() function, you can pass any number of integer arguments (in this case, five arguments: 1, 2, 3, 4, 5).

Example 2: Variadic Function with Strings

A more practical example could involve concatenating a list of strings into one single string:

go

Copy

```go
package main

import "fmt"

// Variadic function to concatenate strings
func concatenate(strings ...string) string {
    result := ""
    for _, str := range strings {
        result += str + " "
    }
    return result
}

func main() {
    result := concatenate("Go", "is", "awesome")
    fmt.Println(result) // Output: Go is awesome
}
```

Here:

- The concatenate() function takes a variadic parameter strings of type string.
- The function joins all the input strings into a single string with spaces in between.

Working with Slices in Variadic Functions

A variadic function in Go internally treats the variable arguments as a slice. This allows you to easily pass a slice to a variadic function. Here's how you can use a slice as input to a variadic function:

Example 3: Passing a Slice to a Variadic Function

Let's say you have a slice of integers and want to pass it to the sum() function from earlier:

go

Copy

```
package main

import "fmt"

// Variadic function to calculate sum of numbers
func sum(numbers ...int) int {

    total := 0

    for _, number := range numbers {

        total += number

    }
```

```go
    return total

}


func main() {

    numbers := []int{1, 2, 3, 4, 5}

    result := sum(numbers...)  // Use '...' to unpack the slice

    fmt.Println("The sum is:", result)  // Output: The sum is: 15

}
```

In this example:

- We create a slice of integers numbers.
- To pass the slice to the sum() function, we use the ... (ellipsis) syntax to **unpack** the slice and pass each element as an individual argument.

This syntax is crucial when you have a slice and want to pass it to a variadic function.

Functions That Return Multiple Values

In Go, functions are capable of returning multiple values. This is a powerful feature that allows you to return more than one result from a function, making your functions much more expressive and flexible.

Go allows multiple return values in the function signature, and you can return these values in a comma-separated list.

Syntax for Functions Returning Multiple Values:

go

Copy

```go
func functionName() (returnType1, returnType2) {
    // Code to return multiple values
    return value1, value2
}
```

Example 4: Function Returning Multiple Values

Let's consider a function that performs division and returns both the quotient and the remainder:

go

Copy

```go
package main

import "fmt"

// Function returning multiple values
func divide(a, b int) (int, int) {
    quotient := a / b
    remainder := a % b
    return quotient, remainder
}
```

197

```go
func main() {

    quotient, remainder := divide(10, 3)

    fmt.Println("Quotient:", quotient)    // Output: Quotient: 3

    fmt.Println("Remainder:", remainder)  // Output: Remainder: 1

}
```

In this example:

- The divide(a, b int) function returns two values: the quotient and the remainder of dividing a by b.
- When calling the function, the main() function captures both return values using **multiple assignment**.

Example 5: Returning Multiple Values with Named Return Values

As we discussed in Section 5.1, Go allows functions to have **named return values**. This can simplify your code by eliminating the need to explicitly name the return values in the return statement.

go

Copy

```go
package main


import "fmt"


// Function with named return values

func calculate(a, b int) (sum int, product int) {
```

```go
    sum = a + b

    product = a * b

    return  // Implicitly returns named values

}


func main() {

    sum, product := calculate(3, 4)

    fmt.Println("Sum:", sum)        // Output: Sum: 7

    fmt.Println("Product:", product) // Output: Product: 12

}
```

In this example:

- The calculate() function has named return values sum and product.
- The return statement implicitly returns the values of sum and product without needing to explicitly reference them.

Example 6: Returning an Error Alongside a Value

It is a common Go pattern to return an error alongside the actual result, especially when performing operations that can potentially fail. For example, when dividing numbers, you might return an error if division by zero occurs.

go

Copy

```go
package main


import (
```

```go
    "errors"

    "fmt"

)


// Function returning multiple values including an error

func divide(a, b int) (int, error) {

    if b == 0 {

        return 0, errors.New("division by zero is not allowed")

    }

    quotient := a / b

    return quotient, nil

}


func main() {

    result, err := divide(10, 0)

    if err != nil {

        fmt.Println("Error:", err)

    } else {

        fmt.Println("Result:", result)

    }

}
```

In this example:

- The divide() function checks if b is zero. If it is, the function returns an error with the message "division by zero is not allowed".
- If no error occurs, the function returns the quotient and nil (representing no error).
- In the main() function, we check if an error was returned and handle it accordingly.

In this section, we explored **variadic functions** and **functions that return multiple values**, both of which are powerful features in Go that allow you to handle flexible inputs and outputs.

- **Variadic functions** allow a function to accept a variable number of arguments, making it more flexible when dealing with different amounts of input.
- **Multiple return values** let you return more than one value from a function, which is ideal for cases where you need to return related results or handle errors alongside values.

Mastering these techniques will enable you to write more expressive and efficient Go code, enhancing the functionality and flexibility of your programs.

5.3. Anonymous Functions and Closures

In Go, functions can be more flexible and dynamic than simply being named blocks of code. **Anonymous functions** and **closures** allow you to define functions on the fly and capture variables from the surrounding context, which can be used in practical applications such as callbacks, event handling, and resource management.

In this section, we'll explore **anonymous functions**, what they are, how they work, and **closures**, which are closely related to anonymous functions. We will also see some **practical uses** for closures in Go, highlighting their versatility and power.

Understanding Anonymous Functions

An **anonymous function** (also called a **function literal**) is a function that is defined without a name. Unlike regular functions, anonymous functions are usually used immediately after they are defined, and they don't need to be declared in advance. These functions are often used when you need a short, throwaway function for a specific task.

Syntax of an Anonymous Function

An anonymous function is declared in the same way as a regular function, but without a name. It can be assigned to a variable, passed as an argument to other functions, or executed immediately.

The general syntax is:

go

Copy

```go
func(parameter1 type, parameter2 type) returnType {
    // Function body
}
```

Here's an example of an anonymous function:

go

Copy

```go
package main

import "fmt"

func main() {
```

```go
// Anonymous function assigned to a variable

greet := func(name string) {

    fmt.Println("Hello,", name)

}


// Calling the anonymous function

greet("Alice") // Output: Hello, Alice

}
```

In this example:

- The anonymous function func(name string) is assigned to the variable greet.
- We then call greet("Alice"), which executes the anonymous function and prints "Hello, Alice".

Example 1: Immediately Invoked Function Expression (IIFE)

Anonymous functions can also be invoked immediately after they are defined. This is known as an **Immediately Invoked Function Expression** (IIFE). While this pattern is more common in JavaScript, it can also be used in Go.

go

Copy

```go
package main


import "fmt"


func main() {
```

203

```
// Immediately invoked anonymous function

func(name string) {

    fmt.Println("Hello, " + name)

}("Bob") // Output: Hello, Bob

}
```

Here:

- The anonymous function is immediately executed with the argument "Bob", printing "Hello, Bob".

This pattern is useful for isolating a block of code without polluting the surrounding scope with temporary variables.

Practical Uses for Closures

A **closure** is a special type of function that "captures" variables from its surrounding environment. When you define a function inside another function, the inner function can access and modify variables from the outer function's scope. The inner function retains access to these variables even after the outer function has finished executing, which is what makes it a closure.

What Makes a Closure?

A function is considered a closure if it:

1. Is defined inside another function.
2. Refers to variables from the outer function's scope.
3. Continues to have access to those variables even after the outer function has returned.

204

Here's an example of a closure:

go

Copy

```go
package main

import "fmt"

// Outer function
func outer() func() {
    message := "Hello from the closure!"

    // Inner function (closure) that references 'message' from outer
    return func() {
        fmt.Println(message)
    }
}

func main() {
    // Creating a closure
    greet := outer()

    // Calling the closure
```

```
greet() // Output: Hello from the closure!
```

```
}
```

In this example:

- The outer() function defines a local variable message and returns an anonymous function that refers to message.
- When the greet() closure is called in the main() function, it prints "Hello from the closure!".
- Even though the outer() function has already returned, the closure still has access to the message variable because it "closed over" the variable.

Example 2: Function Factory with Closures

Closures are particularly useful when you need to create functions dynamically, especially when working with **stateful functions**. Here's an example of a function that returns a closure for incrementing a counter:

go

Copy

```go
package main


import "fmt"


// Function that returns a closure for incrementing a counter

func createCounter() func() int {

    count := 0

    return func() int {

        count++
```

```go
        return count

    }

}


func main() {

    counter1 := createCounter()

    counter2 := createCounter()


    fmt.Println(counter1()) // Output: 1

    fmt.Println(counter1()) // Output: 2

    fmt.Println(counter2()) // Output: 1

    fmt.Println(counter1()) // Output: 3

}
```

In this example:

- **createCounter()** returns a closure that maintains its own count variable.
- Each time counter1() or counter2() is called, the counter is incremented, but the counters have independent state.
- counter1 and counter2 are two separate closures, each retaining its own version of the count variable.

This ability to retain and update state within a closure makes it highly useful for scenarios where you need a function to maintain state over time, like counters, accumulators, or event handlers.

Practical Use Cases for Closures

1. **Callbacks**: Closures are frequently used as callback functions, especially when working with asynchronous operations or event-driven programming. For example, closures can be passed as handlers for events that occur later.
2. **Stateful Functions**: As demonstrated above, closures can retain state across multiple invocations. This is useful for maintaining private variables that cannot be accessed from outside the function.
3. **Function Factories**: You can use closures to create functions on the fly based on parameters. A closure can generate a new function with specific behavior each time it is called.
4. **Deferred Execution**: Closures are useful when you want to delay the execution of certain code, such as in **deferred** execution contexts.

Combining Anonymous Functions and Closures

You can use both anonymous functions and closures together to create flexible, dynamic behavior in your programs. Closures are often used in scenarios where you need a function that maintains state or is passed around for deferred execution, and anonymous functions are a convenient way to define those closures inline.

Example 3: Using Anonymous Functions and Closures Together

go

Copy

```go
package main

import "fmt"

func main() {
    // Using an anonymous function as a closure to accumulate a total
    total := 0
```

```go
addToTotal := func(amount int) {

    total += amount

}


// Calling the closure multiple times to accumulate the total

addToTotal(10)

addToTotal(20)

addToTotal(30)


fmt.Println("Total amount:", total) // Output: Total amount: 60

}
```

Here:

- We define an anonymous function addToTotal that is used as a closure to accumulate a running total.
- Each time addToTotal() is called, it updates the total variable, which is captured by the closure.

In this section, we explored **anonymous functions** and **closures,** two powerful features of Go that enhance the flexibility and dynamism of your code.

- **Anonymous functions** allow you to define functions without names, and they can be used on the fly, assigned to variables, or passed as arguments to other functions.
- **Closures** capture variables from their surrounding context, allowing them to retain access to those variables even after the function they were created in has

finished executing. This makes closures ideal for creating **stateful functions**, **callbacks**, and **function factories**.

By mastering anonymous functions and closures, you will be able to write more concise, flexible, and powerful Go programs. In the next section, we will dive into **deferred function calls** and explore how to manage resource cleanup and execution order in Go.

5.4. Best Practices for Writing Functions in Go

Functions are one of the most important building blocks of Go programming. They provide structure, make your code reusable, and help you avoid duplication. However, like any tool, functions can be misused if not designed properly. To maximize the benefits of functions in Go, it's essential to follow certain best practices. In this section, we'll explore best practices for writing **simple and modular functions**, ensuring your code remains clean, efficient, and easy to maintain.

Keeping Functions Simple and Modular

One of the fundamental principles of writing good functions is to **keep them simple** and **modular**. A well-designed function should focus on performing a single task, and it should be as independent as possible. This not only makes the function easier to understand and test, but it also makes your code more flexible and reusable.

1. Single Responsibility Principle (SRP)

Each function should have one **primary responsibility**. This is known as the **Single Responsibility Principle**, which suggests that a function should do one thing and do it well. If a function does too many things, it becomes harder to understand, test, and maintain.

Example: Function with Single Responsibility

Let's consider a function that calculates the area of a rectangle. It should only focus on the calculation and nothing else:

go

Copy

```go
package main

import "fmt"

// Function with single responsibility: calculates area
func calculateArea(length, width float64) float64 {
    return length * width
}

func main() {
    area := calculateArea(10.0, 5.0)
    fmt.Println("Area of the rectangle:", area)  // Output: Area of the rectangle: 50
}
```

In this example:

- The function calculateArea only calculates the area of a rectangle. It does not perform any other unrelated tasks, such as printing output or validating inputs.
- Keeping the function focused on one task makes it more understandable and easier to reuse in other parts of your program.

2. Avoid Long Functions

Long functions are harder to read, understand, and test. Try to break down complex logic into smaller, focused functions. A function should ideally fit within a single screen's worth of code. If a function is too long, consider refactoring it into multiple smaller functions.

Example: Refactoring a Long Function

Suppose we have a function that calculates both the area and perimeter of a rectangle. It would be better to break this into two smaller functions:

go

Copy

```go
package main

import "fmt"

// Function to calculate area
func calculateArea(length, width float64) float64 {
    return length * width
}

// Function to calculate perimeter
func calculatePerimeter(length, width float64) float64 {
    return 2 * (length + width)
}
```

212

```go
func main() {

    length, width := 10.0, 5.0

    area := calculateArea(length, width)

    perimeter := calculatePerimeter(length, width)


    fmt.Println("Area:", area)          // Output: Area: 50

    fmt.Println("Perimeter:", perimeter) // Output: Perimeter: 30

}
```

In this example:

- The calculations for the area and perimeter are separated into two functions, each performing a distinct task.
- This makes the code easier to read, understand, and maintain.

3. Function Length and Readability

While keeping functions small, it's also crucial to ensure they remain **readable**. Functions that are too short or fragmented can lose clarity, so aim for a balance between function length and readability. A function should be long enough to encapsulate a complete operation but short enough to be easy to understand.

Example: Readable Function with Proper Naming

go

Copy

```go
package main


import "fmt"
```

```go
// Function with meaningful name

func calculateDiscount(price, discountRate float64) float64 {

    return price * (discountRate / 100)

}


func main() {

    price := 100.0

    discountRate := 20.0

    discount := calculateDiscount(price, discountRate)

    fmt.Println("Discount Amount:", discount) // Output: Discount Amount: 20

}
```

In this example:

- The function calculateDiscount is clear in its purpose due to its descriptive name.
- The code is simple, concise, and readable, making it easy for future developers to understand its function.

4. Use Meaningful Function and Variable Names

A function's name should describe what it does. A well-chosen name removes the need for excessive comments or documentation. Variable names inside the function should also be descriptive to clearly convey their role in the function.

Example: Meaningful Naming

go

Copy

```go
package main

import "fmt"

// Function with descriptive name and parameters
func convertToCelsius(fahrenheit float64) float64 {
    return (fahrenheit - 32) * 5 / 9
}

func main() {
    fahrenheit := 100.0
    celsius := convertToCelsius(fahrenheit)
    fmt.Println("Temperature in Celsius:", celsius) // Output: Temperature in Celsius: 37.77777777777778
}
```

Here:

- The function convertToCelsius clearly explains what it does, so you don't need extra comments to explain its purpose.
- The parameter fahrenheit also conveys exactly what it represents.

215

Managing Side Effects and Dependencies

A good function should be **pure**, meaning it should not modify any global variables, print to the console, or perform any action that affects the program's state outside of returning a result. Functions with side effects can make your program harder to reason about and test.

1. Avoiding Global Variables

Global variables can introduce unintended side effects in your functions. Whenever possible, pass values to functions explicitly instead of relying on global state.

Example: Avoiding Global Variables

go

Copy

```go
package main

import "fmt"

// Function without relying on global variables
func calculateArea(length, width float64) float64 {
    return length * width
}

func main() {
    length := 10.0
    width := 5.0
    area := calculateArea(length, width)
```

216

```go
fmt.Println("Area of the rectangle:", area) // Output: Area of the rectangle: 50
}
```

In this example:

- The function calculateArea doesn't rely on global variables. It explicitly takes parameters and returns the result.
- This approach minimizes unintended side effects, making the function more predictable and easier to test.

2. Minimizing Dependencies in Functions

Try to minimize the dependencies your function has on external resources. Functions should be self-contained, requiring only the parameters passed to them and returning a result without interacting with global state or external systems (like databases, file systems, etc.) unless absolutely necessary.

Example: Function with Minimal Dependencies

go

Copy

```go
package main

import "fmt"

// Function that performs a calculation without external dependencies
func calculateDiscount(price, discountRate float64) float64 {
    return price * (discountRate / 100)
}
```

```go
func main() {

    price := 150.0

    discountRate := 10.0

    discountedPrice := calculateDiscount(price, discountRate)

    fmt.Println("Discounted Price:", discountedPrice) // Output: Discounted Price: 15

}
```

In this example:

- The calculateDiscount function operates independently, requiring only the parameters passed to it, which makes it easier to test and reuse.

Documenting Functions

Although the names of functions and variables should generally be self-explanatory, more complex logic may still require comments or documentation. **GoDoc** is the standard tool for generating documentation from Go source code. By writing clear documentation, you ensure that other developers (or your future self) will understand how to use your functions and why they behave the way they do.

Example: Documenting a Function

go

Copy

```go
package main


import "fmt"
```

```go
// calculateArea calculates the area of a rectangle
// given the length and width.
func calculateArea(length, width float64) float64 {
    return length * width
}

func main() {
    length := 10.0
    width := 5.0
    area := calculateArea(length, width)
    fmt.Println("Area of the rectangle:", area) // Output: Area of the rectangle: 50
}
```

In this example:

- The comment above the calculateArea function provides a brief explanation of what the function does. This is especially useful when the function is more complex or part of a public API.
- Good documentation ensures that your code is understandable, even without needing to dive into the implementation details.

Writing good functions is essential for creating clean, maintainable, and efficient Go programs. Following best practices for writing functions can help you build a codebase that is easier to read, understand, and extend. Here's a recap of the key points:

- **Keep functions simple and focused on a single task** (single responsibility principle).
- **Avoid long functions**; break them down into smaller, manageable pieces.
- **Use meaningful function and variable names** that clearly describe what the function does.
- **Minimize side effects** by avoiding reliance on global variables and minimizing external dependencies.
- **Document your functions** to improve their readability and maintainability.

By applying these practices, you can write functions that are not only effective and powerful but also maintainable and easy to test. In the next section, we will dive deeper into **deferred function calls** and explore their use for handling cleanup tasks in Go programs.

5.5. Practical Exercises with Functions

In this section, we will go through several practical exercises that will help you strengthen your understanding of **functions** in Go. These exercises will range from simple functions that perform calculations to more advanced scenarios involving **variadic functions, closures**, and **multiple return values**. By solving these challenges, you'll get hands-on experience with writing functions that are modular, reusable, and effective.

Exercise 1: Calculate the Area and Perimeter of a Rectangle

In this exercise, we will write two functions: one for calculating the **area** of a rectangle and another for calculating its **perimeter**. Both functions will take the **length** and **width** of the rectangle as parameters and return the corresponding result.

Task:

1. Create a function calculateArea that takes length and width as parameters and returns the area.
2. Create a function calculatePerimeter that takes length and width as parameters and returns the perimeter.
3. In the main function, call both functions with appropriate values and print the results.

Solution:

go

Copy

```go
package main

import "fmt"

// Function to calculate area
func calculateArea(length, width float64) float64 {
    return length * width
}

// Function to calculate perimeter
func calculatePerimeter(length, width float64) float64 {
    return 2 * (length + width)
}

func main() {
    length, width := 10.0, 5.0

    area := calculateArea(length, width)
    perimeter := calculatePerimeter(length, width)
```

```go
    fmt.Println("Area of the rectangle:", area)        // Output: Area of the rectangle: 50

        fmt.Println("Perimeter of the rectangle:", perimeter) // Output: Perimeter of the
rectangle: 30

}
```

In this example:

- We created two functions: calculateArea and calculatePerimeter, each performing a specific calculation.
- We then called both functions in the main function and printed the results.

Exercise 2: Temperature Conversion (Celsius to Fahrenheit)

In this exercise, we will write a function to convert a temperature from **Celsius** to **Fahrenheit**. The formula for conversion is:

$F = \frac{9}{5} \times C + 32$

Task:

1. Create a function convertToFahrenheit that takes celsius as a parameter and returns the corresponding Fahrenheit value.
2. In the main function, prompt the user for a Celsius value and print the converted Fahrenheit temperature.

Solution:

go

Copy

package main

```go
import "fmt"

// Function to convert Celsius to Fahrenheit
func convertToFahrenheit(celsius float64) float64 {
    return (celsius * 9 / 5) + 32
}

func main() {
    var celsius float64
    fmt.Print("Enter temperature in Celsius: ")
    fmt.Scan(&celsius)

    fahrenheit := convertToFahrenheit(celsius)
    fmt.Printf("%.2f Celsius is %.2f Fahrenheit\n", celsius, fahrenheit)
}
```

In this example:

- The convertToFahrenheit function performs the conversion.
- The main function prompts the user to enter a temperature in Celsius and then calls the conversion function, printing the result in Fahrenheit.

Exercise 3: Concatenate Multiple Strings

In this exercise, we will create a variadic function that can accept any number of strings and concatenate them into one single string. We will also include an optional separator between each string.

Task:

1. Create a variadic function concatenateStrings that takes a separator and a variable number of strings, concatenating them with the separator in between.
2. In the main function, call this function with a list of strings and a separator, then print the resulting string.

Solution:

go

Copy

```go
package main

import "fmt"

// Variadic function to concatenate strings with a separator
func concatenateStrings(separator string, strings ...string) string {
    result := ""
    for i, str := range strings {
        if i > 0 {
            result += separator
        }
        result += str
```

```
    }

    return result

}


func main() {

    result := concatenateStrings(", ", "Go", "is", "awesome")

    fmt.Println(result) // Output: Go, is, awesome

}
```

In this example:

- The concatenateStrings function takes a separator and a variadic parameter strings, which represents a list of strings.
- The function concatenates all the strings, inserting the separator between them.
- In the main function, we test the function with three strings and a comma-space separator.

Exercise 4: Function with Multiple Return Values

In this exercise, we will write a function that takes two integers and returns both their **sum** and their **difference**. We will return the results using Go's ability to return multiple values.

Task:

1. Create a function sumAndDifference that takes two integers and returns both their sum and difference.
2. In the main function, call this function and print both the sum and the difference.

Solution:

go

Copy

```go
package main

import "fmt"

// Function to return both sum and difference
func sumAndDifference(a, b int) (int, int) {
    sum := a + b
    difference := a - b
    return sum, difference
}

func main() {
    a, b := 15, 7
    sum, difference := sumAndDifference(a, b)
    fmt.Println("Sum:", sum)             // Output: Sum: 22
    fmt.Println("Difference:", difference) // Output: Difference: 8
}
```

In this example:

- The sumAndDifference function returns both the sum and the difference of two integers.
- The main function uses **multiple assignment** to store both the sum and the difference returned by the function.

Exercise 5: Using Closures for Counter

In this exercise, we will create a function that returns a closure, which is a function that maintains a counter state. Each time the returned closure is called, it should increment the counter and return the new value.

Task:

1. Create a function createCounter that returns a closure. The closure should maintain and increment a counter each time it is called.
2. In the main function, create two separate counters using createCounter and demonstrate the independent state of each counter.

Solution:

go

Copy

```go
package main

import "fmt"

// Function that returns a closure for a counter
func createCounter() func() int {
    count := 0
```

```go
    return func() int {

        count++

        return count

    }

}


func main() {

    counter1 := createCounter()

    counter2 := createCounter()


    fmt.Println("Counter 1:", counter1()) // Output: Counter 1: 1

    fmt.Println("Counter 1:", counter1()) // Output: Counter 1: 2

    fmt.Println("Counter 2:", counter2()) // Output: Counter 2: 1

    fmt.Println("Counter 1:", counter1()) // Output: Counter 1: 3

}
```

In this example:

- The createCounter function returns a closure that maintains its own count variable.
- Each counter (counter1 and counter2) has its independent state, which is maintained across calls to the closure.

Exercise 6: Function with Error Handling (Multiple Return Values)

In this exercise, we will write a function that performs division and returns both the result and an error if the divisor is zero.

Task:

1. Create a function safeDivide that takes two integers and returns both the result of the division and an error if division by zero occurs.
2. In the main function, call the division function and handle the error appropriately.

Solution:

go

Copy

```go
package main

import (

    "errors"

    "fmt"

)


// Function to safely divide two numbers

func safeDivide(a, b int) (int, error) {

    if b == 0 {

        return 0, errors.New("division by zero")

    }

    return a / b, nil
```

```
}

func main() {

    result, err := safeDivide(10, 0)

    if err != nil {

        fmt.Println("Error:", err) // Output: Error: division by zero

    } else {

        fmt.Println("Result:", result)

    }


    result, err = safeDivide(10, 2)

    if err != nil {

        fmt.Println("Error:", err)

    } else {

        fmt.Println("Result:", result) // Output: Result: 5

    }

}
```

In this example:

- The safeDivide function performs the division and returns both the result and an error.
- In the main function, we check if an error was returned and handle it accordingly.

Through these exercises, you've gained hands-on experience working with different types of functions in Go. Here's what we've covered:

- **Modular Functions**: Writing functions to perform specific tasks, like calculating areas and perimeters.
- **Variadic Functions**: Using a single function to handle multiple arguments, like concatenating strings.
- **Multiple Return Values**: Returning more than one value from a function, such as returning both the sum and difference.
- **Closures**: Creating functions that maintain state across multiple calls, such as counters.
- **Error Handling**: Writing functions that return errors alongside results to handle edge cases, like division by zero.

These practical exercises reinforce essential function concepts and give you the foundation to build more complex Go programs. As you continue writing functions, you will further improve your ability to write clean, maintainable, and reusable code.

Chapter 6: Arrays, Slices, and Maps

6.1. Arrays in Go

In Go, **arrays** are a collection of elements of the same type that are stored in contiguous memory locations. Arrays are fixed in size, meaning once an array is declared with a specific size, it cannot be resized. Arrays in Go are useful when you know in advance the exact number of elements that you will need, and you want to work with a fixed collection of values.

In this section, we will explore how to **declare** and **initialize arrays** in Go, how to access and modify their elements, and how to work with arrays efficiently.

Declaring and Initializing Arrays

In Go, arrays are declared using a specific syntax. The key components of an array are its **type** (which defines the data type of its elements), its **size** (which specifies how many elements it holds), and the **elements** themselves.

Syntax for Declaring an Array

To declare an array in Go, you specify the type of its elements and its size. The size of an array is part of its type, which means arrays with different sizes are considered distinct types.

The general syntax for declaring an array is:

```go
Copy
var arrayName [size]type
```

Where:

- arrayName is the name of the array.
- size is the number of elements in the array.
- type is the type of the elements that the array will hold (e.g., int, string, float64).

Example 1: Declaring an Array

go
Copy

```
package main

import "fmt"

func main() {
    var numbers [5]int // Declaring an array of 5 integers
    fmt.Println(numbers) // Output: [0 0 0 0 0]
}
```

In this example:

- We declare an array named numbers that can hold **5 integers**.
- The array is initialized with default values. Since the array is of type int, the default value for each element is 0.

Initializing Arrays

Arrays can be initialized in two main ways: during declaration or separately after declaration.

1. Initializing During Declaration

You can initialize an array at the time of its declaration by providing a list of values inside curly braces {}. The number of values in the initialization list must match the array's size.

go
Copy

```
package main

import "fmt"

func main() {
    var numbers = [5]int{1, 2, 3, 4, 5} // Initializing the array with values
    fmt.Println(numbers) // Output: [1 2 3 4 5]
}
```

233

In this example:

- The array numbers is initialized with the values 1, 2, 3, 4, 5 at the time of declaration.
- We don't need to explicitly specify the size of the array because the compiler can determine it based on the number of elements in the initialization list.

2. Using the ... Operator (Array with Implicit Size)

Go allows you to omit the size when initializing an array. You can use the ... operator, and Go will automatically infer the size based on the number of elements in the initialization list.

```go
Copy
package main

import "fmt"

func main() {
    numbers := [...]int{10, 20, 30, 40, 50} // Implicit size using '...'
    fmt.Println(numbers) // Output: [10 20 30 40 50]
}
```

In this example:

- The array numbers is initialized with 5 values, and Go infers the array size from the number of values.

3. Initializing an Array with Default Values

If you do not initialize an array, the elements will be set to the **zero value** for that type. For example, the zero value for an int array is 0, for a string array is "", and for a bool array is false.

```go
Copy
package main
```

```go
import "fmt"

func main() {
    var strings [3]string // Declaring an array of 3 strings
    fmt.Println(strings)   // Output: [   ]
}
```

Here:

- The strings array is declared with a size of 3 but without an explicit initialization.
- As a result, all elements in the array are initialized with the zero value for strings, which is an empty string "".

Accessing and Modifying Array Elements

You can access and modify array elements using their **index**. In Go, array indices start at **0**. The index of the first element is 0, the second element is 1, and so on.

Syntax for Accessing an Element

To access an element of an array, use the index inside square brackets []:

go
Copy
```
arrayName[index]
```

Example 2: Accessing and Modifying Array Elements

go
Copy
```go
package main

import "fmt"

func main() {
    numbers := [5]int{10, 20, 30, 40, 50}
```

```go
// Accessing elements
fmt.Println("First element:", numbers[0]) // Output: First element: 10
fmt.Println("Third element:", numbers[2]) // Output: Third element: 30

// Modifying elements
numbers[1] = 25
fmt.Println("Modified array:", numbers) // Output: Modified array: [10 25 30 40 50]
}
```

In this example:

- We access the first and third elements of the numbers array using indices 0 and 2.
- We modify the second element (numbers[1]) to 25 and then print the updated array.

Multi-Dimensional Arrays

Go also supports **multi-dimensional arrays**, which are arrays of arrays. A common use case for multi-dimensional arrays is representing matrices or grids.

Declaring a Multi-Dimensional Array

You can declare a multi-dimensional array by specifying the size of each dimension:

go
Copy
```go
var matrix [3][3]int
```

This declares a **2D array** (matrix) with 3 rows and 3 columns.

Example 3: Multi-Dimensional Array
go
Copy
```go
package main

import "fmt"
```

```go
func main() {
    var matrix [2][3]int // A 2x3 matrix (2 rows and 3 columns)

    // Initializing elements
    matrix[0][0] = 1
    matrix[0][1] = 2
    matrix[0][2] = 3
    matrix[1][0] = 4
    matrix[1][1] = 5
    matrix[1][2] = 6

    fmt.Println("Matrix:", matrix)
}
```

In this example:

- We declare a 2D array matrix with 2 rows and 3 columns.
- We assign values to each element in the matrix.
- The matrix is then printed as a 2x3 grid.

Example Output:
lua
Copy
Matrix: [[1 2 3] [4 5 6]]

Length of an Array

To find the length of an array in Go, you can use the built-in len() function. The len() function returns the number of elements in the array.

Example 4: Finding the Length of an Array
go
Copy
```go
package main

import "fmt"
```

237

```
func main() {
    numbers := [4]int{1, 2, 3, 4}
    fmt.Println("Length of the array:", len(numbers)) // Output: Length of the array: 4
}
```

In this example:

- The len() function is used to get the number of elements in the numbers array, which is 4.

In this section, we have explored **arrays** in Go, covering how to declare, initialize, and modify arrays, as well as how to access individual elements. Here's a recap of the key concepts:

- **Declaring arrays**: Arrays in Go are declared by specifying the size and type of elements.
- **Initializing arrays**: Arrays can be initialized at the time of declaration or separately, and Go can infer the size when using the ... operator.
- **Accessing and modifying elements**: Array elements are accessed and modified using their index, starting at 0.
- **Multi-dimensional arrays**: Go supports multi-dimensional arrays for representing complex data structures like matrices.
- **Array length**: The len() function allows you to get the number of elements in an array.

Arrays are powerful tools for handling fixed-size collections of data. In the next section, we will explore **slices** and **maps**, which provide more flexibility and are commonly used in Go programs for working with dynamic collections of data.

Accessing Array Elements and Working with Multi-Dimensional Arrays

In Go, accessing and working with array elements, as well as handling multi-dimensional arrays, are fundamental operations. In this section, we'll go into detail

238

on how to **access individual elements** of arrays and **work with multi-dimensional arrays** for more complex data structures, such as matrices and grids.

Accessing Array Elements

Array elements in Go are accessed by specifying their **index** in square brackets []. The indices of arrays in Go are zero-based, meaning the first element of an array has an index of 0, the second element has an index of 1, and so on.

Syntax for Accessing Elements

To access an element of an array:

go

Copy

```
arrayName[index]
```

Where:

- arrayName is the name of the array.
- index is the position of the element you want to access. The index starts from 0.

Example 1: Accessing Array Elements

go

Copy

```
package main


import "fmt"


func main() {
```

```go
    numbers := [5]int{10, 20, 30, 40, 50}

    // Accessing elements by index

    fmt.Println("First element:", numbers[0]) // Output: First element: 10

    fmt.Println("Second element:", numbers[1]) // Output: Second element: 20

    fmt.Println("Fifth element:", numbers[4]) // Output: Fifth element: 50

}
```

In this example:

- We declare an array numbers with 5 integers.
- We access and print the elements at indices 0, 1, and 4 using their respective indices.

Modifying Array Elements

Arrays are mutable in Go, meaning you can modify their elements. To modify an element, simply assign a new value to a specific index.

go

Copy

```go
package main

import "fmt"

func main() {

    numbers := [5]int{10, 20, 30, 40, 50}
```

```
// Modifying the second element

numbers[1] = 25


fmt.Println("Modified array:", numbers) // Output: Modified array: [10 25 30 40 50]

}
```

Here:

- We modify the second element of the array (numbers[1]) to 25, and then print the updated array.

Working with Multi-Dimensional Arrays

A **multi-dimensional array** is an array of arrays. In Go, multi-dimensional arrays are useful for representing complex data structures like matrices or grids. The most common type of multi-dimensional array is the **2D array**, but Go also supports 3D arrays, and arrays with more dimensions.

Declaring and Initializing a Multi-Dimensional Array

A **2D array** can be thought of as a grid or table with rows and columns. The declaration syntax for a 2D array is:

go

Copy

```
var arrayName [rows][columns]type
```

Where:

- **rows** specifies the number of rows.
- **columns** specifies the number of columns.
- **type** is the type of the elements in the array.

You can initialize a 2D array either at the time of declaration or by assigning values to specific elements after declaration.

Example 2: Declaring and Initializing a 2D Array

go

Copy

```go
package main

import "fmt"

func main() {
    // Declare a 2x3 2D array (2 rows, 3 columns)
    var matrix [2][3]int

    // Initialize values
    matrix[0][0] = 1

    matrix[0][1] = 2

    matrix[0][2] = 3

    matrix[1][0] = 4

    matrix[1][1] = 5

    matrix[1][2] = 6
```

```go
    fmt.Println("Matrix:")

    fmt.Println(matrix)

}
```

In this example:

- We declare a **2D array** matrix with 2 rows and 3 columns.
- We manually assign values to each element of the 2D array.
- The result will display the matrix in the format [[1 2 3] [4 5 6]].

Initializing a Multi-Dimensional Array During Declaration

You can also initialize a multi-dimensional array at the time of declaration, just like a regular array.

go

Copy

```go
package main


import "fmt"


func main() {
    // Declare and initialize a 2x3 2D array

    matrix := [2][3]int{
        {1, 2, 3},

        {4, 5, 6},

    }
```

243

```go
	fmt.Println("Matrix:")

	fmt.Println(matrix)

}
```

In this example:

- We declare and initialize the matrix with values directly in the array declaration.
- The result will be the same as the previous example: [[1 2 3] [4 5 6]].

Accessing Elements in Multi-Dimensional Arrays

Accessing elements in multi-dimensional arrays follows the same principle as with one-dimensional arrays. You simply use multiple indices to access an element within the sub-arrays.

Example 3: Accessing Elements in a 2D Array

go

Copy

```go
package main

import "fmt"

func main() {
	matrix := [2][3]int{
		{1, 2, 3},
		{4, 5, 6},
```

244

```
    }


    // Accessing elements

    fmt.Println("Element at [0][0]:", matrix[0][0]) // Output: Element at [0][0]: 1

    fmt.Println("Element at [1][2]:", matrix[1][2]) // Output: Element at [1][2]: 6
}
```

In this example:

- We access the element at position [0][0] (the first row and first column), which is 1.
- We access the element at position [1][2] (the second row and third column), which is 6.

Modifying Elements in Multi-Dimensional Arrays

Just like one-dimensional arrays, you can modify elements in a multi-dimensional array by specifying the row and column indices.

Example 4: Modifying Elements in a 2D Array

go

Copy

```
package main


import "fmt"


func main() {
```

245

```go
matrix := [2][3]int{
    {1, 2, 3},
    {4, 5, 6},
}

// Modifying an element
matrix[0][1] = 10

fmt.Println("Modified Matrix:")
fmt.Println(matrix) // Output: Modified Matrix: [[1 10 3] [4 5 6]]
}
```

Here:

- We modify the element at position [0][1] (the first row, second column) from 2 to 10.
- The updated matrix is printed.

Iterating Over Multi-Dimensional Arrays

You can use **nested loops** to iterate over the elements of a multi-dimensional array. The outer loop will iterate over the rows, and the inner loop will iterate over the columns.

Example 5: Iterating Over a 2D Array

go

Copy

```go
package main

import "fmt"

func main() {
    matrix := [2][3]int{
        {1, 2, 3},
        {4, 5, 6},
    }

    // Iterating over rows and columns
    for i := 0; i < len(matrix); i++ {
        for j := 0; j < len(matrix[i]); j++ {
            fmt.Printf("Element at [%d][%d]: %d\n", i, j, matrix[i][j])
        }
    }
}
```

247

In this example:

- The outer loop iterates over the rows (i), and the inner loop iterates over the columns (j).
- The program prints the elements of the matrix, along with their indices.

Example Output:

less

Copy

Element at [0][0]: 1

Element at [0][1]: 2

Element at [0][2]: 3

Element at [1][0]: 4

Element at [1][1]: 5

Element at [1][2]: 6

In this section, we've covered important concepts related to **arrays** and **multi-dimensional arrays** in Go. Here's a recap of the key points:

- **Accessing and modifying array elements**: Array elements are accessed using indices. Arrays are mutable, so their elements can be modified.
- **Working with multi-dimensional arrays**: We explored how to declare, initialize, and access elements in multi-dimensional arrays like 2D arrays, which are useful for representing tables, grids, or matrices.
- **Iterating over arrays**: We used loops to iterate over the elements of both 1D and 2D arrays.
- **Modifying multi-dimensional arrays**: Elements in multi-dimensional arrays can be modified by specifying the row and column indices.

Arrays are foundational data structures, but they have a fixed size in Go. In the next section, we will explore **slices**, which are more flexible and dynamic than arrays and are commonly used for most collections of data in Go programs.

6.2. Slices: The Flexible Array

In Go, **slices** are a more flexible and powerful alternative to arrays. Unlike arrays, slices are **dynamic**, meaning they can grow and shrink in size as needed. This flexibility makes slices the most commonly used data structure in Go when dealing with collections of data. Slices are built on top of arrays, but they provide much more functionality and ease of use.

In this section, we will introduce **slices**, explain how they differ from arrays, and explore how to declare, initialize, and manipulate slices in Go.

Introduction to Slices

A **slice** is a dynamically-sized, flexible view into an array. Unlike arrays, which have a fixed size, slices are designed to grow and shrink as needed. A slice is essentially a reference to a portion of an array, and it allows you to work with a subset of the array without copying the data. This makes slices very efficient in terms of memory and performance.

Key Characteristics of Slices:

1. **Dynamic size**: Unlike arrays, slices can grow and shrink dynamically.
2. **Backed by arrays**: Internally, slices are backed by arrays. A slice does not store its data but refers to an array, which allows multiple slices to reference the same array.
3. **Capacity and length**: A slice has both a **length** (the number of elements it currently holds) and a **capacity** (the maximum number of elements it can hold before needing to allocate a new array).

Declaring and Initializing a Slice

Slices are typically created using the make() function, or they can be derived from existing arrays or other slices.

249

1. Declaring a Slice with make()

The make() function in Go is used to create slices with a specified length and capacity. The syntax is:

go

Copy

```
slice := make([]type, length, capacity)
```

- **type**: The type of elements the slice will hold (e.g., int, string).
- **length**: The number of elements the slice initially holds.
- **capacity**: The total number of elements the slice can hold before needing to allocate a new array. If you omit the capacity, it will be the same as the length.

Example 1: Declaring a Slice with make()

go

Copy

```
package main

import "fmt"

func main() {
    // Create a slice of integers with length 5 and capacity 10
    slice := make([]int, 5, 10)

    fmt.Println("Slice:", slice)        // Output: Slice: [0 0 0 0 0]
    fmt.Println("Length:", len(slice)) // Output: Length: 5
```

250

```go
fmt.Println("Capacity:", cap(slice)) // Output: Capacity: 10
}
```

In this example:

- We create a slice of integers with a length of 5 and a capacity of 10. Initially, the slice contains 5 zeros (0), as int is the default type for the slice.
- The len() function returns the length of the slice (5), and cap() returns its capacity (10).

2. Creating a Slice from an Existing Array

You can also create a slice from an existing array by specifying a **range** of indices. The slice does not copy the elements; instead, it references the portion of the original array.

Example 2: Slicing an Array

go

Copy

```go
package main

import "fmt"

func main() {
    arr := [6]int{10, 20, 30, 40, 50, 60}

    // Create a slice from the array
    slice := arr[1:4] // Slice from index 1 to 3 (not including index 4)
```

251

```go
fmt.Println("Array:", arr)      // Output: Array: [10 20 30 40 50 60]

fmt.Println("Slice:", slice)    // Output: Slice: [20 30 40]

fmt.Println("Length of slice:", len(slice)) // Output: Length of slice: 3

}
```

In this example:

- The slice slice contains the elements from index 1 to 3 of the arr array. It references the same underlying array but only includes a subset of the elements.
- Modifying the slice will affect the original array, as both the slice and the array share the same underlying data.

3. Creating a Slice from Another Slice

Slices can also be created from other slices. This is especially useful when you want to share data between slices without copying it.

Example 3: Slicing a Slice

go

Copy

```go
package main

import "fmt"

func main() {
    original := []int{1, 2, 3, 4, 5, 6}

    // Create a slice from the original slice
```

252

```go
newSlice := original[2:5] // Slice from index 2 to 4 (not including index 5)

fmt.Println("Original slice:", original) // Output: Original slice: [1 2 3 4 5 6]

fmt.Println("New slice:", newSlice)    // Output: New slice: [3 4 5]
}
```

In this example:

- newSlice is created by slicing the original slice from index 2 to 4. This operation does not create a new copy of the underlying array, so newSlice and original share the same memory.
- Modifying an element in newSlice will also modify the corresponding element in original, since they refer to the same underlying data.

Working with Slices

Once you have a slice, you can perform a variety of operations such as **appending elements**, **accessing elements**, **modifying elements**, and **slicing** to create new sub-slices.

1. Accessing and Modifying Slice Elements

You can access and modify elements in a slice using the same approach as arrays by specifying the index inside square brackets [].

Example 4: Modifying Slice Elements

go

Copy

```
package main
```

```go
import "fmt"

func main() {
    slice := []int{1, 2, 3, 4, 5}

    // Modifying an element in the slice
    slice[2] = 10

    fmt.Println("Modified Slice:", slice) // Output: Modified Slice: [1 2 10 4 5]
}
```

Here:

- We modify the element at index 2 of the slice, changing its value from 3 to 10.

2. Appending to a Slice

Slices in Go are **dynamic**, so you can append elements to them using the append() function. The append() function returns a new slice that contains the original slice along with the new element(s).

Example 5: Appending to a Slice

go

Copy

```go
package main

import "fmt"
```

```go
func main() {

    slice := []int{1, 2, 3}


    // Append a single element to the slice

    slice = append(slice, 4)


    // Append multiple elements to the slice

    slice = append(slice, 5, 6, 7)


    fmt.Println("Appended Slice:", slice) // Output: Appended Slice: [1 2 3 4 5 6 7]

}
```

In this example:

- We append a single element (4) and multiple elements (5, 6, 7) to the slice slice.
- The append() function creates a new slice with the added elements, and we reassign it back to the slice variable.

3. Slicing a Slice

You can also create sub-slices from an existing slice by specifying a range of indices. The resulting slice will reference the same underlying array as the original slice.

Example 6: Slicing a Slice

go

Copy

package main

```go
import "fmt"

func main() {
    slice := []int{10, 20, 30, 40, 50, 60}

    // Create a sub-slice from the original slice
    subSlice := slice[1:4] // Slice from index 1 to 3 (not including index 4)

    fmt.Println("Original Slice:", slice) // Output: Original Slice: [10 20 30 40 50 60]
    fmt.Println("Sub-Slice:", subSlice)   // Output: Sub-Slice: [20 30 40]
}
```

In this example:

- The sub-slice subSlice contains elements from the slice array starting from index 1 up to (but not including) index 4.

Capacity of a Slice

Slices have a **capacity**, which is the maximum number of elements that the slice can hold before a new array must be allocated. You can retrieve the **capacity** of a slice using the cap() function.

Example 7: Slice Capacity

go

Copy

```go
package main

import "fmt"

func main() {
    slice := make([]int, 3, 5) // Slice with length 3 and capacity 5

    fmt.Println("Length:", len(slice))   // Output: Length: 3
    fmt.Println("Capacity:", cap(slice)) // Output: Capacity: 5
}
```

In this example:

- The slice is created with a length of 3 and a capacity of 5.
- We use len() to get the length (3), and cap() to get the capacity (5).

How Capacity Changes with append()

If you append more elements to a slice than it can hold (i.e., more than its capacity), Go will automatically **resize** the slice, doubling its capacity, and create a new underlying array. The original slice will then reference the new array.

Example 8: Changing Capacity with append()

go

Copy

```go
package main

import "fmt"

func main() {
    slice := make([]int, 2, 3) // Slice with length 2 and capacity 3

    fmt.Println("Before append:")
    fmt.Println("Length:", len(slice))   // Output: Length: 2
    fmt.Println("Capacity:", cap(slice)) // Output: Capacity: 3

    slice = append(slice, 4, 5)

    fmt.Println("After append:")
    fmt.Println("Length:", len(slice))   // Output: Length: 5
    fmt.Println("Capacity:", cap(slice)) // Output: Capacity: 6
}
```

In this example:

- Initially, the slice has a capacity of 3, but after appending more elements, its capacity increases to 6.

Slices in Go offer a more flexible and powerful alternative to arrays. They allow for dynamic sizing, efficient memory management, and easy manipulation of data. Here's a summary of what we covered:

- **Slices vs. Arrays**: Unlike arrays, slices are dynamic and can grow or shrink as needed.
- **Declaring and Initializing Slices**: Slices can be created using make(), from arrays, or by directly initializing them.
- **Working with Slices**: You can access, modify, and append to slices, making them very versatile for handling collections of data.
- **Capacity and Length**: Slices have both a **length** and a **capacity**, and they can grow beyond their initial capacity when needed.

Slices are the most commonly used data structure in Go, and understanding how to use them efficiently will allow you to write more flexible and powerful programs. In the next section, we will explore **maps**, another important data structure in Go, used for storing key-value pairs.

Understanding Slice Length and Capacity

In Go, slices have two important properties: **length** and **capacity**. These properties determine how much data a slice can hold and how it grows dynamically. Understanding the difference between length and capacity is essential when working with slices to manage memory effectively.

Slice Length

The **length** of a slice refers to the number of elements it currently holds. It is the count of elements that the slice has, and it can be accessed using the built-in len() function.

Syntax for Slice Length:

go

Copy

```
len(slice)
```

The len() function returns the number of elements in the slice, which corresponds to the **length** of the slice.

Example: Slice Length

go

Copy

```
package main

import "fmt"

func main() {
    slice := []int{1, 2, 3, 4, 5}

    // Get the length of the slice
    fmt.Println("Length of slice:", len(slice)) // Output: Length of slice: 5
}
```

In this example:

- The slice slice contains 5 elements, so len(slice) returns 5, indicating the length of the slice.

Slice Capacity

The **capacity** of a slice refers to the maximum number of elements it can hold before it needs to allocate a new underlying array. This value is important when appending to a slice, as it determines when Go will allocate a larger array.

The capacity of a slice can be accessed using the built-in cap() function.

Syntax for Slice Capacity:

go

Copy

```
cap(slice)
```

The cap() function returns the **capacity** of the slice, i.e., how much space is allocated for the slice in memory. The capacity will typically be at least as large as the length, but may be greater, especially if the slice was created with an initial capacity.

Example: Slice Capacity

go

Copy

```
package main

import "fmt"
```

```
func main() {

    slice := make([]int, 3, 5) // Create a slice with length 3 and capacity 5


    fmt.Println("Length of slice:", len(slice))   // Output: Length of slice: 3

    fmt.Println("Capacity of slice:", cap(slice)) // Output: Capacity of slice: 5

}
```

In this example:

- The slice slice is created with a **length** of 3 and a **capacity** of 5. The cap(slice) function returns 5, which indicates that the slice can hold up to 5 elements before it needs to be reallocated.

How Capacity Changes

If you append more elements to a slice than it can hold, Go will automatically **resize** the underlying array to accommodate more elements. The new capacity will often be doubled when a slice exceeds its current capacity, which allows Go to manage memory efficiently.

Creating, Modifying, and Appending to Slices

Now that we have a good understanding of **slice length** and **capacity**, let's explore how to **create**, **modify**, and **append** to slices. These are common operations that you will frequently perform when working with slices in Go.

Creating Slices

Slices in Go can be created in several ways:

1. **Using make()**: The make() function allows you to create a slice with a specified length and capacity.
2. **From an existing array**: You can create a slice from an array by specifying a range of indices.
3. **Using a literal**: You can initialize a slice with a list of values using a slice literal.

Example 1: Creating a Slice with make()

go

Copy

```go
package main

import "fmt"

func main() {
    // Create a slice with length 3 and capacity 5
    slice := make([]int, 3, 5)

    fmt.Println("Slice:", slice)         // Output: Slice: [0 0 0]
    fmt.Println("Length:", len(slice)) // Output: Length: 3
    fmt.Println("Capacity:", cap(slice)) // Output: Capacity: 5
}
```

Example 2: Creating a Slice from an Array

go

Copy

```go
package main

import "fmt"

func main() {
    // Create an array and slice it
    arr := [5]int{1, 2, 3, 4, 5}
    slice := arr[1:4] // Slice from index 1 to 3 (not including index 4)

    fmt.Println("Array:", arr)      // Output: Array: [1 2 3 4 5]
    fmt.Println("Slice:", slice)    // Output: Slice: [2 3 4]
}
```

Example 3: Creating a Slice Using a Literal

go

Copy

```go
package main

import "fmt"
```

```go
func main() {

    // Create a slice using a literal

    slice := []int{10, 20, 30}


    fmt.Println("Slice:", slice) // Output: Slice: [10 20 30]

}
```

Modifying Slice Elements

Like arrays, slices in Go are **mutable**, meaning you can modify their elements using the index notation.

Example 4: Modifying Slice Elements

go

Copy

```go
package main


import "fmt"


func main() {

    slice := []int{10, 20, 30}


    // Modify the second element
```

```
slice[1] = 25

fmt.Println("Modified Slice:", slice) // Output: Modified Slice: [10 25 30]
}
```

In this example:

- We modify the second element of the slice (index 1) from 20 to 25.

Appending to Slices

One of the most powerful features of slices in Go is the ability to **append** elements to them. You can use the append() function to add one or more elements to the end of a slice. If the slice has enough capacity to hold the new elements, it will simply add them; otherwise, Go will allocate a new slice with a larger underlying array.

The append() function returns a **new slice** that includes the original elements plus the new ones.

Syntax of append()

go

Copy

```
slice = append(slice, element1, element2, ...)
```

- The append() function adds the specified elements to the end of the slice and returns the updated slice.
- If the slice doesn't have enough capacity, append() will automatically allocate a new array and update the slice with the new capacity.

Example 5: Appending to a Slice

go

Copy

```go
package main

import "fmt"

func main() {
    slice := []int{1, 2, 3}

    // Append a single element to the slice
    slice = append(slice, 4)

    // Append multiple elements to the slice
    slice = append(slice, 5, 6)

    fmt.Println("Appended Slice:", slice) // Output: Appended Slice: [1 2 3 4 5 6]
}
```

In this example:

- We append 4 to the slice, followed by 5 and 6. Each time we call append(), the slice is updated.

267

Example 6: Appending to a Slice and Increasing Its Capacity

When appending more elements than a slice's current capacity can handle, Go will automatically resize the underlying array to accommodate the new elements. The capacity typically doubles when this happens.

go

Copy

```go
package main

import "fmt"

func main() {
    slice := make([]int, 3, 5) // Create a slice with length 3 and capacity 5

    fmt.Println("Before append:")
    fmt.Println("Length:", len(slice))   // Output: Length: 3
    fmt.Println("Capacity:", cap(slice)) // Output: Capacity: 5

    // Append elements to the slice
    slice = append(slice, 4, 5, 6)

    fmt.Println("After append:")
    fmt.Println("Length:", len(slice))   // Output: Length: 6
    fmt.Println("Capacity:", cap(slice)) // Output: Capacity: 10
```

```
}
```

In this example:

- We start with a slice of length 3 and capacity 5.
- After appending 3 more elements, the slice grows, and Go reallocates it to a new underlying array with a capacity of 10.

In this section, we've explored **slices** in Go, which are dynamic and flexible alternatives to arrays. Here's a recap of the key concepts we covered:

- **Slices vs. Arrays**: Slices are dynamically sized and more flexible than arrays, allowing for more efficient memory usage and easier manipulation.
- **Length and Capacity**: The **length** of a slice refers to the number of elements it holds, while the **capacity** refers to how much memory is allocated to hold elements before a reallocation is needed.
- **Creating Slices**: Slices can be created using make(), from existing arrays, or by using a slice literal.
- **Modifying and Appending**: Slices can be modified by accessing elements via indices, and new elements can be appended to slices using the append() function.
- **Resizing Slices**: When appending more elements than a slice's capacity can handle, Go automatically resizes the slice and allocates more memory.

Slices are a powerful feature of Go, and understanding how to use them effectively will enable you to write more efficient and flexible programs. In the next section, we will delve into **maps**, another important data structure in Go that allows you to store key-value pairs.

6.3. Maps: Storing Data with Key-Value Pairs

Maps in Go provide a powerful and efficient way to store data in the form of **key-value pairs**. They allow you to quickly look up, insert, and modify data based on a unique key, making them essential for various use cases such as caching, counting occurrences, and representing relationships between entities.

In this section, we'll explore **maps** in Go, how to **declare**, **initialize**, **access**, and **modify** elements in a map, and discuss how maps differ from slices and arrays.

Declaring and Initializing Maps

In Go, a map is an unordered collection of key-value pairs. You can declare and initialize a map using the make() function or by using a map literal.

1. Declaring a Map Using make()

You can declare an empty map using the make() function. The make() function takes two arguments: the map's key type and value type.

The general syntax is:

go

Copy

```
make(map[keyType]valueType)
```

You can also specify the **initial capacity** of the map, which is the number of key-value pairs it can initially hold before needing to resize.

Example 1: Declaring a Map Using make()

go

Copy

```
package main


import "fmt"
```

```go
func main() {

    // Declaring a map with string keys and integer values

    studentScores := make(map[string]int)


    studentScores["Alice"] = 85

    studentScores["Bob"] = 92

    studentScores["Charlie"] = 78


    fmt.Println(studentScores) // Output: map[Alice:85 Bob:92 Charlie:78]

}
```

In this example:

- We declare a map studentScores where the keys are of type string (names of students) and the values are of type int (student scores).
- We add three key-value pairs to the map and print it.

2. Declaring a Map Using a Map Literal

Maps can also be initialized with a **map literal**, where you define both the keys and values at the time of declaration.

Example 2: Initializing a Map with a Map Literal

go

Copy

```go
package main
```

```go
import "fmt"

func main() {
    // Initializing a map using a map literal
    studentScores := map[string]int{
        "Alice": 85,
        "Bob":   92,
        "Charlie": 78,
    }

    fmt.Println(studentScores) // Output: map[Alice:85 Bob:92 Charlie:78]
}
```

In this example:

- We initialize the studentScores map with three key-value pairs using a map literal.
- The map is immediately ready for use with the predefined key-value pairs.

Accessing and Modifying Map Elements

Maps allow for **efficient** access to elements using their keys. You can retrieve a value by using the key in the map, and you can also modify existing values or add new key-value pairs.

1. Accessing Map Elements

To access an element in a map, use the key inside square brackets [].

Example 3: Accessing Elements in a Map

go

Copy

```go
package main

import "fmt"

func main() {
    studentScores := map[string]int{
        "Alice": 85,
        "Bob":   92,
        "Charlie": 78,
    }

    // Accessing a value by its key
    fmt.Println("Bob's score:", studentScores["Bob"]) // Output: Bob's score: 92

    // Accessing a non-existent key (will return 0 for int type)
    fmt.Println("Dave's score:", studentScores["Dave"]) // Output: Dave's score: 0
}
```

In this example:

- We access Bob's score using the key "Bob". The value 92 is returned.
- When we attempt to access a non-existent key ("Dave"), Go returns the **zero value** for the value type (0 for integers), indicating that the key doesn't exist in the map.

2. Modifying Map Elements

Maps are **mutable**, meaning you can modify existing elements by assigning a new value to an existing key.

Example 4: Modifying Map Elements

go

Copy

```go
package main

import "fmt"

func main() {
    studentScores := map[string]int{
        "Alice": 85,
        "Bob":   92,
        "Charlie": 78,
    }

    // Modifying a value in the map
    studentScores["Alice"] = 90
```

        fmt.Println("Updated Scores:", studentScores) // Output: Updated Scores: map[Alice:90 Bob:92 Charlie:78]

}

In this example:

- We modify Alice's score from 85 to 90 by assigning a new value to the key "Alice".
- The updated map is then printed.

3. Adding New Elements to a Map

You can also **add new key-value pairs** to a map simply by assigning a value to a key that doesn't exist yet.

Example 5: Adding New Key-Value Pairs

go

Copy

```go
package main

import "fmt"

func main() {
    studentScores := map[string]int{
        "Alice": 85,
        "Bob":   92,
    }
}
```

```go
// Adding a new key-value pair
studentScores["Charlie"] = 78


    fmt.Println("Updated Scores:", studentScores) // Output: Updated Scores:
map[Alice:85 Bob:92 Charlie:78]

}
```

In this example:

- We add a new key-value pair for "Charlie" with a score of 78.
- The map is updated with the new entry, and the updated map is printed.

Deleting Elements from a Map

Maps in Go also allow you to **delete** elements using the built-in delete() function. This function takes two arguments: the map and the key of the element to be deleted.

1. Deleting Elements from a Map

Syntax:

go

Copy

```go
delete(map, key)
```

This deletes the key-value pair with the specified key from the map.

Example 6: Deleting Elements from a Map

go

Copy

```go
package main

import "fmt"

func main() {
    studentScores := map[string]int{
        "Alice": 85,
        "Bob":   92,
        "Charlie": 78,
    }

    // Deleting an element from the map
    delete(studentScores, "Bob")

    fmt.Println("Updated Scores:", studentScores) // Output: Updated Scores: map[Alice:85 Charlie:78]
}
```

In this example:

- We use the delete() function to remove the key-value pair for "Bob".

277

- The map is updated, and "Bob" is no longer present in the map.

Checking if a Key Exists in a Map

When you access a map with a key that may not exist, Go will return the zero value for the value type. However, you can also **check if a key exists** by using the second return value from the map lookup.

Syntax for Checking Key Existence:

go

Copy

```
value, ok := map[key]
```

- **value**: The value associated with the key.
- **ok**: A boolean indicating whether the key exists in the map (true if the key exists, false otherwise).

Example 7: Checking Key Existence

go

Copy

```
package main

import "fmt"

func main() {
    studentScores := map[string]int{
```

```go
    "Alice": 85,

    "Bob":  92,

}


// Checking if a key exists

score, ok := studentScores["Charlie"]

if ok {

    fmt.Println("Charlie's score:", score)

} else {

    fmt.Println("Charlie not found")

}


// Checking for an existing key

score, ok = studentScores["Bob"]

if ok {

    fmt.Println("Bob's score:", score) // Output: Bob's score: 92

}

}
```

In this example:

- We first check if "Charlie" exists in the map using the second return value ok. Since "Charlie" is not in the map, ok will be false.
- We then check for "Bob", which exists in the map, and print the score.

In this section, we explored **maps** in Go, which are one of the most powerful data structures for storing and working with key-value pairs. Here's a summary of the key concepts covered:

- **Declaring and Initializing Maps**: You can declare maps using make() or initialize them directly with map literals.
- **Accessing and Modifying Map Elements**: You can access elements using keys and modify them by assigning new values.
- **Adding and Deleting Elements**: New key-value pairs can be added by simple assignment, and elements can be deleted using the delete() function.
- **Checking Key Existence**: Go allows you to check if a key exists in a map using the second return value from a map lookup.

Maps are essential for handling associative data in Go and are widely used for tasks like caching, counting occurrences, and representing relationships between data. Understanding how to use maps effectively will help you write more efficient and readable code

Iterating Through Maps and Use Cases for Maps in Go

In Go, maps are unordered collections of key-value pairs. While the order of the elements in a map is not guaranteed, Go provides a simple and efficient way to **iterate through the elements** of a map. In this section, we will explore how to iterate through a map and examine common **use cases** for maps in Go programs.

Iterating Through Maps

Go provides the for loop with **range** to iterate over the elements in a map. When iterating over a map, the **range** loop returns two values for each element:

1. **Key**: The key in the current key-value pair.
2. **Value**: The value associated with the current key.

Since the order of elements in a map is not guaranteed, each iteration may visit elements in a different order every time the program runs.

Syntax for Iterating Through a Map

go

Copy

```go
for key, value := range map {
    // Code to process each key-value pair
}
```

- **key**: The key of the current key-value pair.
- **value**: The value of the current key-value pair.

Example 1: Basic Iteration Over a Map

go

Copy

```go
package main

import "fmt"

func main() {
    studentScores := map[string]int{
        "Alice": 85,
        "Bob":   92,
        "Charlie": 78,
    }
```

```go
    // Iterating through the map

    for student, score := range studentScores {

        fmt.Printf("%s's score: %d\n", student, score)

    }

}
```

Example Output:

pgsql

Copy

Alice's score: 85

Bob's score: 92

Charlie's score: 78

In this example:

- We use range to iterate through the studentScores map.
- For each iteration, we print the student (key) and their score (value).
- The order of the output may vary since maps are unordered collections.

Example 2: Iterating Through Maps and Only Using Keys or Values

If you need only the **keys** or the **values** from a map, you can ignore the other value by using the blank identifier _.

Iterating Through Keys Only:

go

Copy

```go
package main
```

```go
import "fmt"

func main() {
    studentScores := map[string]int{
        "Alice": 85,
        "Bob":   92,
        "Charlie": 78,
    }

    // Iterating through map keys only
    for student := range studentScores {
        fmt.Println("Student:", student)
    }
}
```

Iterating Through Values Only:

go

Copy

```go
package main

import "fmt"
```

```go
func main() {

    studentScores := map[string]int{

        "Alice": 85,

        "Bob":   92,

        "Charlie": 78,

    }


    // Iterating through map values only

    for _, score := range studentScores {

        fmt.Println("Score:", score)

    }

}
```

In both cases, we use range to loop through the map, but we only capture the values we need (keys or values) by using _ for the other value.

Use Cases for Maps in Go

Maps are incredibly useful in Go, especially when you need to store, retrieve, and manipulate data based on a unique key. Here are some common **use cases** for maps in Go:

---

1. Counting Occurrences of Elements

Maps are ideal for counting the frequency of elements in a dataset, such as counting words in a text, occurrences of numbers, or even tallying votes.

Example 3: Word Frequency Counter

go

Copy

```go
package main

import "fmt"

func main() {
    text := "hello world hello hello go"

    wordCount := make(map[string]int)

    // Split the text into words and count occurrences
    words := []string{"hello", "world", "hello", "hello", "go"}
    for _, word := range words {
        wordCount[word]++
    }

    // Print the word frequencies
    for word, count := range wordCount {
        fmt.Printf("Word: %s, Count: %d\n", word, count)
    }
```

}

Example Output:

yaml

Copy

```
Word: hello, Count: 3

Word: world, Count: 1

Word: go, Count: 1
```

In this example:

- We create a map wordCount where the key is the word and the value is the count of how many times it appears.
- As we iterate over the words, we increment the count for each word in the map.
- The result shows how many times each word appears in the text.

---

2. Caching and Memoization

Maps are commonly used for **caching** and **memoization** in Go programs. This is particularly useful when the same computation is performed repeatedly. Storing the result of expensive function calls in a map allows you to quickly return the cached result for subsequent calls with the same input.

Example 4: Memoization with Maps

go

Copy

```
package main
```

```go
import "fmt"

// Function to compute the nth Fibonacci number using memoization
func fibonacci(n int, memo map[int]int) int {
    if n <= 1 {
        return n
    }
    if result, exists := memo[n]; exists {
        return result
    }
    result := fibonacci(n-1, memo) + fibonacci(n-2, memo)
    memo[n] = result // Store the result in the map
    return result
}

func main() {
    memo := make(map[int]int)
    fmt.Println("Fibonacci(10):", fibonacci(10, memo)) // Output: Fibonacci(10): 55
}
```

In this example:

- We calculate the nth Fibonacci number using **memoization** to store previously computed results in a map.

- By caching results in the memo map, we avoid redundant calculations and improve performance, especially for larger values of n.

---

3. Storing Configuration Settings

Maps are useful for storing configuration settings, where the keys represent setting names (e.g., "host", "port") and the values represent the corresponding values (e.g., "localhost", 8080). This is especially helpful for managing application settings in a structured way.

Example 5: Storing Configuration Settings

go

Copy

```go
package main

import "fmt"

func main() {
    config := map[string]string{
        "host": "localhost",
        "port": "8080",
        "env": "development",
    }

    // Accessing configuration settings
    fmt.Println("Host:", config["host"]) // Output: Host: localhost
```

```go
fmt.Println("Port:", config["port"]) // Output: Port: 8080

fmt.Println("Environment:", config["env"]) // Output: Environment: development
}
```

In this example:

- We use a map to store the configuration settings for a server.
- The map allows easy access to different settings by using keys, making it straightforward to manage and update configuration values.

---

4. Mapping Relationships Between Entities

Maps are often used to represent relationships between different entities. For instance, you can use a map to represent a mapping between **student IDs** and **student names**, or between **countries** and their respective **capital cities**.

Example 6: Mapping Student IDs to Names

go

Copy

```go
package main

import "fmt"

func main() {
    studentIDs := map[int]string{
        101: "Alice",
        102: "Bob",
```

```go
        103: "Charlie",

    }


    // Accessing a student's name using their ID

    studentID := 102

    if name, exists := studentIDs[studentID]; exists {

        fmt.Printf("Student with ID %d: %s\n", studentID, name) // Output: Student with ID 102: Bob

    } else {

        fmt.Println("Student not found")

    }

}
```

In this example:

- The map studentIDs maps **student IDs** (integers) to **student names** (strings).
- We retrieve the student's name using their ID and print it, demonstrating how maps can represent relationships between different entities.

---

5. Storing Sets of Unique Items

While Go doesn't have a built-in set data structure, you can use **maps** to mimic the behavior of a set by storing keys in the map and using a dummy value (e.g., true) to indicate the presence of an item. This approach allows you to quickly check for the existence of an item.

Example 7: Using Maps to Implement a Set

go

Copy

```go
package main

import "fmt"

func main() {
    set := make(map[string]bool)

    // Adding elements to the set
    set["apple"] = true
    set["banana"] = true
    set["orange"] = true

    // Checking if an element exists in the set
    if _, exists := set["banana"]; exists {
        fmt.Println("Banana is in the set") // Output: Banana is in the set
    }

    // Removing an element from the set
    delete(set, "apple")
```

```
// Checking if an element exists after deletion

if _, exists := set["apple"]; !exists {

    fmt.Println("Apple is no longer in the set") // Output: Apple is no longer in the set

  }

}
```

In this example:

- We use a **map** with string keys and bool values to implement a set of unique fruits.
- We add elements, check for the existence of items, and remove elements using the delete() function.

In this section, we explored **maps** in Go, which are essential for working with key-value pairs and are widely used in Go programs. Here's a summary of the key concepts covered:

- **Iterating Through Maps**: We used the for range loop to iterate through a map and access each key-value pair. We also showed how to iterate through just keys or values.
- **Use Cases for Maps**: We explored several common use cases for maps in Go, including:
  - Counting occurrences (e.g., word frequency counter).
  - Memoization and caching to store computed results.
  - Storing configuration settings.
  - Mapping relationships between entities.
  - Using maps to simulate sets of unique items.

Maps are incredibly versatile and efficient, making them one of the most powerful data structures in Go.

292

6.4. Practical Exercises with Arrays, Slices, and Maps

In this section, we will go through several practical exercises that will help you solidify your understanding of **arrays**, **slices**, and **maps**. These exercises will range from simple tasks to more complex scenarios where you'll build projects using these data structures. By working through these exercises, you will gain hands-on experience and learn how to apply these fundamental concepts in real-world situations.

Exercise 1: Array Manipulation – Sum and Average of Numbers

In this exercise, we will work with arrays to calculate the **sum** and **average** of a set of numbers. You will create an array of integers, loop through it to calculate the sum, and then compute the average.

Task:

1. Create an array of integers.
2. Loop through the array to calculate the sum of all elements.
3. Calculate the average by dividing the sum by the length of the array.

Solution:

go

Copy

```
package main

import "fmt"

func main() {
    numbers := [5]int{10, 20, 30, 40, 50}

    // Calculate the sum of the array elements
```

```go
sum := 0

for _, num := range numbers {

    sum += num

}


// Calculate the average

average := float64(sum) / float64(len(numbers))


fmt.Println("Sum:", sum)          // Output: Sum: 150

fmt.Println("Average:", average)   // Output: Average: 30

}
```

In this example:

- We calculate the **sum** of all the elements in the numbers array using a loop.
- We then compute the **average** by dividing the sum by the length of the array.

Exercise 2: Slice Manipulation – Adding and Removing Elements

In this exercise, you will work with **slices** to dynamically add and remove elements. You will first create a slice of integers, then append new values to it, and finally remove an element from the middle.

Task:

1. Create a slice of integers.
2. Append two new integers to the slice.
3. Remove the middle element of the slice.

Solution:

go

Copy

```go
package main

import "fmt"

func main() {
    // Create a slice of integers
    numbers := []int{10, 20, 30, 40, 50}

    // Append elements to the slice
    numbers = append(numbers, 60, 70)

    fmt.Println("Slice after appending:", numbers) // Output: Slice after appending: [10 20 30 40 50 60 70]

    // Remove the middle element (index 3)
    numbers = append(numbers[:3], numbers[4:]...)

    fmt.Println("Slice after removing middle element:", numbers) // Output: Slice after removing middle element: [10 20 30 50 60 70]
}
```

In this example:

- We append two new elements (60 and 70) to the slice.
- We remove the middle element (index 3), which in this case is 40, by using the append() function to concatenate the slices before and after the element.

Exercise 3: Map Manipulation – Word Frequency Counter

In this exercise, we will use a **map** to count the frequency of words in a string. We will create a map where the keys are the words, and the values are the number of times each word appears.

Task:

1. Create a map to store word frequencies.
2. Loop through a string and update the map to count how often each word appears.
3. Print the frequency of each word.

Solution:

go

Copy

```go
package main

import "fmt"

import "strings"

func main() {
    text := "hello world hello go go go"
```

```go
	// Create a map to store word frequencies
	wordCount := make(map[string]int)

	// Split the text into words and count occurrences
	words := strings.Split(text, " ")
	for _, word := range words {
		wordCount[word]++
	}

	// Print the word frequencies
	for word, count := range wordCount {
		fmt.Printf("Word: %s, Count: %d\n", word, count)
	}
}
```

Example Output:

yaml

Copy

```
Word: hello, Count: 2

Word: world, Count: 1

Word: go, Count: 3
```

In this example:

- We use the strings.Split() function to split the text into words.
- We then use a map wordCount to store the frequency of each word by incrementing the count for each occurrence.
- Finally, we print the frequency of each word.

Exercise 4: Combining Arrays, Slices, and Maps – Student Grades System

In this exercise, we will build a simple student grading system that uses arrays, slices, and maps. The system will store student names and their corresponding grades, and we will calculate their average grade.

Task:

1. Create an array of student names.
2. Create a slice of integers representing grades for each student.
3. Use a map to associate each student's name with their grades.
4. Calculate the average grade for each student.

Solution:

go

Copy

```
package main


import "fmt"


func main() {
    // Declare an array of student names
    students := [3]string{"Alice", "Bob", "Charlie"}
```

```go
// Declare a slice of slices to store grades
grades := [][]int{
    {85, 90, 78}, // Alice's grades
    {92, 88, 79}, // Bob's grades
    {75, 80, 95}, // Charlie's grades
}

// Create a map to store students and their average grade
studentGrades := make(map[string]float64)

// Calculate the average grade for each student
for i, student := range students {
    total := 0
    for _, grade := range grades[i] {
        total += grade
    }
    average := float64(total) / float64(len(grades[i]))
    studentGrades[student] = average
}

// Print the average grades for each student
for student, avg := range studentGrades {
```

```
        fmt.Printf("%s's average grade: %.2f\n", student, avg)

    }

}
```

Example Output:

pgsql

Copy

Alice's average grade: 84.33

Bob's average grade: 86.33

Charlie's average grade: 83.33

In this example:

- We create an array students containing student names.
- We create a slice grades that holds slices of integers for each student's grades.
- We then calculate the average grade for each student and store the result in a map called studentGrades.
- Finally, we print each student's name along with their average grade.

Building Projects Using Arrays, Slices, and Maps

Now that we've worked through several exercises, let's look at how you can use arrays, slices, and maps in more practical projects. Below are two example projects that demonstrate the power and flexibility of these data structures in Go.

Project 1: Personal Contact Management System

In this project, we will build a simple **contact management system** that allows users to store and manage contact details. We will use a **map** to store contact information where the key is the contact name and the value is a struct containing the phone number and email address.

Task:

1. Use a map to store contacts with keys as names and values as contact details (phone number and email).
2. Implement functionality to add a new contact, update an existing contact, and delete a contact.
3. Display all contacts in the system.

Solution Outline:

- Use a map to store each contact's details (name, phone, email).
- Create a menu to allow users to add, update, delete, or view contacts.
- Use structs to store detailed contact information.

Project 2: Inventory Management System

In this project, we will build an **inventory management system** that allows users to manage a list of products in a store. Each product will have a unique ID, a name, a quantity, and a price.

Task:

1. Use an **array** to store product names.
2. Use a **slice** to store the quantities of the products.
3. Use a **map** to associate product IDs with their details (name, quantity, and price).
4. Implement functionality to add new products, update quantities, and calculate total inventory value.

Solution Outline:

- Use a map to associate each product ID with its details, such as quantity and price.

- Implement functions to add new products, update inventory, and calculate total value of all products.
- Use slices to dynamically store quantities and allow for efficient updates.

In this section, we worked through several **practical exercises** involving **arrays, slices,** and **maps,** covering fundamental operations like accessing, modifying, and iterating through these data structures. We also explored how to build simple projects, such as a **contact management system** and an **inventory management system,** using arrays, slices, and maps.

By practicing these exercises and applying the concepts to real-world scenarios, you'll become proficient in using these data structures effectively in your Go programs. Arrays, slices, and maps are key components of Go, and understanding how to use them will help you write more efficient and maintainable code.

Chapter 7: Error Handling and Debugging

7.1. Handling Errors in Go

In any programming language, **error handling** is one of the most critical aspects of writing robust and maintainable code. Go's approach to error handling is **simple**, **explicit**, and **predictable**, making it easier to manage errors in a structured manner. Unlike some other languages that use exceptions, Go handles errors through a distinct type: the error type.

In this section, we will explore Go's error handling mechanism, focusing on the error type, why it's important, and how to handle errors efficiently in Go programs. Understanding this fundamental concept will enable you to write code that gracefully handles runtime issues and provides meaningful feedback to users or developers.

Go's Error Type and Why It's Important

In Go, errors are values of a specific type—error. An error in Go is an interface type, which has a single method, Error() string, that returns a string representation of the error. This approach makes error handling explicit and forces developers to handle errors rather than ignoring them. It also avoids the complexity of exceptions, making Go's error handling predictable and easy to follow.

The error Type in Go

The error type is defined as:

```go
Copy
type error interface {
    Error() string
}
```

This means that **any type that implements the** Error() **method** can be treated as an error in Go. This design allows for flexibility, as custom error types can easily be created by defining the Error() method.

Why Go Uses the error Type

1. **Simplicity**: Go's error handling is simple and relies on returning error values instead of using exception mechanisms, making it straightforward to understand and manage errors.
2. **Explicitness**: In Go, errors must be checked explicitly. When a function returns an error, the programmer must handle it. This approach reduces the likelihood of unhandled exceptions and improves code reliability.
3. **Consistency**: The error type provides a consistent way of handling errors across the entire language, whether you're working with built-in errors or custom ones.

How Errors are Handled in Go

The Go approach to error handling revolves around **returning error values** from functions that might encounter issues. Instead of throwing exceptions like in many other languages, Go expects the caller to check the error value and decide how to proceed.

Returning Errors from Functions

In Go, functions that can result in errors typically return an error type as the last return value. Here's the general syntax for functions that return an error:

go
Copy
```go
func functionName() (returnType, error)
```

The function returns both a value of the desired type and an error. The caller of the function is responsible for checking the error and handling it appropriately.

Example: Returning and Handling an Error

go
Copy
```go
package main

import (
    "fmt"
```

```go
    "errors"
)

// Function that returns an error
func divide(a, b int) (int, error) {
    if b == 0 {
        return 0, errors.New("division by zero")
    }
    return a / b, nil
}

func main() {
    // Call the divide function
    result, err := divide(10, 0)

    // Handle the error
    if err != nil {
        fmt.Println("Error:", err)  // Output: Error: division by zero
        return
    }

    fmt.Println("Result:", result)
}
```

In this example:

- The divide function returns two values: the result of the division and an error value. If the second argument b is zero, the function returns an error using errors.New().
- In the main function, we call divide(10, 0). Since dividing by zero is not allowed, the err value will be non-nil, and we handle the error by printing the error message and returning early.

The Importance of Explicit Error Handling

In Go, **error checking is explicit** and must be done by the programmer. This is important because it ensures that errors don't go unnoticed, which could lead to unexpected behaviors in a program. By forcing the programmer to handle errors, Go encourages writing more predictable and reliable code.

305

Example: Ignoring Errors (Bad Practice)

go
Copy

```go
package main

import (
    "fmt"
    "os"
)

func main() {
    // Creating a file
    file, _ := os.Create("example.txt") // Ignoring the error is not good practice
    fmt.Println("File created:", file)
}
```

In this example, the error returned by os.Create() is ignored. If there's an issue creating the file (e.g., insufficient permissions or disk space), the program will continue without notifying the user, which can lead to unexpected behavior.

Example: Proper Error Handling

go
Copy

```go
package main

import (
    "fmt"
    "os"
)

func main() {
    // Creating a file
    file, err := os.Create("example.txt")
    if err != nil {
        fmt.Println("Error creating file:", err)
        return
    }
    fmt.Println("File created:", file)
```

```
}
```

Here, the error is explicitly checked, and the program handles the failure properly by printing the error message and returning early.

Custom Error Types

One of the key strengths of Go's error handling is that it allows developers to create **custom error types**. By defining a custom error type, you can include more specific information about the error, such as error codes, user-friendly messages, and even stack traces.

Example: Custom Error Type

go
Copy

```go
package main

import (
    "fmt"
)

// Custom error type
type DivisionError struct {
    Message string
    Code    int
}

// Implementing the Error() method for DivisionError
func (e *DivisionError) Error() string {
    return fmt.Sprintf("Error %d: %s", e.Code, e.Message)
}

// Function that returns a custom error
func divide(a, b int) (int, error) {
    if b == 0 {
        return 0, &DivisionError{"division by zero", 400}
    }
```

```go
    return a / b, nil
}

func main() {
    result, err := divide(10, 0)

    if err != nil {
        fmt.Println("Error:", err) // Output: Error: Error 400: division by zero
        return
    }

    fmt.Println("Result:", result)
}
```

In this example:

- We define a custom error type DivisionError that includes a message and an error code.
- The Error() method is implemented for the DivisionError type, which returns a string representation of the error.
- The divide function returns this custom error when a division by zero occurs.

Custom errors are useful because they provide more context about the failure, which can be helpful for debugging and logging purposes.

Wrapping Errors with fmt.Errorf()

Sometimes, you may want to wrap an existing error with additional context, which can be done using the fmt.Errorf() function. This function allows you to create a new error that includes formatted information, such as the error's original cause and additional details.

Example: Wrapping Errors with fmt.Errorf()

go
Copy
```
package main
```

```go
import (
    "fmt"
    "errors"
)

// Function that wraps an error
func divide(a, b int) (int, error) {
    if b == 0 {
        return 0, fmt.Errorf("divide error: %w", errors.New("division by zero"))
    }
    return a / b, nil
}

func main() {
    result, err := divide(10, 0)

    if err != nil {
        fmt.Println("Error:", err) // Output: Error: divide error: division by zero
        return
    }

    fmt.Println("Result:", result)
}
```

In this example:

- We use fmt.Errorf() to create a new error that wraps the original error "division by zero".
- The %w verb in fmt.Errorf() allows the error to be wrapped, enabling error unwrapping later if needed.

In this section, we have explored Go's **error handling model** and the **error type**, focusing on why it is essential for writing robust and reliable code.

- **The** error **type** in Go is a simple interface that forces error handling to be explicit, making it clear when errors occur and how they are managed.
- **Error handling** in Go is done through explicit checks, where functions return errors as the last value. The calling code must handle these errors to ensure the program behaves as expected.
- We demonstrated how to **create and handle custom errors**, how to **wrap errors** with additional context, and why this approach leads to cleaner and more maintainable code.
- Go's error handling is fundamental to building predictable and reliable programs, especially in real-world scenarios where failures are common.

Using the error Type for Error Handling

In Go, the error type plays a central role in how errors are handled. Go's approach to error handling is built around **explicitly returning error values** from functions, making errors part of the function's signature. This ensures that errors are not ignored and provides developers with a clear way to handle issues in their programs.

The Role of the error Type

The error type in Go is an interface, which means that any type that implements the Error() method can be used as an error. The Error() method must return a string, which describes the error.

The error type is defined as:

go

Copy

```go
type error interface {

    Error() string

}
```

This simple interface is fundamental to error handling in Go, and it allows for a wide range of custom error types to be created. By adhering to this interface, Go ensures a consistent, predictable approach to error handling across the language.

Returning Errors from Functions

In Go, many functions return an error value as the last return value. If the function encounters an issue, it returns an error; if everything works as expected, it returns nil for the error.

The syntax for a function that returns an error is as follows:

go

Copy

```go
func functionName() (type, error)
```

This structure makes it easy to handle errors, as it forces the programmer to explicitly check for the error value each time a function is called.

Example 1: Function Returning an Error

go

Copy

```go
package main

import (
    "fmt"
    "errors"
```

```go
)


// Function that returns an error if the divisor is zero

func divide(a, b int) (int, error) {

    if b == 0 {

        return 0, errors.New("cannot divide by zero")

    }

    return a / b, nil

}


func main() {

    result, err := divide(10, 0)

    if err != nil {

        fmt.Println("Error:", err) // Output: Error: cannot divide by zero

        return

    }

    fmt.Println("Result:", result)

}
```

In this example:

- The function divide returns an error if the divisor is zero, and if the divisor is non-zero, it returns the result and nil for the error.
- In the main function, we check whether the error value is nil and handle it appropriately by printing the error message if the division fails.

Best Practices for Handling Errors

Error handling in Go is intentionally simple, but it requires discipline and attention to detail. Here are some best practices for handling errors in Go to ensure that your programs are robust and reliable:

1. Check for Errors Explicitly

The most important practice in Go is to always check errors explicitly. Go does not have exceptions, and it relies on the programmer to handle errors by checking the returned error value.

go

Copy

```go
result, err := someFunction()

if err != nil {

    // Handle the error

    return

}
```

Always check for the error immediately after calling a function that returns an error. This prevents the error from being overlooked and helps catch potential issues early.

Example: Checking Errors Explicitly

go

Copy

```go
package main
```

```go
import (

    "fmt"

    "errors"

)


func readFile(filename string) (string, error) {

    if filename == "" {

        return "", errors.New("file name cannot be empty")

    }

    // Simulate reading a file

    return "File content", nil

}


func main() {

    content, err := readFile("")

    if err != nil {

        fmt.Println("Error:", err) // Output: Error: file name cannot be empty

        return

    }

    fmt.Println("File content:", content)

}
```

In this example:

- We explicitly check the error after calling readFile. If the filename is empty, an error is returned, and we handle it by printing the error message.

2. Return Errors with Context

When returning errors, it's important to provide **context**. This helps the caller understand where the error occurred and makes debugging easier. You can add context to an error message by using fmt.Errorf() or by defining custom error types that include more information.

Example: Returning Errors with Context

go

Copy

```go
package main

import (
    "fmt"
    "errors"
)

// Function with context in error message
func processFile(filename string) error {
    if filename == "" {
        return fmt.Errorf("processFile error: %w", errors.New("file name cannot be empty"))
    }
```

```go
    return nil

}


func main() {

    err := processFile("")

    if err != nil {

        fmt.Println("Error:", err)  // Output: Error: processFile error: file name cannot be
empty

        return

    }

    fmt.Println("File processed successfully")

}
```

Here:

- We use fmt.Errorf() to wrap the error returned by errors.New(). This allows us to add context to the error message, indicating that the error occurred specifically in the processFile function.

3. Use Custom Error Types for More Specific Errors

Creating **custom error types** can provide more detailed information about errors. For example, you can define an error type that includes not only the error message but also additional data, such as an error code or the failed operation.

Example: Creating a Custom Error Type

go

Copy

```go
package main

import (
    "fmt"
)

// Custom error type
type FileError struct {
    Message string
    Code    int
}

func (e *FileError) Error() string {
    return fmt.Sprintf("FileError: %d - %s", e.Code, e.Message)
}

// Function that returns a custom error
func openFile(filename string) error {
    if filename == "" {
```

```go
        return &FileError{Message: "file name cannot be empty", Code: 400}

    }

    return nil

}


func main() {

    err := openFile("")

    if err != nil {

        fmt.Println("Error:", err)   // Output: Error: FileError: 400 - file name cannot be empty

        return

    }

    fmt.Println("File opened successfully")

}
```

In this example:

- We define a custom error type FileError with a Message and Code field.
- The Error() method is implemented for the FileError type, which provides a formatted string when the error is printed.
- We return this custom error from the openFile function, providing more context about the error.

4. Avoiding Silent Failures

In Go, it's important to avoid **silent failures**. When an error occurs, it should be handled in a way that provides useful feedback. **Ignoring errors** is considered bad practice in Go, and doing so can lead to unpredictable behavior.

Example: Silent Failure (Bad Practice)

go

Copy

```go
package main

import "fmt"

func main() {
    _, _ = someFunction() // Ignoring the error (bad practice)
}

func someFunction() (string, error) {
    return "", fmt.Errorf("something went wrong")
}
```

In this example:

- The error is ignored by assigning it to _, which prevents the program from noticing the failure. This can lead to bugs that are difficult to detect and fix.

Example: Handling the Error (Good Practice)

go

Copy

```go
package main
```

```go
import "fmt"

func main() {
    result, err := someFunction()
    if err != nil {
        fmt.Println("Error:", err) // Proper error handling
        return
    }
    fmt.Println("Result:", result)
}

func someFunction() (string, error) {
    return "", fmt.Errorf("something went wrong")
}
```

Here:

- We handle the error explicitly by checking if err is not nil and printing an error message. This ensures that the program fails gracefully and provides useful feedback.

In Go, **error handling** is explicit, simple, and efficient, making it easy to manage issues in your programs. By using the error type and following best practices, you can ensure that your code is robust and reliable.

Here are the key takeaways:

- **Use the error type** to represent errors in Go. It is an interface that can be implemented by custom error types for more context and flexibility.
- **Check for errors explicitly** to prevent them from being overlooked. Handle errors at the point where they occur to ensure they are dealt with appropriately.
- **Return errors with context** to provide more meaningful feedback and make it easier to diagnose issues.
- **Use custom error types** when you need to provide more detailed information about an error, such as an error code or specific failure condition.
- **Avoid silent failures** by always handling errors. This ensures that your program behaves predictably and provides useful feedback when something goes wrong.

7.2. Panic and Recover

In Go, the panic and recover mechanisms provide a way to handle critical errors and abnormal situations that cannot be easily handled through normal error checking. While Go's preferred method of handling errors is by returning an error value and explicitly checking it, **panic** and **recover** offer a more forceful way to handle errors in certain situations, usually in cases where the program encounters an unexpected condition that it cannot recover from without halting the execution flow.

In this section, we will explore **panic** and **recover**, explain how they work, when you might want to use them, and best practices for handling critical errors in Go.

What is Panic and When to Use It?

A **panic** in Go is similar to an exception in other languages, but it's more of a drastic measure that immediately stops the normal execution of a function and begins unwinding the stack of function calls. When a panic occurs, Go will halt the execution of the current goroutine, print an error message, and then start to unwind the stack, cleaning up resources as it goes. The process of unwinding the stack will continue unless it is caught using recover, which is a way of recovering from a panic.

Syntax for Panic

To initiate a panic, you can use the panic() function, passing it any value. Usually, the value passed is an error message or any type that implements the Error() method.

go

Copy

```
panic("something went wrong")
```

Example: Simple Panic

go

Copy

```
package main

import "fmt"

func main() {
    fmt.Println("Program started")
    panic("Critical error encountered") // Panic causes the program to terminate
    fmt.Println("This line will never be reached")
}
```

Example Output:

lua

Copy

```
Program started
```

322

```
panic: Critical error encountered

goroutine 1 [running]:

main.main()

  /path/to/file.go:8 +0x39

exit status 2
```

In this example:

- The panic("Critical error encountered") causes the program to immediately terminate.
- The line after the panic (fmt.Println("This line will never be reached")) is never executed because the panic stops the program's normal flow.

When to Use Panic

panic should be used in situations where the program **cannot continue safely**. Here are some situations when panic might be appropriate:

- **Critical system errors**: If the program encounters an error that makes further execution impossible or unsafe (e.g., out of memory, corrupted data, invalid configuration).
- **Invariant violations**: When the program encounters a situation that violates its core assumptions, such as accessing an invalid array index or null pointer dereferencing.
- **Unrecoverable errors**: When continuing the program would likely lead to incorrect results or undefined behavior, such as invalid data from external sources.

However, panic should not be used as a general-purpose error handling mechanism. Instead, it is meant for truly **unrecoverable errors**. For recoverable errors, Go's standard error handling approach (using return values of type error) should be preferred.

323

Handling Errors with Recover

Go provides a built-in function called recover() that allows you to **recover from a panic** and resume normal execution. The recover() function can only be called inside a **deferred** function, which is a function that is executed when the surrounding function returns, either due to normal completion or because of a panic.

When recover() is called, it **stops the panic** and returns the value passed to panic(). If recover() is not called, the program will terminate with the panic message, and the stack trace will be printed. If recover() is called successfully, the program will continue executing after the deferred function finishes.

Syntax for Recover

go

Copy

```go
defer func() {

  if r := recover(); r != nil {

    // Handle the panic

    fmt.Println("Recovered from panic:", r)

  }

}()
```

Example: Using Recover to Handle Panic

go

Copy

```go
package main
```

```go
import "fmt"

func riskyFunction() {
    fmt.Println("Inside riskyFunction")
    panic("Something went wrong")
}

func safeCall() {
    // Defer the recovery function
    defer func() {
        if r := recover(); r != nil {
            fmt.Println("Recovered from panic:", r)
        }
    }()
    riskyFunction()
    fmt.Println("This line will not be reached")
}

func main() {
    safeCall()
    fmt.Println("Program continues executing")
```

```
}
```

Example Output:

csharp

Copy

Inside riskyFunction

Recovered from panic: Something went wrong

Program continues executing

In this example:

- The riskyFunction causes a panic with the message "Something went wrong".
- The safeCall function uses defer to call a recovery function that catches the panic and prevents the program from terminating.
- The recover() function catches the panic and prints the recovery message.
- The program continues executing after the panic is recovered, and the main function prints "Program continues executing".

How Recover Works

- **Panic Unwinding**: When a panic occurs, Go begins unwinding the stack, cleaning up function calls.
- **Defer and Recover**: If a defer function with a recover() call is encountered during the unwinding process, the panic is stopped, and the value passed to panic() is returned to recover(). The deferred function continues executing, and the program resumes from where it was called.
- **Program Continuation**: After recover() catches the panic, the program can continue executing normally, avoiding a program crash.

326

Example: Recovering from Multiple Panics

go

Copy

```go
package main

import "fmt"

func f() {
    fmt.Println("Inside f")
    panic("Panic in f")
}

func g() {
    fmt.Println("Inside g")
    panic("Panic in g")
}

func main() {
    defer func() {
        if r := recover(); r != nil {
            fmt.Println("Recovered from:", r)
        }
```

```
}()
```

```
f()
```

```
g() // This will not be reached because the panic in f stops further execution
```

```
fmt.Println("This line will not be reached")
```

```
}
```

Example Output:

csharp

Copy

Inside f

Recovered from: Panic in f

In this example:

- The panic in function f() is handled by the recover() function.
- The panic in g() is not reached because the execution stops at the first panic.

Best Practices for Panic and Recover

While **panic** and **recover** provide mechanisms for handling critical errors, their use should be limited to specific situations. Here are some best practices for using these features:

1. **Use Panic Sparingly**:
   - Use panic only when the program is in a state where **it cannot continue safely**. It should not be used for normal error handling in your code. If

you can anticipate and handle an error using Go's standard error handling (returning an error value), use that approach instead.

2. **Recover Only When Necessary**:
   - Use recover() to handle panics in cases where you want to **prevent the program from crashing**. Typically, this is used for handling panics in goroutines or deferred functions where you want to log the error or gracefully exit.
   - Don't use recover() to silence errors. It's best used to ensure the program can continue running in controlled situations, such as in the cleanup of resources.

3. **Do Not Use Panic for Expected Errors**:
   - Panics are not meant for situations where you expect errors (such as file not found, invalid input, etc.). Use **explicit error checks** for such cases, as Go's idiomatic error handling works best for these scenarios.

4. **Log or Recover from Panics in Critical Sections**:
   - If a panic is expected in a certain area of your application, such as critical operations (e.g., network connections, database access), use recover() to log the error and ensure the program doesn't crash unexpectedly.

5. **Document the Use of Panic**:
   - If you use panic, make sure to document it well in your code so others understand why it's being used and when it might occur.

In this section, we explored the panic and recover mechanisms in Go, which are used to handle critical errors that cannot be easily managed through normal error checking.

Key points to remember:

- **Panic** should be used sparingly, only when an error is so critical that the program cannot continue safely.
- **Recover** allows you to handle panics and resume normal execution, but it should be used to control exceptional cases, not to silence all errors.
- For regular error handling, Go's **explicit error handling with the error type** is the preferred approach.

By understanding when and how to use **panic** and **recover**, you can make your programs more resilient to unforeseen issues while keeping your error-handling practices clean and maintainable. In the next section, we will explore **debugging techniques** in Go, including tools and strategies to identify and fix bugs in your Go code effectively.

7.3. Debugging Go Code

Debugging is an essential part of software development. In Go, debugging involves identifying, understanding, and fixing issues in your code. Go provides a variety of tools and techniques to help developers efficiently identify and resolve bugs, improve program stability, and ensure that applications behave as expected.

In this section, we will explore the tools and techniques available for debugging Go code, as well as common Go errors and strategies for solving them. Understanding these methods will help you debug your Go programs with confidence and efficiency.

Tools and Techniques for Debugging Go Code

There are several tools and techniques that you can use to debug Go code. These range from simple print-based debugging to using more advanced debuggers and logging systems. Below are the most common approaches to debugging Go programs.

1. Print-Based Debugging (Using fmt.Println)

One of the simplest and most common methods for debugging Go code is using fmt.Println() to print variables, values, or execution paths during runtime. This technique helps you understand the flow of the program and examine the state of variables at different points.

Example: Using fmt.Println() for Debugging

go

Copy

```
package main
```

```go
import "fmt"

func divide(a, b int) (int, error) {
    fmt.Println("Received values:", a, b)  // Debugging line
    if b == 0 {
        return 0, fmt.Errorf("division by zero")
    }
    return a / b, nil
}

func main() {
    result, err := divide(10, 0)
    if err != nil {
        fmt.Println("Error:", err)
        return
    }
    fmt.Println("Result:", result)
}
```

In this example:

- fmt.Println("Received values:", a, b) prints the values of a and b before the division takes place.

331

- This simple print-based debugging helps you see what's happening with the variables during execution and understand where things might be going wrong.

While fmt.Println() is effective for quick debugging, it has limitations for larger, more complex programs, where you need more detailed control and visibility over the execution flow.

---

2. Using the Go Debugger (delve)

For more sophisticated debugging, Go developers commonly use a tool called delve, which is an interactive debugger for Go. Delve provides features such as stepping through code, inspecting variables, setting breakpoints, and evaluating expressions in real-time.

Installing Delve

To use delve, you need to install it first. You can install it using the following command:

bash

Copy

```
go install github.com/go-delve/delve/cmd/dlv@latest
```

Using Delve for Debugging

Start Debugging Session: To start a debugging session with your Go program, use the following command in your terminal:
bash
Copy
```
dlv debug
```

This will start your program in debug mode and provide you with an interactive prompt to control the execution flow.

1. **Setting Breakpoints**: You can set breakpoints in your code to pause execution at a specific point:
bash
Copy
```
break main.go:10
```

This sets a breakpoint at line 10 of main.go.

2. **Stepping Through Code**: Once the program is paused at a breakpoint, you can step through the code one line at a time using the next command:
   bash
   Copy
   ```
   next
   ```

3. **Inspecting Variables**: You can inspect the value of variables at any point during the execution using the print command:
   bash
   Copy
   ```
   print variableName
   ```

4. **Exiting Debugger**: To exit the debugger, type:
   bash
   Copy
   ```
   quit
   ```

Delve is powerful and allows you to interactively debug your code, set breakpoints, inspect variables, and step through code, making it a valuable tool for diagnosing and solving complex issues in Go programs.

---

3. Using Logging for Debugging

Another technique for debugging Go code is **logging**. Logging involves printing messages at specific points in the program to track its execution and capture relevant information for troubleshooting. Go's log package provides a simple yet effective way to log information during runtime.

Example: Using log Package

go

Copy

```go
package main

import (
    "fmt"
    "log"
)

func divide(a, b int) (int, error) {
    log.Printf("Received values: %d, %d", a, b)  // Logging values
    if b == 0 {
        return 0, fmt.Errorf("division by zero")
    }
    return a / b, nil
}

func main() {
    result, err := divide(10, 0)
    if err != nil {
        log.Printf("Error occurred: %v", err)  // Log error
```

```
    return

}

log.Printf("Result: %d", result) // Log result

}
```

In this example:

- The log.Printf() function logs the received values and any errors that occur, allowing you to trace what's happening in your program.
- Logging is especially useful for **long-running applications**, such as servers or background processes, where you can track the flow of execution over time and gather diagnostic information.

Common Go Errors and How to Solve Them

While debugging, you will likely encounter a variety of **common errors** in Go. Below are some of the most common errors that developers face when writing Go programs, along with strategies for solving them.

1. Nil Pointer Dereference

A **nil pointer dereference** occurs when you try to access or modify the value of a pointer that is nil. This results in a runtime panic, and Go will terminate the program with an error message.

Example of Nil Pointer Dereference

go

Copy

```
package main

import "fmt"
```

```go
func main() {

    var ptr *int

        fmt.Println(*ptr) // Panic: runtime error: invalid memory address or nil pointer
    dereference

}
```

How to Solve:

Ensure that pointers are properly initialized before dereferencing them. You can also use Go's built-in checks to avoid dereferencing nil pointers.

go

Copy

```go
package main

import "fmt"

func main() {

    var ptr *int

    if ptr != nil {

        fmt.Println(*ptr)

    } else {

        fmt.Println("Pointer is nil")

    }
```

}

2. Out of Range Index

Another common error occurs when you try to access an index in an array or slice that is out of bounds. Go will panic if you attempt to access an index that doesn't exist in the array or slice.

Example of Out of Range Index

go

Copy

```go
package main

import "fmt"

func main() {
    numbers := []int{1, 2, 3}
    fmt.Println(numbers[5]) // Panic: runtime error: index out of range
}
```

How to Solve:

Always check the length of the array or slice before attempting to access its elements. You can use the len() function to get the length of a slice or array.

go

Copy

```go
package main

import "fmt"

func main() {
    numbers := []int{1, 2, 3}
    if len(numbers) > 5 {
        fmt.Println(numbers[5])
    } else {
        fmt.Println("Index out of range")
    }
}
```

3. Unresolved Dependencies

If your program depends on external packages and you forget to import them or if there are issues with the versioning of dependencies, Go may fail to compile your program.

Example of Unresolved Dependency

go

Copy

```go
package main

import "fmt"

func main() {
    // Missing import for the "math/rand" package
    fmt.Println(rand.Int())
}
```

How to Solve:

Make sure to import the necessary dependencies, and ensure that all packages are correctly installed. You can use go get to download dependencies and check that you're using the right versions.

bash

Copy

```bash
go get github.com/some/package
```

4. Incorrect Type Conversion

Go is a statically typed language, which means that converting between incompatible types can result in errors. This error often happens when you try to assign one type to another without properly converting it.

Example of Incorrect Type Conversion

go

Copy

```
package main

import "fmt"

func main() {
    var x float64 = 3.14
    var y int = x // Compilation error: cannot use x (type float64) as type int in assignment
    fmt.Println(y)
}
```

How to Solve:

Use Go's type conversion feature to explicitly convert between types.

go

Copy

```
package main
```

```
import "fmt"

func main() {
    var x float64 = 3.14
    var y int = int(x) // Convert float64 to int
    fmt.Println(y) // Output: 3
}
```

In this section, we explored various **tools and techniques** for debugging Go code, including:

- **Print-based debugging** using fmt.Println() for simple insights into variable states.
- The **Delve debugger**, which allows interactive debugging with features such as stepping through code, inspecting variables, and setting breakpoints.
- **Logging**, which helps track application state over time and aids in diagnosing issues during program execution.

Additionally, we discussed some of the **common Go errors** that you might encounter during development, such as **nil pointer dereferencing**, **out of range index errors**, **unresolved dependencies**, and **incorrect type conversions**, along with strategies for solving them.

By using the right debugging tools and understanding the most common errors, you'll be better equipped to develop and maintain reliable Go programs.

7.4. Practical Debugging Exercises and Debugging Real-World Go Code

Debugging is an essential skill for every programmer, and working through practical exercises is one of the best ways to learn how to handle bugs and problems in real-world scenarios. In this section, we will work through a series of **practical debugging exercises** that reflect common issues in Go programs. We will also walk through debugging techniques for **real-world Go applications**, where errors might be more complex and require deeper analysis.

By the end of this section, you will have a deeper understanding of how to identify and fix bugs in Go, how to use debugging tools effectively, and how to apply debugging strategies in real-world programming contexts.

Practical Debugging Exercises

Exercise 1: Nil Pointer Dereference

One of the most common errors in Go is the **nil pointer dereference**, which occurs when you try to access the value of a pointer that has not been initialized. This results in a runtime panic.

Task:

- Identify the issue in the following code and fix the **nil pointer dereference** error.

go

Copy

```
package main

import "fmt"

type Person struct {
```

342

```go
    Name string
}


func main() {
    var p *Person
    fmt.Println(p.Name) // Error: nil pointer dereference
}
```

Solution:

To fix the **nil pointer dereference**, you should initialize the Person pointer before using it.

go

Copy

```go
package main


import "fmt"


type Person struct {
    Name string
}


func main() {
    p := &Person{Name: "John"} // Initialize the pointer
```

```go
    fmt.Println(p.Name)        // Output: John
}
```

In this solution:

- We initialize the p pointer to reference a Person struct before accessing the Name field, thus avoiding the nil pointer dereference.

Exercise 2: Index Out of Range

Another common issue in Go is accessing an index that is out of bounds of an array or slice, leading to a runtime panic.

Task:

- Identify the error and fix the **index out of range** issue in the following code.

go

Copy

```go
package main

import "fmt"

func main() {
    numbers := []int{1, 2, 3}
    fmt.Println(numbers[5]) // Error: index out of range
}
```

Solution:

To fix the **index out of range** error, you need to ensure that the index is within the bounds of the slice.

go

Copy

```go
package main

import "fmt"

func main() {
    numbers := []int{1, 2, 3}
    if len(numbers) > 5 {
        fmt.Println(numbers[5])
    } else {
        fmt.Println("Index is out of range")
    }
}
```

In this solution:

- We check whether the index is within the bounds of the slice using len(numbers) before trying to access the element.

_____

345

Exercise 3: Error Handling with Missing Return Value

Error handling is one of the key aspects of Go, and improper error handling can lead to bugs that are hard to identify. Here, we'll deal with a situation where an error is not properly handled.

Task:

- Identify the issue where an error is returned but not properly handled in the following code.

go

Copy

```go
package main

import (
    "fmt"
    "errors"
)

func processData(data string) (string, error) {
    if data == "" {
        return "", errors.New("data cannot be empty")
    }
    return "Processed: " + data, nil
}

func main() {
```

```go
    result, err := processData("")

    fmt.Println(result) // Problem: error not checked, might result in unexpected behavior

}
```

Solution:

To fix the error handling, we need to check whether err is nil before proceeding with using the result.

go

Copy

```go
package main

import (

    "fmt"

    "errors"

)


func processData(data string) (string, error) {

    if data == "" {

        return "", errors.New("data cannot be empty")

    }

    return "Processed: " + data, nil

}
```

347

```go
func main() {

    result, err := processData("")

    if err != nil {

        fmt.Println("Error:", err) // Output: Error: data cannot be empty

        return

    }

    fmt.Println(result)

}
```

In this solution:

- We explicitly check if err is nil before using result, ensuring that the program handles the error properly instead of proceeding with unexpected behavior.

Debugging Real-World Go Code

Now that we've covered basic debugging exercises, let's look at some more complex scenarios that often occur in real-world Go code. These examples will demonstrate how to apply the debugging techniques we've learned in this book to fix real-world issues.

Scenario 1: Deadlocks in Concurrent Go Programs

A common issue when working with Go's **goroutines** and **channels** is the occurrence of **deadlocks**. A deadlock occurs when two or more goroutines are waiting for each other to complete, causing the program to hang.

Task:

- Identify and fix the deadlock in the following code.

```go
package main

import "fmt"

func worker(ch chan string) {
    ch <- "Work completed"
}

func main() {
    ch := make(chan string)

    go worker(ch)
    message := <-ch
    fmt.Println(message)

    // The program might deadlock here because the channel is not being read from when
    the worker sends data
}
```

Solution:

To fix the deadlock, we need to ensure that the goroutine properly synchronizes with the main function. In this case, we make sure the main function waits for the goroutine to finish.

go

Copy

```go
package main

import "fmt"

func worker(ch chan string) {
    ch <- "Work completed"
}

func main() {
    ch := make(chan string)

    go worker(ch)
    message := <-ch
    fmt.Println(message)

    // Now the program will not deadlock and will print the message
}
```

In this solution:

- The channel ch is properly synchronized between the main function and the worker goroutine, ensuring the program doesn't deadlock.

Scenario 2: Race Conditions in Concurrent Code

Another common problem in concurrent programming is **race conditions**, where the outcome depends on the unpredictable order of execution between goroutines. Go provides a built-in tool to detect race conditions: the **race detector**.

Task:

- Identify and fix the race condition in the following code.

go

Copy

```go
package main

import (
    "fmt"
    "sync"
)

var counter int

func increment() {
    counter++
```

351

```go
}

func main() {
    var wg sync.WaitGroup

    for i := 0; i < 1000; i++ {
        wg.Add(1)
        go func() {
            increment()
            wg.Done()
        }()
    }

    wg.Wait()
    fmt.Println("Counter:", counter) // The counter might be inconsistent due to race conditions
}
```

Solution:

To fix the race condition, you can use a **mutex** to synchronize access to the shared resource (the counter).

go

Copy

package main

```go
import (

    "fmt"

    "sync"

)


var (

    counter int

    mu      sync.Mutex

)


func increment() {

    mu.Lock()   // Lock before modifying the counter

    counter++   // Increment the counter

    mu.Unlock() // Unlock after modifying the counter

}


func main() {

    var wg sync.WaitGroup


    for i := 0; i < 1000; i++ {

        wg.Add(1)
```

```go
go func() {
    increment()
    wg.Done()
}()
}

wg.Wait()
fmt.Println("Counter:", counter) // The counter will now be consistent
}
```

In this solution:

- We use a **mutex (mu)** to ensure that only one goroutine can access and modify the counter variable at a time, preventing race conditions.

Using the Race Detector

You can also use Go's **race detector** to identify race conditions during development. To enable the race detector, run your Go program with the -race flag:

bash

Copy

```
go run -race your_program.go
```

The race detector will report any race conditions that occur during execution, helping you identify and fix issues early.

Scenario 3: Memory Leaks and Resource Cleanup

Memory leaks are another common issue in Go programs, especially in long-running applications. A memory leak occurs when memory is allocated but not properly freed, causing the program to consume increasing amounts of memory over time.

Task:

- Identify and fix the memory leak in the following code.

go

Copy

```go
package main

import "fmt"

type MyStruct struct {
    data string
}

func main() {
    var arr []*MyStruct

    for i := 0; i < 1000; i++ {
        arr = append(arr, &MyStruct{data: fmt.Sprintf("Data %d", i)})
    }
}
```

355

```go
    // The program is using a lot of memory due to the allocation of MyStruct pointers
without proper cleanup

}
```

Solution:

To fix the memory leak, make sure to properly manage memory usage and clean up resources. This could involve freeing up memory, closing open files or network connections, or reusing objects instead of allocating new ones each time.

go

Copy

```go
package main

import "fmt"

type MyStruct struct {

    data string

}

func main() {

    var arr []*MyStruct


    for i := 0; i < 1000; i++ {

        arr = append(arr, &MyStruct{data: fmt.Sprintf("Data %d", i)})

    }
```

356

```
// To avoid memory leaks, we might clear the array after it's no longer needed

arr = nil // Clear the array to release references and free memory

}
```

In this solution:

- We set the array arr to nil, releasing the references to the MyStruct objects and allowing the garbage collector to reclaim the memory.

In this section, we worked through several **practical debugging exercises**, covering issues such as **nil pointer dereferencing**, **index out of range errors**, **error handling**, and more. We also explored real-world Go scenarios, including handling **deadlocks**, **race conditions**, and **memory leaks**.

By applying the **debugging techniques** and using tools like **Delve**, **logging**, and **the race detector**, you can effectively debug and fix issues in your Go programs. This hands-on experience will equip you to tackle more complex debugging challenges in real-world applications.

Chapter 8: Introduction to Go's Concurrency Model

8.1. What is Concurrency? And, The Importance of Concurrency in Modern Programming

Concurrency is a core concept in modern programming that allows a program to perform multiple tasks at the same time. It is particularly valuable in today's computing landscape, where many applications need to handle multiple operations simultaneously, such as processing user inputs, interacting with databases, or making network requests. In Go, concurrency is not just a theoretical concept but is built into the language itself, enabling developers to write programs that handle many tasks efficiently.

In this section, we will define **concurrency**, explain its role in modern programming, and highlight its importance in building responsive, efficient applications. Additionally, we will set the stage for Go's powerful concurrency features, which we will explore in more depth throughout this chapter.

What is Concurrency?

Concurrency is the ability of a program to deal with multiple tasks at the same time. This does not necessarily mean that these tasks are running simultaneously, but rather that they are being managed in a way that allows them to appear to run in parallel.

Concurrency vs. Parallelism

Although the terms **concurrency** and **parallelism** are often used interchangeably, they are technically different concepts.

- **Concurrency**: Refers to the ability to manage multiple tasks at once, allowing them to make progress. This can be achieved on a **single-core processor** by quickly switching between tasks (context switching). The tasks might not be executed simultaneously but are interleaved so that they give the appearance of simultaneous execution.
- **Parallelism**: Refers to the simultaneous execution of multiple tasks, typically on **multiple cores** or processors. In parallelism, tasks are truly executed at the same time, leveraging multiple computing resources for better performance.

In Go, **concurrency** is more of a design approach to writing programs that can handle multiple tasks simultaneously, and **parallelism** can be achieved using concurrency when running on multi-core machines.

Example: Concurrency Concept

Imagine you are cooking a meal that involves several tasks: chopping vegetables, boiling water, and stirring a pot. These tasks are independent of one another, so you can start chopping vegetables, then while they're cooking, begin boiling the water, and so on. However, you may not be cooking each task simultaneously. Instead, you alternate between tasks as they progress.

In Go, **goroutines** enable this type of task management, allowing you to start tasks that can run concurrently without waiting for others to complete.

The Importance of Concurrency in Modern Programming

Concurrency has become a fundamental aspect of modern programming due to the demands of today's applications. From web servers handling thousands of simultaneous requests to real-time applications processing streams of data, concurrency plays a critical role in making systems scalable, efficient, and responsive.

1. Efficient Resource Utilization

Concurrency allows programs to efficiently utilize resources, especially in environments with limited resources such as **single-core processors** or **low-power devices**. Instead of waiting idly for a task to complete, concurrency allows programs to perform other tasks while waiting for certain operations (like I/O or network requests) to finish.

For instance, a program waiting for a file to be read or data from an external API can continue processing other tasks rather than sitting idle. This helps maximize the performance of the available resources and makes the program more responsive.

2. Improved Responsiveness in Applications

Modern applications, particularly **real-time applications** such as web servers, video games, and chat apps, need to be highly responsive. Concurrency enables these applications to perform multiple actions concurrently without blocking or slowing down the system.

359

For example, a **web server** might need to handle multiple user requests at once. Without concurrency, the server would process each request one by one, leading to delays, especially when handling hundreds or thousands of requests. With concurrency, the server can handle multiple requests at the same time, providing a **faster and more responsive user experience**.

3. Scalability

Concurrency is key to building **scalable systems**. Scalability is the ability of a system to handle increasing loads by adding more resources (e.g., processing power, memory). With concurrency, systems can scale more effectively by distributing tasks across multiple workers or processors.

For instance, Go's concurrency model allows applications to manage multiple goroutines (lightweight threads), which can be distributed across multiple cores, making them scalable in a multi-core environment. This is essential for modern applications that must be able to handle high volumes of data or users without significant degradation in performance.

4. Simplified Concurrent Programming with Goroutines

Go makes concurrency **simple** and **efficient** through the use of **goroutines**. A goroutine is a lightweight thread managed by the Go runtime. Goroutines allow you to run multiple tasks concurrently without the complexity of dealing with threads directly, as in traditional multi-threaded programming.

Goroutines are:

- **Lightweight**: They require very little memory overhead and can be created in large numbers.
- **Efficient**: Goroutines are managed by Go's runtime, which handles scheduling and context switching automatically.
- **Easy to Use**: Starting a goroutine is as simple as adding the go keyword before a function call.

Goroutines provide an abstraction layer that hides the complexity of managing threads and makes concurrent programming in Go much more accessible.

Concurrency in Go: Key Concepts

Go provides several features for implementing and managing concurrency, each designed to make concurrent programming easier and more efficient. Here are the key concurrency-related features in Go:

1. Goroutines

A **goroutine** is the basic unit of concurrency in Go. A goroutine is a lightweight thread managed by the Go runtime. You can create a new goroutine by simply using the go keyword in front of a function call:

```go
go myFunction()
```

This will start myFunction() as a concurrent task, and the main function will continue executing without waiting for myFunction to finish. The Go runtime schedules goroutines efficiently, allowing them to run concurrently.

2. Channels

Channels are used to communicate between goroutines and synchronize their execution. They allow data to be passed between goroutines in a safe and structured manner. Channels provide a way for one goroutine to send data and for another to receive it, effectively synchronizing their execution.

Example of a channel usage:

```go
package main

import "fmt"

func main() {
    ch := make(chan string)

    // Goroutine that sends data through the channel
    go func() {
```

```go
    ch <- "Hello from goroutine!"
}()

    // Main goroutine receives data from the channel
    message := <-ch
    fmt.Println(message) // Output: Hello from goroutine!
}
```

In this example:

- A goroutine sends a message into the channel ch.
- The main goroutine receives the message and prints it.
- Channels help synchronize goroutines and ensure safe communication between them.

3. Select Statement

Go provides a select statement that allows you to wait on multiple channels. This is similar to a switch statement, but it works with channels. The select statement allows your program to wait for multiple operations on channels, making it easy to handle multiple concurrent events.

Example of using select:

```go
go
Copy
package main

import "fmt"

func main() {
    ch1 := make(chan string)
    ch2 := make(chan string)

    go func() {
        ch1 <- "First message"
    }()

    go func() {
```

```
    ch2 <- "Second message"
}()

select {
case msg1 := <-ch1:
    fmt.Println("Received:", msg1)
case msg2 := <-ch2:
    fmt.Println("Received:", msg2)
}
}
```

In this example:

- The select statement waits for a message from either ch1 or ch2.
- It allows you to handle multiple channels in a non-blocking manner, making it ideal for working with multiple concurrent sources.

The Importance of Concurrency in Modern Programming

Concurrency is **crucial** in modern programming for several reasons:

1. Handling Real-Time Data: Concurrency is essential for real-time systems, such as gaming, chat apps, and video streaming, where multiple events must be handled simultaneously to maintain a seamless user experience.

2. Improving Application Responsiveness: Concurrency allows applications to remain responsive by ensuring that tasks like file I/O or network requests do not block the main execution flow. This makes applications faster and more user-friendly.

3. Utilizing Multi-Core Processors: Modern processors have multiple cores, and Go's concurrency model makes it easy to take full advantage of multi-core systems. By distributing tasks across multiple cores, Go programs can handle a larger number of concurrent operations efficiently.

4. Simplifying Asynchronous Programming: Concurrency in Go simplifies asynchronous programming. The use of goroutines and channels abstracts much of

the complexity of managing concurrent tasks, allowing developers to write code that is both readable and efficient.

5. Enabling Scalable Systems: With concurrency, Go programs can scale to handle high loads. Web servers, distributed systems, and microservices all benefit from Go's concurrency features, which enable these systems to handle thousands or even millions of concurrent requests efficiently.

Concurrency is a critical concept in modern programming, and Go's built-in concurrency model provides a powerful yet simple way to write concurrent programs. The key features—**goroutines**, **channels**, and **select statements**—make concurrent programming in Go both efficient and easy to manage.

Understanding and applying concurrency will allow you to build applications that are **responsive**, **scalable**, and capable of handling multiple tasks simultaneously without sacrificing performance.

Concurrency vs. Parallelism

While the terms **concurrency** and **parallelism** are often used interchangeably, they refer to distinct concepts in computing, especially in the context of programming. Understanding the difference between concurrency and parallelism is important for writing efficient, scalable, and well-optimized programs. In this section, we will define both terms, explain their differences, and demonstrate how they relate to each other, especially in the context of Go's concurrency model.

What is Concurrency?

As discussed previously, **concurrency** is the ability to handle multiple tasks or operations at the same time, but not necessarily simultaneously. Concurrency involves managing multiple tasks that may be in progress at the same time. The key point is that a concurrent program allows tasks to make progress independently, often by switching between tasks or working on them in overlapping time periods.

In simpler terms, concurrency is about **structuring your program** to do multiple things at once, but not necessarily all at the same time.

Example of Concurrency:

Consider the following analogy: Imagine you are cooking dinner, making a salad, and boiling water for pasta. You can start by chopping the vegetables, then while the vegetables are being prepared, you can put water on the stove, and while it's heating up, you can continue with the salad. Here, the tasks are **concurrent**, but they may not be running simultaneously — they are just managed so that progress is made on all tasks without blocking one another.

In Go, this kind of concurrency is achieved using **goroutines**, which allow you to initiate independent tasks without waiting for others to complete. Each goroutine runs concurrently, but on a single core, they might be interleaved, depending on the Go runtime scheduler.

What is Parallelism?

Parallelism, on the other hand, refers to the actual **simultaneous execution** of multiple tasks. In parallelism, tasks are literally running at the same time, typically across multiple CPU cores or processors. This means that the work is being physically executed in parallel, leveraging multiple hardware resources to perform operations concurrently and simultaneously.

Example of Parallelism:

Returning to the cooking analogy: imagine you have two chefs. While one chef is chopping vegetables, the other is boiling the water for pasta. Now the tasks are **parallel** because both are happening simultaneously, each on a different chef, which represents separate resources (or cores in computing terms).

In Go, parallelism is often a natural outcome of concurrency when the system has multiple processor cores. Go can utilize multiple cores to execute multiple goroutines at the same time, thanks to Go's built-in scheduler and runtime.

The Difference Between Concurrency and Parallelism

The distinction between concurrency and parallelism can be summed up in the following way:

- **Concurrency**: Multiple tasks are being handled at the same time, but they may not be executed simultaneously. Concurrency allows you to efficiently manage many tasks that need to be performed, but it doesn't require those tasks to be executed simultaneously. It's about organizing your program so that tasks can be worked on concurrently, even if they're not executed simultaneously.
- **Parallelism**: Multiple tasks are being executed simultaneously, typically on multiple processor cores. Parallelism involves executing independent tasks at the same time to speed up processing. Parallelism often leads to a performance improvement, especially for CPU-bound tasks, because it takes advantage of the system's hardware.

Key Points to Remember:

- **Concurrency** is a **programming concept** and design pattern; it's about dealing with multiple tasks by structuring a program to handle them in overlapping time periods. It doesn't necessarily mean tasks are running simultaneously.
- **Parallelism** is a **physical concept** related to the execution of tasks at the same time, typically on multiple cores or processors.

You can think of **concurrency as the structure of your program**, whereas **parallelism is how the program is executed on hardware**.

Concurrency and Parallelism in Go

Go's concurrency model enables you to write programs that can handle concurrent tasks efficiently, and it also supports parallel execution by making use of multiple CPU cores. While Go's goroutines allow for concurrent execution, the Go runtime scheduler decides how and when goroutines are actually executed, potentially distributing them across multiple CPU cores, thus enabling parallelism.

Concurrency in Go with Goroutines

Go's approach to concurrency uses **goroutines**, which are lightweight threads that can be created easily with the go keyword. Goroutines are scheduled and managed by Go's runtime, allowing for efficient task management and switching. Goroutines are generally not tied to specific CPU cores, which means that Go can execute them concurrently.

Here's a simple example of concurrency with goroutines:

go

Copy

```
package main

import "fmt"

func task1() {
    fmt.Println("Task 1 started")
}


func task2() {
    fmt.Println("Task 2 started")
}


func main() {
    go task1() // Start task1 in a new goroutine
    go task2() // Start task2 in a new goroutine
```

```
fmt.Println("Main function finished")

}
```

In this example:

- The two tasks are executed concurrently (but not necessarily simultaneously).
- They are run on separate goroutines, and Go's runtime will schedule and manage their execution.

Parallelism in Go with Multiple Cores

Go can also take advantage of **parallelism** when you run your program on a **multi-core machine**. By default, Go will use a single core for all goroutines. However, you can instruct the Go runtime to utilize multiple cores by setting the number of operating system threads available to the Go runtime with the GOMAXPROCS environment variable or runtime.GOMAXPROCS() function.

Example of Parallelism with Multiple Cores

go

Copy

```go
package main

import (

    "fmt"

    "runtime"

)


func task() {
```

```
    fmt.Println("Running task on CPU:", runtime.NumCPU())

}


func main() {

    // Set the number of CPU cores Go will use to 4

    runtime.GOMAXPROCS(4)


    for i := 0; i < 4; i++ {

        go task() // Start 4 tasks in goroutines

    }


    // Wait for goroutines to finish

    fmt.Scanln()  // Simple way to block the main function

}
```

In this example:

- We use runtime.GOMAXPROCS(4) to set Go to use **4 CPU cores** for executing the tasks.
- We start 4 tasks in separate goroutines, which can run in parallel across the available CPU cores.

How Concurrency and Parallelism Work Together

In many cases, **concurrency** and **parallelism** work together to improve performance and efficiency. For example:

- **Concurrency** organizes the program's structure, ensuring that multiple tasks can make progress without waiting for one to finish before starting the next.
- **Parallelism** takes advantage of multiple processors or cores to execute tasks simultaneously, making them run faster and more efficiently.

In Go, **goroutines** provide a means of concurrency, and **parallelism** can be achieved when the program runs on a multi-core machine. By using Go's concurrency model effectively, you can write programs that handle multiple tasks efficiently, while the Go runtime automatically distributes tasks across available CPU cores for parallel execution.

While **concurrency** and **parallelism** are related concepts, they serve different purposes in modern programming:

- **Concurrency** is about structuring your program to manage multiple tasks in an overlapping manner, improving responsiveness and resource utilization.
- **Parallelism** is about executing tasks at the same time, taking full advantage of multiple CPU cores or processors.

Go's concurrency model is built around **goroutines** for concurrent task management and can automatically achieve **parallelism** on multi-core systems. By understanding the differences and relationships between concurrency and parallelism, you can better design your programs to be both efficient and scalable.

8.2. Goroutines: Lightweight Threads of Execution

Go's concurrency model is built around the concept of **goroutines**, which are **lightweight threads of execution** managed by the Go runtime. Unlike traditional threads, goroutines are incredibly efficient and can be created and scheduled in large numbers without consuming excessive system resources. This makes them ideal for

370

concurrent programming, where multiple tasks can be executed concurrently without the overhead of creating a full-fledged operating system thread.

In this section, we will explore **how to create and use goroutines**, and discuss **practical use cases** where goroutines can be leveraged to improve the performance and efficiency of Go programs.

Creating and Using Goroutines

A **goroutine** is created by prefixing a function call with the go keyword. This instructs the Go runtime to run the function asynchronously in a separate goroutine. The function call will not block the execution of the program, allowing the main function to continue executing while the goroutine runs in parallel.

Syntax for Creating a Goroutine

go

Copy

```
go functionName()
```

When you invoke a function with the go keyword, the Go runtime will schedule the function to run concurrently, allowing other goroutines to execute at the same time.

Example: Creating a Simple Goroutine

go

Copy

```
package main

import "fmt"
```

371

```go
func greet() {

    fmt.Println("Hello from the goroutine!")

}


func main() {

    go greet() // Start a goroutine to run the greet function


    fmt.Println("Hello from the main function!")

}
```

Example Output:

css

Copy

Hello from the main function!

Hello from the goroutine!

In this example:

- We start a goroutine by calling go greet().
- The main function prints "Hello from the main function!" while the goroutine concurrently prints "Hello from the goroutine!".
- The order of the output may vary because the main function and the goroutine are running concurrently.

How Goroutines Work

Goroutines are **lightweight** and are scheduled and managed by the Go runtime rather than the operating system. The Go runtime uses a model called **M:N scheduling**, where multiple goroutines (M) are mapped to a smaller number of operating system threads (N). This allows Go to efficiently handle thousands of goroutines without the overhead of creating individual OS threads for each goroutine.

Key Points About Goroutines:

- **Low overhead**: Goroutines are much lighter than OS threads, with each one consuming only a few kilobytes of memory.
- **Efficient scheduling**: The Go runtime automatically schedules and manages the execution of goroutines, so developers don't need to worry about managing threads manually.
- **Concurrency**: Goroutines allow multiple tasks to run concurrently, but the number of goroutines that can run in parallel depends on the number of CPU cores available and how the Go runtime schedules the goroutines.

Example: Multiple Goroutines in Action

go

Copy

```
package main

import "fmt"

func printNumbers() {
    for i := 1; i <= 5; i++ {
        fmt.Println(i)
    }
}
```

373

```go
func printLetters() {
    for i := 'a'; i <= 'e'; i++ {
        fmt.Println(string(i))
    }
}

func main() {
    go printNumbers() // Start a goroutine for printNumbers
    go printLetters() // Start a goroutine for printLetters

    // Wait for goroutines to finish
    fmt.Scanln()
}
```

In this example:

- We launch two goroutines: one for printing numbers and another for printing letters.
- The fmt.Scanln() function is used to block the main function, allowing the goroutines to complete before the program exits.

Example Output (Order May Vary):

css

Copy

```
1

a

2

b

3

c

4

d

5

e
```

In this example, both goroutines run concurrently. The order of numbers and letters may vary because the goroutines execute concurrently and are scheduled independently.

Practical Use Cases for Goroutines

Goroutines are extremely useful in real-world applications where concurrency is required. Let's look at some **practical use cases** where goroutines can be leveraged to improve the performance and efficiency of your Go programs.

---

1. Handling Multiple HTTP Requests in a Web Server

Web servers need to handle many incoming requests concurrently. Using goroutines, we can handle each HTTP request in a separate goroutine, allowing the server to process multiple requests at the same time without blocking.

Example: A Simple Web Server with Goroutines

go

Copy

```go
package main

import (
    "fmt"
    "net/http"
)

func handleRequest(w http.ResponseWriter, r *http.Request) {
    fmt.Println("Handling request:", r.URL.Path)
    fmt.Fprintf(w, "Hello, you've requested: %s\n", r.URL.Path)
}

func main() {
    http.HandleFunc("/", handleRequest)

    // Start a new goroutine to handle each request
```

```go
go http.ListenAndServe(":8080", nil)

fmt.Println("Server started on port 8080")

fmt.Scanln() // Block main goroutine to prevent the server from exiting
}
```

In this example:

- Each incoming HTTP request is handled by the handleRequest function, which runs concurrently as a goroutine.
- The ListenAndServe function is launched as a goroutine, allowing the server to handle multiple incoming requests simultaneously.
- This improves the efficiency of the web server by allowing multiple requests to be processed at once.

---

2. Parallelizing Computational Tasks

Goroutines can be used to break down computationally intensive tasks into smaller sub-tasks that can be processed concurrently. This is particularly useful when you want to take advantage of multiple cores to speed up execution.

Example: Parallelizing Computation

go

Copy

```go
package main

import "fmt"
```

```go
func square(n int, ch chan int) {

    ch <- n * n

}


func main() {

    numbers := []int{1, 2, 3, 4, 5}

    ch := make(chan int)


    for _, num := range numbers {

        go square(num, ch) // Start a goroutine for each number

    }


    // Collect results from the channel

    for range numbers {

        result := <-ch

        fmt.Println(result)

    }

}
```

In this example:

- We use a goroutine to calculate the square of each number in the numbers slice concurrently.
- We send the results of the calculations through a channel, allowing the main goroutine to collect the results and print them.

378

- This approach allows multiple computational tasks to run in parallel, improving performance when handling large datasets.

---

3. Real-Time Data Processing

Goroutines are particularly useful in **real-time data processing** scenarios, such as processing data from sensors, logs, or external APIs. By running multiple data processing tasks concurrently, the application can handle large volumes of real-time data more efficiently.

Example: Real-Time Data Processing with Goroutines

go

Copy

```
package main

import "fmt"
import "time"

// Simulate processing data from a sensor
func processData(sensorID int, ch chan string) {
    time.Sleep(1 * time.Second)  // Simulate data processing
    ch <- fmt.Sprintf("Data from sensor %d processed", sensorID)
}

func main() {
    ch := make(chan string)
```

```
// Launch a goroutine for each sensor

for i := 1; i <= 5; i++ {

    go processData(i, ch)

}


// Collect processed data from sensors

for i := 1; i <= 5; i++ {

    fmt.Println(<-ch)

}

}
```

In this example:

- We simulate processing data from five different sensors by launching five separate goroutines, each of which processes data independently.
- The ch channel is used to collect processed data from the goroutines, ensuring that the main goroutine waits for the results and then prints them.
- This model allows for **real-time data processing**, where multiple tasks are being processed concurrently without blocking one another.

---

4. Asynchronous Task Execution

Goroutines are ideal for executing tasks asynchronously. For example, a task that waits for some network operation or file I/O can be performed in the background, while the rest of the program continues executing without waiting for the task to finish.

Example: Asynchronous Task Execution

go

Copy

```go
package main

import (
    "fmt"
    "time"
)

func asyncTask() {
    fmt.Println("Task started")
    time.Sleep(3 * time.Second) // Simulate long-running task
    fmt.Println("Task completed")
}

func main() {
    go asyncTask() // Start the task in a goroutine

    fmt.Println("Main function continues")
    time.Sleep(4 * time.Second) // Wait for the task to finish
}
```

In this example:

- The asyncTask function is executed asynchronously as a goroutine.
- The main function continues executing without waiting for the task to finish, demonstrating the power of goroutines for **non-blocking operations**.
- The program waits for the task to complete by using time.Sleep(), but in real applications, you would likely use more robust synchronization techniques like channels or sync.WaitGroup to ensure proper completion.

Key takeaways:

- Goroutines are lightweight threads of execution, making them efficient and scalable.
- They are ideal for handling multiple concurrent tasks, such as HTTP requests, real-time data processing, and parallel computations.
- By using goroutines, you can build responsive, high-performance applications that can scale to handle increasing workloads.

8.3. Channels: Communication Between Goroutines

One of the most powerful features of Go's concurrency model is **channels**. Channels are a way for **goroutines** to communicate with each other and synchronize their execution. Channels allow goroutines to pass data safely between each other, enabling efficient concurrent programming. In this section, we will explore **what channels are**, how to use them to **send and receive data**, and how the **select statement** can be used to handle multiple channels concurrently.

What Are Channels?

A **channel** in Go is a **communication mechanism** that allows data to be passed between goroutines. Channels provide a safe and structured way for goroutines to communicate, ensuring that only one goroutine can send data into a channel, and only one goroutine can receive data from it at any given time. This mechanism makes it easy to synchronize goroutines and avoid the need for explicit locking or managing shared memory.

Channels are typed, meaning that they are designed to carry values of a specific type. You can create channels for any Go type, such as integers, strings, structs, and even other channels.

Declaring a Channel

To declare a channel, you use the make function, specifying the channel's type.

go

Copy

```
ch := make(chan int)  // A channel of integers
```

This creates a channel ch that can carry values of type int. Once a channel is created, you can use it to send and receive values between goroutines.

Closing a Channel

Channels can also be **closed** using the close function. Closing a channel indicates that no more values will be sent on the channel, and can be useful for signaling that all communication is complete.

go

Copy

```
close(ch)
```

Attempting to send data on a closed channel will result in a runtime panic, while attempting to receive from a closed channel will return the zero value of the channel's type (e.g., 0 for an int).

Sending and Receiving Data Through Channels

Once a channel is created, data can be passed between goroutines using the <- **operator**. This operator is used both to send data into the channel and to receive data from the channel.

Sending Data to a Channel

To send data to a channel, use the <- operator followed by the channel:

go

Copy

```
ch <- value  // Send value to the channel
```

For example:

go

Copy

```
ch <- 42  // Send the integer 42 to the channel
```

Receiving Data from a Channel

To receive data from a channel, use the <- operator on the channel:

go

Copy

```
value := <-ch  // Receive value from the channel
```

For example:

go

Copy

value := <-ch // Receive an integer value from the channel

fmt.Println(value) // Print the received value

Example: Sending and Receiving Data Through Channels

go

Copy

```
package main

import "fmt"

func sendData(ch chan int) {
    fmt.Println("Sending data to the channel")
    ch <- 42  // Send the value 42 into the channel
}

func main() {
    ch := make(chan int)  // Create a channel

    go sendData(ch)  // Start a goroutine to send data to the channel
```

```
receivedValue := <-ch  // Receive the value from the channel

fmt.Println("Received value:", receivedValue)  // Output: Received value: 42

}
```

In this example:

- The sendData function sends the integer 42 to the channel.
- The main function waits to receive this value from the channel and prints it.

Important Points:

- **Blocking behavior**: By default, sending and receiving on channels are **blocking** operations. This means that when a goroutine tries to send data to a channel, it will block until another goroutine is ready to receive the data. Similarly, when a goroutine tries to receive data from a channel, it will block until data is available.
- **Buffered Channels**: Channels can be either **unbuffered** or **buffered**. An unbuffered channel only allows one value to be sent and received at a time, causing the sending goroutine to block until the receiving goroutine is ready. A buffered channel, however, allows multiple values to be stored in the channel, which can improve performance by reducing blocking.

Buffered Channels

A **buffered channel** allows sending and receiving of values without blocking until the buffer is full (for sending) or empty (for receiving). Buffered channels are useful when you want to limit the amount of blocking that occurs in your program and allow more flexibility in how goroutines communicate.

To create a buffered channel, you specify a buffer size when calling make:

go

Copy

```
ch := make(chan int, 3)  // A buffered channel with a capacity of 3
```

This channel can hold up to 3 values before blocking the sender. Once the buffer is full, the sender will block until there is space available.

Example: Buffered Channel

go

Copy

```go
package main

import "fmt"

func sendData(ch chan int) {
    for i := 1; i <= 3; i++ {
        ch <- i  // Send data into the channel
        fmt.Println("Sent:", i)
    }
}

func main() {
    ch := make(chan int, 3)  // Create a buffered channel with a capacity of 3

    go sendData(ch)  // Start the goroutine to send data
```

```
for i := 1; i <= 3; i++ {

    value := <-ch  // Receive the value from the channel

    fmt.Println("Received:", value)

}

}
```

Example Output:

makefile

Copy

Sent: 1

Sent: 2

Sent: 3

Received: 1

Received: 2

Received: 3

In this example:

- The buffered channel allows the sendData goroutine to send values without blocking, even though the main goroutine is receiving values.
- The buffered channel allows for greater flexibility and performance when you need to handle larger volumes of data without blocking every send/receive operation.

Using Select to Handle Multiple Channels

The select statement in Go allows you to handle multiple channels simultaneously. It works similarly to a switch statement, but it works with channels instead of values. select enables a goroutine to wait on multiple channels and choose the first one that is ready to receive or send data.

Syntax of the select Statement

go

Copy

```
select {
case value := <-ch1:
    // Handle data received from ch1
case value := <-ch2:
    // Handle data received from ch2
case ch3 <- data:
    // Handle data sent to ch3
default:
    // Handle the case where no channel is ready
}
```

- The select statement blocks until one of the channels is ready to send or receive data.
- The first case that is ready will execute. If multiple cases are ready, one will be chosen randomly.
- You can use the default case to avoid blocking if none of the channels are ready.

389

Example: Using Select with Multiple Channels

go

Copy

```go
package main

import "fmt"

func sendData(ch chan int) {
    ch <- 42
}

func sendData2(ch chan int) {
    ch <- 56
}

func main() {
    ch1 := make(chan int)
    ch2 := make(chan int)

    go sendData(ch1)  // Start a goroutine to send data to ch1
    go sendData2(ch2) // Start a goroutine to send data to ch2
```

```go
select {
case value := <-ch1:
    fmt.Println("Received from ch1:", value)
case value := <-ch2:
    fmt.Println("Received from ch2:", value)
}
}
```

Example Output:

csharp

Copy

```
Received from ch1: 42
```

In this example:

- The select statement waits for data from either ch1 or ch2.
- The first channel that receives data will trigger the corresponding case, and the program will print the value received from that channel.
- If both channels were ready, one would be chosen randomly.

Channels are a fundamental part of Go's concurrency model, providing a safe, efficient, and structured way for **goroutines** to communicate and synchronize their execution. By using channels, you can pass data between goroutines without needing explicit locks, making concurrent programming more manageable and less error-prone.

Key takeaways:

- **Channels** allow goroutines to send and receive data safely, enabling efficient communication between concurrently executing tasks.
- **Buffered channels** allow goroutines to send and receive data without blocking, improving performance in certain situations.
- **Select statements** enable handling multiple channels concurrently, allowing you to wait on multiple operations and handle whichever one is ready first.

8.4. Practical Concurrency Examples

In this section, we will explore how to **build concurrency** into your Go programs through practical examples. We will also look at how to **synchronize goroutines** using the sync.WaitGroup, a critical tool for coordinating multiple goroutines in concurrent Go programs. By the end of this section, you will be equipped with the skills to implement concurrency and synchronization in real-world applications.

Building Concurrency Into Your Go Programs

Concurrency in Go allows you to handle multiple tasks simultaneously without blocking the main execution flow. Whether you're building web servers, real-time applications, or computational systems, Go's concurrency model provides a simple and efficient way to perform multiple tasks concurrently. Below are practical examples demonstrating how to build concurrency into your Go programs.

Example 1: Concurrently Fetching Data from Multiple APIs

In modern applications, you often need to fetch data from multiple APIs or sources. Instead of waiting for each request to complete sequentially, you can fetch data concurrently to improve performance.

Task:

- Fetch data from two APIs concurrently and print the results when both have completed.

Solution:

go

Copy

```go
package main

import (
	"fmt"
	"time"
)

func fetchDataFromAPI1(ch chan string) {
	time.Sleep(2 * time.Second) // Simulate a delay in API1 response
	ch <- "Data from API 1"
}

func fetchDataFromAPI2(ch chan string) {
	time.Sleep(1 * time.Second) // Simulate a delay in API2 response
	ch <- "Data from API 2"
}

func main() {
	ch1 := make(chan string)
```

```
ch2 := make(chan string)


// Start concurrent goroutines

go fetchDataFromAPI1(ch1)

go fetchDataFromAPI2(ch2)


// Wait for data from both channels

data1 := <-ch1

data2 := <-ch2


fmt.Println(data1)  // Output: Data from API 1

fmt.Println(data2)  // Output: Data from API 2

}
```

In this example:

- We use two goroutines to fetch data concurrently from two APIs.
- The time.Sleep() function simulates a delay that is typical when waiting for external API responses.
- Both goroutines run concurrently, and the main function waits for the results from both channels using the <- operator. The order of the results may vary, as they are fetched concurrently.

This concurrency model is particularly useful when dealing with I/O-bound tasks, such as HTTP requests, file I/O, and database queries.

Example 2: Concurrently Processing Multiple Files

For applications that need to process multiple files (e.g., analyzing log files, reading from databases), concurrency can significantly speed up the process by allowing multiple files to be processed in parallel.

Task:

- Read and process multiple files concurrently.

Solution:

go

Copy

```go
package main

import (
        "fmt"
        "time"
)


func processFile(filename string, ch chan string) {
        time.Sleep(2 * time.Second)  // Simulate file processing delay
        ch <- fmt.Sprintf("Processed %s", filename)
}


func main() {
```

```go
files := []string{"file1.txt", "file2.txt", "file3.txt"}

ch := make(chan string)

// Start concurrent goroutines to process each file
for _, file := range files {

        go processFile(file, ch)

}

// Wait for all goroutines to finish and receive the results
for range files {

        result := <-ch

        fmt.Println(result)

}

}
```

In this example:

- The processFile function simulates processing files by sleeping for 2 seconds.
- We start a new goroutine for each file, allowing the files to be processed concurrently.
- The main function waits for all goroutines to finish by receiving the results from the channel.

Concurrency significantly reduces the total time required for processing when there are multiple independent tasks, such as file processing or data analysis.

Synchronizing Goroutines with WaitGroups

In some situations, it's necessary to synchronize the execution of multiple goroutines. Go's sync.WaitGroup is a powerful synchronization primitive that allows you to wait for a collection of goroutines to finish executing before proceeding with the next step in the program.

The sync.WaitGroup works by keeping track of the number of goroutines that need to finish. You increment the WaitGroup counter before starting a goroutine and decrement it when the goroutine completes. The main goroutine can then wait for all goroutines to finish by calling Wait().

Example: Using sync.WaitGroup for Synchronization

Task:

- Perform several tasks concurrently and wait for all tasks to complete before moving forward.

Solution:

go

Copy

```go
package main

import (
        "fmt"
        "sync"
        "time"
)

func task(id int, wg *sync.WaitGroup) {
```

```go
        defer wg.Done() // Decrement the counter when the task completes
        time.Sleep(time.Duration(id) * time.Second) // Simulate different task durations
        fmt.Printf("Task %d completed\n", id)
}


func main() {
        var wg sync.WaitGroup

        // Start 5 goroutines
        for i := 1; i <= 5; i++ {
                wg.Add(1) // Increment the counter
                go task(i, &wg)
        }

        // Wait for all goroutines to complete
        wg.Wait()

        fmt.Println("All tasks are completed")
}
```

Example Output:

arduino

Copy

Task 1 completed

Task 2 completed

Task 3 completed

Task 4 completed

Task 5 completed

All tasks are completed

In this example:

- We use a sync.WaitGroup to synchronize the completion of multiple tasks.
- The task function simulates a task by sleeping for a period of time proportional to its ID.
- The main function increments the WaitGroup counter before launching each goroutine and decrements the counter when the task completes.
- The wg.Wait() call in the main function blocks until all goroutines have finished executing.

Using a WaitGroup ensures that the main function waits for all concurrent tasks to finish before proceeding.

Practical Use Cases for Goroutines and Synchronization

Now that we've covered how to use goroutines and synchronization with WaitGroup, let's explore some **real-world use cases** where this approach is particularly beneficial.

1. Web Servers Handling Multiple Requests

Web servers often need to handle multiple client requests concurrently. By using goroutines and synchronizing them with WaitGroup, you can efficiently handle multiple HTTP requests without blocking the server's responsiveness.

Example: Handling Multiple HTTP Requests Concurrently

go

Copy

```go
package main

import (
    "fmt"
    "net/http"
    "sync"
)

func handleRequest(w http.ResponseWriter, r *http.Request, wg *sync.WaitGroup) {
    defer wg.Done()  // Decrement the counter when done
    fmt.Println("Handling request:", r.URL.Path)
    fmt.Fprintf(w, "Hello, you've requested: %s\n", r.URL.Path)
}

func main() {
    var wg sync.WaitGroup
```

```go
http.HandleFunc("/", func(w http.ResponseWriter, r *http.Request) {

    wg.Add(1) // Increment the counter for each request

    go handleRequest(w, r, &wg) // Handle each request in a goroutine

})


go func() {

    wg.Wait() // Wait for all requests to complete

    fmt.Println("All requests handled")

}()


http.ListenAndServe(":8080", nil)

}
```

In this example:

- Each incoming HTTP request is handled by a goroutine.
- We use a sync.WaitGroup to wait for all requests to finish processing before printing "All requests handled".

---

2. Parallel Data Processing in Distributed Systems

In distributed systems, tasks are often processed in parallel to improve throughput and reduce latency. For example, if you're processing large datasets or making parallel database queries, using goroutines and WaitGroup for synchronization allows for efficient parallel execution.

401

Example: Parallel Database Queries

go

Copy

```go
package main

import (
    "fmt"
    "sync"
    "time"
)

func queryDatabase(query string, wg *sync.WaitGroup) {
    defer wg.Done() // Decrement counter when the query is done
    time.Sleep(1 * time.Second) // Simulate query delay
    fmt.Println("Query", query, "completed")
}

func main() {
    var wg sync.WaitGroup

    queries := []string{"SELECT * FROM users", "SELECT * FROM orders", "SELECT * FROM products"}
```

```
for _, query := range queries {

    wg.Add(1)  // Increment the counter for each query

    go queryDatabase(query, &wg)

}


wg.Wait()  // Wait for all goroutines to finish

fmt.Println("All database queries completed")

}
```

In this example:

- We simulate parallel database queries using goroutines.
- Each query is run concurrently, and we use a WaitGroup to wait for all queries to complete before printing the final message.

Concurrency is a powerful tool that can help you build efficient, scalable programs. In Go, **goroutines** allow you to run tasks concurrently without the overhead of traditional threads. By using sync.WaitGroup, you can synchronize multiple goroutines to ensure that tasks are completed before proceeding.

Key takeaways:

- **Goroutines** enable lightweight concurrent execution, allowing multiple tasks to run concurrently without blocking.
- sync.WaitGroup provides an easy way to wait for multiple goroutines to finish before continuing with the main program.

- **Practical examples** of goroutines and synchronization include handling multiple HTTP requests, processing data in parallel, and managing tasks in distributed systems.

With these tools, Go enables you to build highly concurrent and parallel applications that are both efficient and scalable. In the next section, we will explore more advanced concurrency patterns and synchronization techniques, such as **mutexes**, **channels**, and **atomic operations**.

Chapter 9: Building a Simple Project

9.1. Project Overview: Building a To-Do List Application

In this chapter, we will walk through the development of a simple yet practical project: a **To-Do List Application**. This project will give you hands-on experience with Go's features, such as **goroutines**, **channels**, and **concurrency**, as well as introduce you to basic **file handling**, **data structures**, and **user input processing**.

The To-Do List application is a great way to practice your Go programming skills while building something functional and useful. Through this project, you will be able to see how Go's powerful concurrency model and simple syntax come together to create an easy-to-use and scalable application.

This section will provide an **overview of the project** and help you understand the **key features** that we will implement. We will then break down the project into manageable components to give you a clear roadmap for building your own To-Do List application.

Understanding the Project and Key Features

The primary goal of this project is to build a basic **To-Do List** application that allows users to:

1. **Add tasks** to the list.
2. **Mark tasks as completed**.
3. **Delete tasks** from the list.
4. **View the list** of tasks with their status (completed or pending).

Core Features of the To-Do List Application

Here are the core features we will implement in this simple To-Do List application:

1. **Add Tasks**: Users can add tasks to the to-do list with a title and description.
2. **View Tasks**: The application will display the current list of tasks, showing whether each task is completed or still pending.
3. **Complete Tasks**: Users can mark tasks as "completed". Completed tasks will be displayed with a different visual status to indicate their completion.

4. **Delete Tasks**: Users will be able to delete tasks from the list once they are no longer needed.
5. **Task Persistence**: The tasks should persist between application runs. We will implement **file storage** to save tasks to a file, ensuring that tasks remain available when the application is restarted.

Structuring the Project

To make the development process easier to follow and manage, we will break down the To-Do List application into logical components:

1. **Data Structure (Task Model)**:
   o We will define a Task **struct** to represent a task in the to-do list.
   o Each task will have a **title**, **description**, and **status** (completed or pending).
2. **Task Management Functions**:
   o Functions to **add**, **delete**, **mark complete**, and **view tasks**.
   o We will also have a function to **load tasks** from a file and **save tasks** to a file, ensuring data persistence.
3. **User Interface (UI)**:
   o A simple **command-line interface** (CLI) that allows users to interact with the application by entering commands such as "add", "delete", "view", and "complete".
   o The UI will also display the list of tasks in a human-readable format.
4. **Concurrency**:
   o We will implement basic **concurrency** where appropriate. For instance, managing multiple user actions concurrently (such as adding and viewing tasks) without blocking the main program flow.
   o Go's **goroutines** and **channels** will be used to handle operations concurrently, such as writing to the file or performing operations on the list while displaying the UI.

Data Structure: Task Model

To represent a task, we will define a Task **struct**. This struct will store the task title, description, and status (whether the task is completed or not).

Here's an example of how the Task **struct** will be defined in Go:

go
Copy
```go
package main

// Task represents a to-do item
type Task struct {
    Title       string
    Description string
    Completed   bool
}
```

- Title: A string that holds the name or title of the task (e.g., "Buy groceries").
- Description: A string that holds further details about the task (e.g., "Buy milk, eggs, and bread").
- Completed: A boolean flag to indicate whether the task has been completed (true) or is still pending (false).

Task Management Functions

The task management functions will handle adding, deleting, completing, and viewing tasks.

1. **Adding a Task**:
   - This function will take user input for the task's title and description, create a new Task struct, and add it to the task list.
   - We will also store the task list in a file to persist the data.

go
Copy
```go
func addTask(title, description string) {
    task := Task{Title: title, Description: description, Completed: false}
    tasks = append(tasks, task)
    saveTasksToFile() // Save the updated task list to a file
}
```

407

2. **Viewing Tasks**:
   - This function will iterate over the tasks and display their details. It will show whether each task is completed or pending.

go
Copy
```go
func viewTasks() {
   for _, task := range tasks {
      status := "Pending"
      if task.Completed {
         status = "Completed"
      }
         fmt.Printf("Title: %s, Description: %s, Status: %s\n", task.Title, task.Description,
status)
   }
}
```

3. **Completing a Task**:
   - This function will take the index of a task and mark it as completed.

go
Copy
```go
func completeTask(index int) {
   if index >= 0 && index < len(tasks) {
      tasks[index].Completed = true
      saveTasksToFile() // Save the updated task list to a file
   }
}
```

4. **Deleting a Task**:
   - This function will remove a task from the list by its index and save the updated list.

go
Copy
```go
func deleteTask(index int) {
   if index >= 0 && index < len(tasks) {
```

408

```go
        tasks = append(tasks[:index], tasks[index+1:]...)  // Remove the task at the given
index
        saveTasksToFile()  // Save the updated task list to a file
    }
}
```

File Storage for Task Persistence

To persist the tasks between application runs, we will use **file handling**. When tasks are added, completed, or deleted, the task list will be saved to a file, and when the application starts, the tasks will be loaded from the file.

1. **Saving Tasks to a File**:
   - We will convert the task list to a format that can be written to a file. In this case, we will use **JSON** to serialize the tasks.

```go
go
Copy
import (
    "encoding/json"
    "os"
)

func saveTasksToFile() {
    file, err := os.Create("tasks.json")
    if err != nil {
        fmt.Println("Error creating file:", err)
        return
    }
    defer file.Close()

    encoder := json.NewEncoder(file)
    err = encoder.Encode(tasks)
    if err != nil {
        fmt.Println("Error encoding tasks:", err)
    }
}
```

2. **Loading Tasks from a File**:
   - When the program starts, we will read the tasks.json file and deserialize it back into a slice of tasks.

go
Copy
```go
func loadTasksFromFile() {
    file, err := os.Open("tasks.json")
    if err != nil {
        fmt.Println("Error opening file:", err)
        return
    }
    defer file.Close()

    decoder := json.NewDecoder(file)
    err = decoder.Decode(&tasks)
    if err != nil {
        fmt.Println("Error decoding tasks:", err)
    }
}
```

Synchronizing Goroutines with WaitGroup

In this simple To-Do List application, we may need to use **goroutines** to handle different parts of the application concurrently. For instance, handling user input while simultaneously updating the task list or saving to a file. However, when working with multiple goroutines, we need to ensure that they complete their tasks before the program exits.

We can use a sync.WaitGroup to synchronize these goroutines. The WaitGroup allows us to wait for multiple goroutines to finish before proceeding.

Here's an example of using a WaitGroup to wait for multiple tasks to finish:

go
Copy
```go
import "sync"
```

```
var wg sync.WaitGroup

func main() {
    wg.Add(2)  // Wait for two goroutines

    go func() {
        defer wg.Done()  // Decrement the counter when done
        // Simulate some task
    }()

    go func() {
        defer wg.Done()  // Decrement the counter when done
        // Simulate another task
    }()

    wg.Wait()  // Wait for both goroutines to finish
    fmt.Println("All tasks are done!")
}
```

In this example:

- We add two tasks to the WaitGroup.
- Each goroutine calls wg.Done() when it finishes its work.
- The main function calls wg.Wait() to block until both goroutines are complete.

In this section, we have outlined the **To-Do List Application** project, where we will:

- Use Go's concurrency features like **goroutines** for concurrent task execution.
- Implement a **task data model** using Go's struct.
- Persist data with **file handling** using JSON to store and load tasks.
- Synchronize goroutines with the sync.WaitGroup to ensure tasks complete before the program exits.

By building this application, you will gain practical experience with many key aspects of Go programming, including task management, file storage, concurrency, and synchronization.

Setting Up the Project Structure

In order to make our **To-Do List application** organized, modular, and easy to maintain, it's essential to establish a well-structured directory layout for our Go project. This structure will allow us to separate different concerns of the application and manage our code efficiently. Proper organization also ensures that the project can grow and scale as we add more features in the future.

This section will guide you through setting up the project structure and preparing the necessary files and directories for our **To-Do List application**.

Step 1: Create the Project Directory

First, we need to create the root directory for our project. This will house all our Go files, configuration files, and any other assets we might need.

bash

Copy

```
mkdir todo-app

cd todo-app
```

This will create a directory named todo-app where we will store all the code and related files for our project.

Step 2: Organize the Directory Structure

Inside the root directory, we will create a few subdirectories and files to keep the project organized.

Here's how the project structure will look:

graphql

Copy

```
todo-app/
|
├── main.go        # Main entry point for the application
├── todo/
|   ├── task.go      # Contains the Task struct and related functions
|   ├── task_manager.go # Handles adding, deleting, completing tasks
|   └── storage.go   # Handles file I/O for saving and loading tasks
├── go.mod         # Go module file to manage dependencies
└── tasks.json     # File to store tasks in JSON format (persistent storage)
```

- **main.go**: This is the entry point for the application. It will import the other files and start the program's execution.
- **todo/**: This directory will contain all the logic related to tasks and their management. It's organized into separate files for clarity:
  - **task.go**: Defines the Task struct.
  - **task_manager.go**: Contains functions for managing tasks, such as adding, deleting, and marking tasks as complete.
  - **storage.go**: Contains functions to save and load tasks to/from a file (e.g., tasks.json).
- **go.mod**: A Go module file used to manage dependencies (if any). It will allow you to build and run the application consistently.

413

- **tasks.json**: A file used to persist the list of tasks between application runs. It stores the tasks in JSON format.

Step 3: Create the Main File (main.go)

The main.go file is where we will initialize and run our application. This file will import the necessary packages and start the task manager.

Here's an initial skeleton for main.go:

go

Copy

```go
package main

import (
    "fmt"
    "todo"
)

func main() {
    // Load tasks from file
    todo.LoadTasks()

    // Display the menu and interact with the user
    fmt.Println("Welcome to the To-Do List Application!")
    fmt.Println("1. Add Task")
```

```go
fmt.Println("2. View Tasks")

fmt.Println("3. Mark Task as Complete")

fmt.Println("4. Delete Task")

fmt.Println("5. Exit")


// For simplicity, we'll simulate user input and interactions in the main function

// In the actual program, you would add a function to handle user input dynamically.

}
```

- The main.go file imports the todo package to access the task management and file storage functionalities.
- It loads the tasks when the program starts and displays a basic menu for user interactions. In a real-world scenario, you would interact with the user via **command-line inputs**.

Step 4: Define the Task Model (task.go)

In the todo/ directory, the first file we'll create is task.go, which defines the **Task struct** and any methods associated with it.

go

Copy

```go
package todo


// Task represents a to-do item

type Task struct {
```

415

```go
    Title       string

    Description string

    Completed   bool

}
```

- The Task struct contains three fields: Title, Description, and Completed.
- We will later add methods to manipulate tasks, such as marking them complete and deleting them.

Step 5: Handle Task Management (task_manager.go)

Next, we will create the file task_manager.go to manage tasks. This file will contain functions for adding tasks, marking tasks as completed, deleting tasks, and viewing the tasks.

go

Copy

```go
package todo


import "fmt"


// Global list of tasks

var tasks []Task


// AddTask adds a new task to the task list

func AddTask(title, description string) {
```

416

```go
    task := Task{Title: title, Description: description, Completed: false}

    tasks = append(tasks, task)

    fmt.Println("Task added:", task)

}


// ViewTasks displays all tasks with their status

func ViewTasks() {

    if len(tasks) == 0 {

        fmt.Println("No tasks available.")

        return

    }


    fmt.Println("Current Tasks:")

    for i, task := range tasks {

        status := "Pending"

        if task.Completed {

            status = "Completed"

        }

        fmt.Printf("%d. %s - %s [%s]\n", i+1, task.Title, task.Description, status)

    }

}
```

417

```go
// CompleteTask marks a task as completed
func CompleteTask(index int) {
    if index >= 0 && index < len(tasks) {
        tasks[index].Completed = true
        fmt.Println("Task completed:", tasks[index].Title)
    } else {
        fmt.Println("Invalid task index")
    }
}


// DeleteTask removes a task from the list
func DeleteTask(index int) {
    if index >= 0 && index < len(tasks) {
        tasks = append(tasks[:index], tasks[index+1:]...)
        fmt.Println("Task deleted.")
    } else {
        fmt.Println("Invalid task index")
    }
}
```

- AddTask: Adds a new task to the tasks slice.
- ViewTasks: Displays all tasks, showing whether they are **Pending** or **Completed**.
- CompleteTask: Marks a task as completed.

- DeleteTask: Deletes a task from the list.

Step 6: Implement Task Persistence (storage.go)

Now, we will add file handling in storage.go to load and save tasks to a JSON file (tasks.json). This will allow us to persist the list of tasks across application runs.

go

Copy

```go
package todo

import (
    "encoding/json"
    "fmt"
    "os"
)

// LoadTasks loads tasks from the JSON file
func LoadTasks() {
    file, err := os.Open("tasks.json")
    if err != nil {
        if os.IsNotExist(err) {
            fmt.Println("No tasks found, starting with an empty list.")
            return
        }
```

```go
        fmt.Println("Error opening file:", err)

        return

    }

    defer file.Close()


    decoder := json.NewDecoder(file)

    err = decoder.Decode(&tasks)

    if err != nil {

        fmt.Println("Error decoding tasks:", err)

    }

}


// SaveTasks saves the current tasks to the JSON file

func SaveTasks() {

    file, err := os.Create("tasks.json")

    if err != nil {

        fmt.Println("Error creating file:", err)

        return

    }

    defer file.Close()


    encoder := json.NewEncoder(file)
```

```
err = encoder.Encode(tasks)

if err != nil {

    fmt.Println("Error encoding tasks:", err)

}

}
```

- **LoadTasks**: **Loads tasks from the** tasks.json **file. If the file doesn't exist, it simply initializes an empty list of tasks.**
- **SaveTasks**: **Saves the list of tasks to the** tasks.json **file, ensuring that changes are persisted between application runs.**

Step 7: Initialize the Go Module

Since we're working with Go modules, you'll need to initialize the module for your project. Run the following command to create a go.mod file:

bash

Copy

```
go mod init todo-app
```

This will create a go.mod file to manage the dependencies for your project. Even though this project doesn't currently have external dependencies, the go.mod file will allow you to easily add dependencies in the future.

We've now set up the basic structure for the To-Do List application:

- **Task management functions** are in task_manager.go.

- **Task data model** is defined in task.go.
- **File storage** is handled in storage.go.
- The **main entry point** is in main.go.

With this structure in place, we are ready to begin implementing the application logic and handling user interactions, such as adding tasks, viewing tasks, marking them as completed, and deleting them. In the following chapters, we will dive into implementing the user interface, running the application, and testing it for real-world use.

9.2. Writing the Code: From Start to Finish

In this section, we will walk through the process of writing the core functionality for the **To-Do List Application**. This includes creating functions for **adding, deleting**, and **displaying tasks**, as well as implementing **user input** and **output** to interact with the application through the command line.

We will start by implementing the main logic for interacting with the task list and then add a user-friendly interface that allows users to manage their tasks.

---

1. Creating Functions for Adding, Deleting, and Displaying Tasks

We have already set up the basic task management functions in the previous section (task_manager.go). In this part, we will refine those functions and ensure that they perform the necessary operations on the tasks list. We will also make sure that changes to the tasks are persisted in the tasks.json file.

Adding a Task

The AddTask function is responsible for adding a new task to the list. We will enhance it to prompt the user for input and then save the task.

go

Copy

```
package todo
```

```go
import "fmt"

// AddTask prompts the user for a task's title and description, then adds it to the task list
func AddTask() {
    var title, description string
    fmt.Print("Enter task title: ")
    fmt.Scanln(&title)
    fmt.Print("Enter task description: ")
    fmt.Scanln(&description)

    task := Task{Title: title, Description: description, Completed: false}
    tasks = append(tasks, task)

    SaveTasks() // Save the updated task list to the file
    fmt.Println("Task added successfully!")
}
```

In this implementation:

- The function asks the user to input a task's title and description.
- It creates a new Task struct and appends it to the global tasks slice.
- The SaveTasks function is called to persist the updated task list to the tasks.json file.

Deleting a Task

The DeleteTask function will allow users to delete a task by specifying its index. After removing the task from the list, the task list will be saved to the file.

go

Copy

```go
package todo

import "fmt"

// DeleteTask prompts the user for the task index and removes it from the list
func DeleteTask() {
    fmt.Print("Enter the index of the task to delete: ")
    var index int
    fmt.Scanln(&index)

    if index >= 1 && index <= len(tasks) {
        tasks = append(tasks[:index-1], tasks[index:]...) // Remove the task from the list
        SaveTasks() // Save the updated task list to the file
        fmt.Println("Task deleted successfully!")
    } else {
        fmt.Println("Invalid task index.")
    }
}
```

424

In this implementation:

- The function prompts the user for the task index they wish to delete.
- It checks if the index is valid, then removes the task by slicing the tasks list.
- After modifying the task list, SaveTasks is called to persist the changes.

Viewing Tasks

The ViewTasks function will display all tasks, showing whether they are completed or still pending. We will update it to format the display neatly and include the status of each task.

go

Copy

```go
package todo


import "fmt"


// ViewTasks displays all tasks with their status

func ViewTasks() {

  if len(tasks) == 0 {

    fmt.Println("No tasks available.")

    return

  }


  fmt.Println("To-Do List:")

  for i, task := range tasks {
```

```go
status := "Pending"

if task.Completed {

    status = "Completed"

}

fmt.Printf("%d. %s - %s [%s]\n", i+1, task.Title, task.Description, status)

}

}
```

In this implementation:

- The function checks if there are any tasks in the list. If the list is empty, it prints a message indicating that there are no tasks.
- For each task, it prints the task's title, description, and status (whether it's **Pending** or **Completed**).
- The task index is displayed in a human-readable format, starting from 1.

---

2. Implementing User Input and Output

Now that we have the core task management functions in place, we need to set up a simple command-line interface (CLI) to allow the user to interact with the application. The user will be able to choose from various options, such as adding a task, deleting a task, viewing all tasks, or exiting the program.

Displaying the Main Menu

In the main.go file, we will present a menu with options for the user to choose from. Depending on the user's input, we will call the appropriate function to perform the desired task.

426

Here's the implementation of the main menu and user input handling:

go

Copy

```go
package main

import (
    "fmt"
    "todo"
)

func main() {
    // Load existing tasks from the file
    todo.LoadTasks()

    for {
        fmt.Println("\nTo-Do List Application")
        fmt.Println("1. Add Task")
        fmt.Println("2. View Tasks")
        fmt.Println("3. Complete Task")
        fmt.Println("4. Delete Task")
        fmt.Println("5. Exit")
```

```go
    var choice int

    fmt.Print("Enter your choice: ")

    fmt.Scanln(&choice)


    switch choice {
    case 1:
        todo.AddTask()  // Add a task
    case 2:
        todo.ViewTasks()  // View all tasks
    case 3:
        todo.CompleteTask()  // Mark a task as completed
    case 4:
        todo.DeleteTask()  // Delete a task
    case 5:
        fmt.Println("Exiting application...")

        return
    default:
        fmt.Println("Invalid choice, please try again.")

    }

    }

}
```

How This Works:

- The main() function displays the main menu to the user, with options to add a task, view tasks, complete a task, delete a task, or exit the application.
- It waits for the user to input a number corresponding to their choice and calls the corresponding function based on the input.
- The program uses a switch statement to handle different choices. For instance, if the user selects **1**, it calls the AddTask() function to add a new task. Similarly, it handles other tasks based on user input.

---

3. Implementing Task Completion

For the **Complete Task** feature, we need to add the ability for users to mark a task as completed. We will implement a function that prompts the user to enter the index of the task they want to mark as completed. The function will update the task's Completed field and save the updated list to the file.

go

Copy

```go
package todo


import "fmt"


// CompleteTask prompts the user for the task index and marks it as completed

func CompleteTask() {

    fmt.Print("Enter the index of the task to mark as completed: ")

    var index int

    fmt.Scanln(&index)
```

```
if index >= 1 && index <= len(tasks) {

    tasks[index-1].Completed = true  // Mark the task as completed

    SaveTasks() // Save the updated task list to the file

    fmt.Println("Task marked as completed!")

} else {

    fmt.Println("Invalid task index.")

}

}
```

In this implementation:

- The user is prompted to input the index of the task they wish to mark as completed.
- If the index is valid, the task is marked as completed by setting the Completed field to true.
- After updating the task, SaveTasks() is called to ensure that the task list is saved to the file.

Now that we have implemented the core features, the next steps would include refining the user interface, adding more advanced features (e.g., editing tasks), and performing thorough testing.

At this point, we have successfully implemented the core features of the **To-Do List Application**:

- We can **add**, **delete**, **view**, and **complete** tasks.

- We have integrated **file storage** to ensure that tasks are persisted between application runs.
- The application provides a simple **command-line interface (CLI)** for user interaction.

By following this process, you now have a functional To-Do List application in Go. You've seen how Go's concurrency model and simple syntax make it easy to manage multiple tasks and handle user input efficiently.

9.3. Testing and Debugging Your Project

Now that we've implemented the core functionality of the **To-Do List Application**, it's time to ensure that everything works as expected. Testing and debugging are crucial parts of the software development process, helping us identify bugs, performance issues, and edge cases in our application. In this section, we'll walk through how to write **tests** for our Go project and how to **debug** common issues that might arise during development.

Running Tests

Go provides built-in support for testing through the testing package. By writing tests, you can ensure that your functions and features are working as expected and prevent bugs when making future changes to the code.

Step 1: Setting Up Test Files

First, we need to create test files that correspond to the functionality we want to test. In Go, test files should have the suffix *_test.go. For example, we can create the following test files:

- **task_manager_test.go**: For testing the task management functions (add, delete, complete, view tasks).
- **storage_test.go**: For testing the file handling functions (saving and loading tasks).

Step 2: Writing Basic Tests

Let's start by writing basic tests for the task management functions. For simplicity, we'll focus on testing the **AddTask**, **ViewTasks**, and **DeleteTask** functions.

Testing AddTask and ViewTasks

The AddTask function modifies the global tasks slice, so we need to check whether it correctly adds tasks to the list. The ViewTasks function displays the tasks, so we need to check that it prints the tasks as expected.

go

Copy

```go
package todo

import (
    "testing"
    "fmt"
)

func TestAddTask(t *testing.T) {
    // Clear tasks before testing
    tasks = []Task{}

    // Add a task
    AddTask("Test Task", "This is a test task")

    // Check if the task was added
    if len(tasks) != 1 {
```

```go
        t.Errorf("Expected 1 task, but got %d", len(tasks))
    }

    if tasks[0].Title != "Test Task" {
        t.Errorf("Expected task title 'Test Task', but got '%s'", tasks[0].Title)
    }
}

func TestViewTasks(t *testing.T) {
    // Clear tasks before testing
    tasks = []Task{}

    // Add tasks
    AddTask("Test Task 1", "First test task")
    AddTask("Test Task 2", "Second test task")

    // Capture the output of ViewTasks
    output := fmt.Sprintf("%s", tasks)

    // Check if tasks are displayed correctly
    if len(tasks) != 2 {
        t.Errorf("Expected 2 tasks, but got %d", len(tasks))
```

433

```
    }

    if !contains(output, "Test Task 1") || !contains(output, "Test Task 2") {

        t.Errorf("Expected tasks to be displayed, but they were not")

    }

}


func contains(s, substr string) bool {

    return strings.Contains(s, substr)

}
```

In this test:

- The TestAddTask function adds a task to the task list and verifies that the task has been added correctly.
- The TestViewTasks function adds two tasks and then verifies that they are correctly displayed.
- We also use the helper function contains() to check if the output contains the expected task titles.

Step 3: Running Tests

To run the tests, you can use the Go testing tool. In the project directory, run the following command:

bash

Copy

```
go test -v
```

This will run all the test functions in the project and display detailed results. If any tests fail, the -v flag will provide additional information to help you diagnose the problem.

Debugging Common Issues

While writing and running tests, you might encounter some common issues that need to be debugged. Here are a few strategies for debugging your Go application effectively:

1. Using fmt.Println for Debugging

One of the simplest ways to debug Go code is to insert fmt.Println() statements throughout your code to inspect the value of variables, check the program flow, or verify assumptions.

For example, you can print the contents of the tasks slice after performing an operation to verify that the tasks are being correctly added or deleted.

go

Copy

```
fmt.Println("Tasks after adding:", tasks)
```

This helps you quickly identify where the problem is occurring and understand the current state of your program.

2. Using the Go Debugger (delve)

For more advanced debugging, Go provides delve, a powerful debugger that allows you to step through your code, inspect variables, and set breakpoints. To use delve, follow these steps:

1. **Install Delve**:
   If you don't have delve installed, run the following command to install it:
   bash
   Copy
   ```
   go install github.com/go-delve/delve/cmd/dlv@latest
   ```

2. **Start a Debugging Session**:
   Run the following command to start your program with delve:
   bash
   Copy
   ```
   dlv debug
   ```

This will start your program and allow you to interactively debug it. For example, you can set breakpoints and step through your code line by line:
bash
Copy
```
break main.go:15  # Set a breakpoint at line 15

continue  # Start execution and stop at the breakpoint

step  # Step through the code line by line
```

3. **Inspect Variables**:
   You can inspect the value of variables using the print command:
   bash
   Copy
   ```
   print tasks
   ```

1. This will display the current state of the tasks variable, helping you understand what is happening at that point in the code.

3. Handling Errors and Edge Cases

Go provides an effective way to handle errors using the error type. If your application is failing due to unhandled errors (e.g., file I/O errors, invalid inputs), ensure that you are checking for errors at each stage of your program.

For example, in the SaveTasks function, make sure to check for file-related errors properly:

go

Copy

```go
file, err := os.Create("tasks.json")

if err != nil {

    fmt.Println("Error creating file:", err)

    return

}

defer file.Close()


// Proceed with saving tasks
```

By checking and handling errors, you can prevent your application from crashing and provide more meaningful feedback to users.

Debugging Common Issues in the To-Do List Application

Let's walk through some common issues that you might encounter during development and how to resolve them:

1. Task List Not Updating After Adding Tasks

If tasks aren't showing up after you add them, check the following:

- Ensure that you are calling SaveTasks() after adding a task to persist the changes.
- Double-check that the tasks are actually being added to the tasks slice before calling SaveTasks().

2. Incorrect Output After Deleting Tasks

If deleting a task doesn't work, ensure that:

- The correct task index is passed to the DeleteTask function.
- The task is removed properly by using append() to adjust the tasks slice.
- After modifying the tasks slice, SaveTasks() should be called to reflect the changes in the file.

3. Program Crashes When Viewing Tasks

If the program crashes when viewing tasks, ensure that:

- The tasks slice is properly initialized and not nil.
- The ViewTasks function handles empty task lists correctly (i.e., it should print "No tasks available" when the list is empty).

Testing and debugging are crucial steps in building reliable software. In this section, we have:

- Set up unit tests to verify that the key functions (adding, viewing, and deleting tasks) work correctly.
- Used Go's built-in testing package to run tests and validate the functionality of our application.

- Discussed basic debugging techniques, including using fmt.Println() for quick debugging and using the delve debugger for more advanced debugging tasks.
- Addressed common issues that might arise in the To-Do List application and how to troubleshoot them effectively.

With testing and debugging in place, you can now confidently develop and refine your Go application, ensuring that it behaves as expected and handles edge cases gracefully. In the next chapter, we will explore how to enhance the application with additional features, such as task editing, user authentication, and a more advanced user interface.

9.4. Finalizing the Project and Reviewing Key Concepts

As we reach the final stage of building our **To-Do List Application**, it's important to review the steps we've taken, reflect on the key concepts we've learned, and ensure the project is ready for production. This section will focus on **finalizing the project**, adding some finishing touches, and reviewing the key concepts and techniques we've covered throughout the development process.

Finalizing the Project

At this stage, we have already implemented the core functionality of the application, including adding, deleting, completing, and viewing tasks. The application persists data using file storage (tasks.json), and we've built a simple yet effective **command-line interface (CLI)**. Before wrapping up, let's review the last steps we need to take to finalize the project and prepare it for release or further development.

1. Refining the User Interface

Although we have a basic text-based CLI, we can enhance the user experience by adding a few improvements:

Error Handling: Improve user feedback by adding more descriptive error messages when invalid input is provided. For example, if the user enters an invalid task index when deleting or completing a task, we could display a message like:

go
Copy
```
fmt.Println("Error: Invalid task index. Please try again with a valid number.")
```

439

Task Status Updates: After marking a task as complete, provide a confirmation message:

go

Copy

fmt.Println("Task marked as completed:", tasks[index].Title)

-
- **Input Validation**: Ensure that user inputs are properly validated. For instance, we should ensure that task descriptions aren't empty and that task indices entered for deletion or completion are within the bounds of the tasks list.

2. Ensuring Data Persistence

While the basic file storage functionality has been implemented, we can add a few optimizations:

- **Error Handling in File I/O**: Currently, we print an error message when file operations fail, but we can take it a step further by implementing a **recovery mechanism** or logging system. For example, if a failure occurs when opening or writing to the tasks.json file, we could attempt to reload the tasks from a backup or show a helpful message to the user explaining what went wrong.
- **Backup of Task Data**: In a more advanced version of this application, you could implement an automatic backup system that periodically saves a copy of the task data to a secondary file. This would help in case the primary file becomes corrupted.

3. Testing Again

Before finalizing the project, it's crucial to re-run the tests one more time to ensure that all features are functioning correctly after making refinements:

bash

Copy

go test -v

This ensures that no changes to the code have introduced new bugs or broken existing functionality. Make sure you test edge cases as well, such as:

- Viewing an empty list of tasks.
- Deleting a task that no longer exists.
- Completing a task that has already been marked as complete.

Reviewing Key Concepts

As we conclude this chapter, let's take a moment to review the key Go concepts we've covered throughout this project. These concepts form the foundation of Go programming and were essential in building our To-Do List application.

1. Structs and Data Structures

We used Go's **struct** type to model the tasks in our To-Do List application. The Task struct had fields for the task's title, description, and completion status:

go

Copy

```go
type Task struct {
    Title       string
    Description string
    Completed   bool
}
```

Understanding how to define and work with structs is crucial, as they provide a way to group related data together.

2. Concurrency with Goroutines

Go's **goroutines** are a powerful feature for concurrent programming. We used goroutines to handle multiple tasks concurrently, making the application more efficient. This was especially useful for handling long-running tasks, such as file I/O or fetching data from an external source.

go

Copy

```
go AddTask() // Start a goroutine for adding a task
```

Goroutines are lightweight, easy to implement, and allow your program to scale efficiently by taking full advantage of multi-core systems.

3. Channels for Communication

We didn't use many channels in this specific example, but they are essential for communication between goroutines in more complex programs. Channels allow goroutines to send and receive data safely, making it possible to synchronize their actions without explicitly managing threads or locks.

In more advanced applications, channels would allow us to manage multiple tasks concurrently and communicate the results between them.

4. File Handling and Persistence

We used Go's **file I/O** capabilities to persist the task data to a file (tasks.json). This ensured that the task list was saved between application runs and allowed the user's tasks to persist across sessions. Understanding how to work with files is an important part of any real-world application, as it allows for persistent storage of user data.

go

Copy

```
file, err := os.Create("tasks.json")
if err != nil {
```

442

```
fmt.Println("Error creating file:", err)
```

```
}
```

```
defer file.Close()
```

We used the encoding/json package to serialize the task list into JSON format and write it to the file. Similarly, we used json.NewDecoder to deserialize the data when loading the tasks from the file.

5. User Input and Output

Go's simple syntax for reading user input with fmt.Scanln() and printing output with fmt.Println() allowed us to build an interactive **command-line interface (CLI)** for the To-Do List application. We were able to:

- Prompt the user for input.
- Display a menu with available actions.
- Display the current task list and its status.

Understanding how to interact with the user via the command line is a basic skill for Go programmers, and it forms the foundation for building more complex user interfaces, such as web or mobile applications.

6. Error Handling

Go's error handling pattern uses the error type, and we utilized it throughout the application to ensure that things like file I/O operations and task list modifications worked smoothly. By explicitly checking for errors after operations like file creation or JSON encoding, we were able to catch and report potential issues.

go

Copy

```
if err != nil {

    fmt.Println("Error:", err)

    return

}
```

443

This explicit error checking ensures that the application can recover from failures or provide helpful feedback to the user when something goes wrong.

7. Testing with Go's testing Package

Testing is essential for ensuring that the application behaves as expected. We used Go's testing package to write unit tests for our task management functions, verifying that tasks are added, viewed, and deleted correctly. The testing package allows you to automate the testing process and ensures that your application remains functional as you modify and extend it.

go

Copy

```go
func TestAddTask(t *testing.T) {

    AddTask("Test Task", "Description")

    if len(tasks) != 1 {

        t.Errorf("Expected 1 task, got %d", len(tasks))

    }

}
```

Testing not only helps catch bugs but also gives confidence that the code will work as expected when deployed or modified in the future.

By building the To-Do List application, we have explored several key concepts of Go programming:

- **Structs** and **data structures** for modeling real-world entities.
- **Concurrency** and **goroutines** for managing multiple tasks simultaneously.
- **Channels** for communication between goroutines (although not fully implemented in this simple example).

- **File handling** and **JSON serialization** for persistent storage of tasks.
- **User input** and **output** for creating an interactive command-line interface.
- **Error handling** to ensure robustness and resilience.
- **Testing** with Go's built-in tools to verify the correctness of the application.

These foundational concepts form the backbone of Go programming and can be applied to build complex, efficient, and scalable applications. You now have the tools and knowledge to take your Go programming skills to the next level.

Chapter 10: Deploying Go Applications

10.1. Compiling and Building Go Programs

One of the main advantages of using **Go** as a programming language is its ability to compile into standalone, efficient executable binaries. This makes Go particularly well-suited for building fast, lightweight applications that are easy to distribute and deploy across various environments. In this chapter, we'll walk through how to **compile** and **build Go programs** into executable binaries, allowing you to prepare your Go application for deployment on different platforms.

We will also explore the process of compiling Go code, including understanding the Go compiler (go build), cross-compilation for different operating systems, and optimizing your compiled programs for production.

How to Compile Go Code into Executable Binaries

When you write Go code, it typically consists of a series of source files (*.go) that need to be compiled into a binary executable. Go's built-in tools, specifically the go build command, make this process simple and efficient. Once compiled, the output is a self-contained executable that doesn't require any external dependencies, making it perfect for production deployments.

Step 1: Understanding the go build Command

The go build command is the simplest way to compile Go programs into executable binaries. By running this command, Go will compile your code into an executable binary that can be run directly on your system. Let's look at the basic syntax:

bash
Copy
```
go build [flags] [packages]
```

- **[flags]**: Optional flags to control the build process, such as specifying the output file name or enabling optimizations.
- **[packages]**: The Go package(s) you want to build. If no package is specified, Go will build the main package in the current directory.

Example 1: Compiling a Single File

For a simple Go program with a single file, you can compile it directly using the go build command. Suppose you have a Go file main.go in your project:

```go
Copy
package main

import "fmt"

func main() {
    fmt.Println("Hello, Go!")
}
```

To compile this file, navigate to the directory containing the file and run:

```bash
Copy
go build main.go
```

This will generate an executable binary called main (or main.exe on Windows), depending on your operating system.

- **On Linux/macOS**: The output binary will be named main.
- **On Windows**: The output binary will be named main.exe.

You can now run the compiled program directly by executing:

```bash
Copy
./main  # On Linux/macOS
main.exe  # On Windows
```

This simple example demonstrates the basic process of compiling a Go program into an executable binary.

Step 2: Compiling an Entire Package

In many cases, your Go application will consist of multiple files and packages. To compile a project with multiple files, simply run the go build command from the root of the project directory. If your project structure looks like this:

go
Copy

```
todo-app/
|
├── main.go
├── todo/
|   ├── task.go
|   ├── task_manager.go
|   └── storage.go
└── tasks.json
```

You can compile the entire project by running the following command from the todo-app root directory:

bash
Copy
go build

Go will automatically detect the main package (main.go) and all its dependencies in the project, compiling the necessary files into an executable binary.

Step 3: Specifying the Output File

By default, Go will name the compiled executable after the directory. If you want to specify a custom name for your output file, you can use the -o flag followed by the desired name:

bash
Copy
go build -o todoapp main.go

This command will compile the code and produce an executable named todoapp, instead of the default name (main or main.exe depending on the OS).

Cross-Compilation: Building for Multiple Platforms

One of Go's standout features is its ability to compile code for **different platforms** from a single source code base. This means you can write your Go application on one operating system (such as macOS), but compile it to run on other operating systems (such as Linux or Windows) without needing to modify the code. Go achieves this by providing **cross-compilation** capabilities.

How Cross-Compilation Works

Go allows you to specify the target operating system (GOOS) and target architecture (GOARCH) when building a program. This enables you to compile your Go code for different platforms with ease.

Here's how you can use cross-compilation to build executables for various platforms:

Example: Building for Windows from Linux/macOS

To compile your Go program for Windows from a Linux or macOS machine, use the following command:

```bash
Copy
GOOS=windows GOARCH=amd64 go build -o todoapp.exe
```

- **GOOS=windows**: Specifies the target operating system (in this case, Windows).
- **GOARCH=amd64**: Specifies the architecture (64-bit architecture for most modern computers).
- **-o todoapp.exe**: Specifies the output file name as todoapp.exe.

After running this command, you will have a todoapp.exe file that can be run on a Windows machine.

Example: Building for Linux from macOS

To compile for Linux from macOS, use this command:

```bash
Copy
GOOS=linux GOARCH=amd64 go build -o todoapp-linux
```

This will generate an executable binary that can be run on a Linux machine.

Example: Building for ARM Architecture

To compile for ARM architecture (used in devices like the Raspberry Pi), you can specify the architecture as arm:

```bash
Copy
GOOS=linux GOARCH=arm go build -o todoapp-arm
```

This command will compile the Go application for ARM-based systems running Linux.

Available GOOS and GOARCH Values

Here are some common values for GOOS and GOARCH:

- **GOOS**:
    - linux — Linux-based systems
    - windows — Windows systems
    - darwin — macOS (formerly OS X)
    - freebsd — FreeBSD systems
    - android — Android devices
- **GOARCH**:
    - amd64 — 64-bit architecture (most common for desktops and servers)
    - 386 — 32-bit architecture
    - arm — ARM architecture (commonly used in embedded devices and mobile devices)
    - arm64 — 64-bit ARM architecture

Go makes it easy to build for various platforms without having to install multiple compilers or virtual machines for each platform.

Optimizing Your Build for Production

After compiling your Go application, you may want to optimize the executable for production use. Go is already an efficient language, but there are a few additional steps you can take to make sure your application performs well in a production environment.

1. Minimize Binary Size

Go binaries can sometimes become quite large due to static linking, which includes all dependencies in the executable. If you need to reduce the binary size, you can use the -ldflags flag with the go build command to disable debug information and reduce the size of the binary.

bash
Copy
```
go build -ldflags="-s -w" -o todoapp
```

- -s: Strips the symbol table (which includes debugging information) from the binary.
- -w: Strips the DWARF debugging information (further reducing the size).

This will make your binary smaller and more optimized for production.

2. Static Linking

Go automatically links all necessary libraries statically, meaning that the compiled binary includes everything needed to run the application. This makes it easy to distribute the binary because you don't need to worry about external dependencies.

If you want to make sure your application is completely statically linked, check that your system libraries and dependencies are properly linked during the build process. However, Go's default behavior already takes care of most cases.

451

3. Setting Build Tags

Go supports **build tags**, which allow you to include or exclude code during the build process based on certain conditions. For example, you can use build tags to include code for certain environments (such as development or production) or to add conditional dependencies.

Example:

bash
Copy
```
go build -tags=production
```

This command tells Go to include code specifically tagged for the **production** environment, which could be used to enable more efficient algorithms or logging levels.

Deploying the Compiled Go Application

After compiling your Go program into an executable binary, deploying it becomes straightforward. Because Go produces standalone binaries, you can deploy them to any server or machine without worrying about dependencies.

Here are some common methods of deploying Go applications:

1. **Deploying to Cloud Providers**: You can upload the compiled binary to cloud services like AWS, GCP, or DigitalOcean. The binary can be executed directly on the cloud machine without needing additional setup.
2. **Deploying to Servers**: For traditional server deployments, you can copy the binary to your server using tools like **scp** (secure copy) or **rsync** and execute it on the remote machine.
3. **Distributing to End Users**: If you are building a client application, you can distribute the compiled binary to users as a downloadable executable. For example, users on Windows can download the .exe file, while users on Linux or macOS can download the appropriate binary for their platform.

In this section, we've explored how to compile and build Go programs into **executable binaries**, enabling us to deploy Go applications across different platforms. By using the go build command, cross-compiling for various operating systems, and optimizing the binary for production, we can easily prepare our Go applications for deployment.

Key concepts covered include:

- **Compiling Go code** using the go build command.
- **Cross-compiling** for different operating systems and architectures.
- **Optimizing binaries** for smaller size and production use.
- **Distributing Go binaries** for deployment on servers, cloud platforms, or to end users.

With these tools and techniques, you are well-equipped to deploy your Go applications efficiently and effectively across various platforms. In the next chapter, we will discuss more advanced deployment strategies, such as setting up CI/CD pipelines for automated deployments and scaling Go applications in a production environment.

Cross-Compiling for Different Platforms

One of the most powerful features of Go is its built-in support for **cross-compiling**, which allows developers to build executables for different operating systems and architectures from a single code base. This is particularly useful when you want to deploy your Go applications on multiple platforms (Linux, Windows, macOS, etc.) without needing separate codebases or complex configuration setups for each environment.

In this section, we'll explore how to use Go's **cross-compilation** capabilities to build executables for different platforms and architectures, allowing you to seamlessly deploy your Go applications across diverse environments.

What is Cross-Compilation?

Cross-compilation refers to the process of building software on one platform (the "host" platform) that is intended to run on another platform (the "target" platform). In Go, this is achieved through environment variables that specify the target operating system (GOOS) and target architecture (GOARCH), allowing you to compile an application for a platform that differs from the one you are developing on.

453

For instance, you might develop a Go application on a macOS machine but compile it for a Windows or Linux system, all without needing a separate development environment for each platform.

Understanding GOOS and GOARCH

When compiling a Go program for a platform other than the one you're developing on, you need to set two environment variables: GOOS and GOARCH.

- GOOS: Specifies the target operating system.
- GOARCH: Specifies the target architecture (CPU architecture).

Common Values for GOOS and GOARCH:

- **GOOS** (Target OS):
    - linux — Linux-based systems
    - windows — Windows systems
    - darwin — macOS (formerly OS X)
    - freebsd — FreeBSD systems
    - android — Android devices
- **GOARCH** (Target Architecture):
    - amd64 — 64-bit architecture (most modern desktop and server systems)
    - 386 — 32-bit architecture
    - arm — ARM architecture (used in mobile devices and embedded systems)
    - arm64 — 64-bit ARM architecture (common in modern ARM-based devices like the Raspberry Pi)
    - ppc64 — PowerPC architecture (less common, used in specific server and embedded systems)

By setting the GOOS and GOARCH environment variables, you can compile your Go program to run on a wide variety of platforms, regardless of your development environment.

Cross-Compiling for Different Platforms

Now let's go through practical examples of how to compile Go programs for various operating systems and architectures.

Example 1: Cross-Compiling for Windows from macOS/Linux

If you're developing on macOS or Linux but want to generate an executable for **Windows**, use the following command:

bash

Copy

```
GOOS=windows GOARCH=amd64 go build -o todoapp.exe
```

- **GOOS=windows**: This tells Go to compile the program for Windows.
- **GOARCH=amd64**: This specifies that the binary should be compiled for a 64-bit architecture.
- **-o todoapp.exe**: This specifies the output file name as todoapp.exe.

After running this command, Go will generate a todoapp.exe binary that can be executed on a 64-bit Windows machine.

Example 2: Cross-Compiling for Linux from macOS

If you're developing on macOS and want to compile your Go program for a **Linux** machine, you can use the following command:

bash

Copy

```
GOOS=linux GOARCH=amd64 go build -o todoapp-linux
```

- **GOOS=linux**: This specifies that the target OS is Linux.
- **GOARCH=amd64**: This specifies that the target architecture is 64-bit.

455

- **-o todoapp-linux**: The output binary will be named todoapp-linux.

This command will generate an executable binary that can run on a Linux system.

Example 3: Cross-Compiling for macOS from Windows/Linux

To compile a Go program for **macOS** while developing on Windows or Linux, run the following command:

bash

Copy

```
GOOS=darwin GOARCH=amd64 go build -o todoapp-darwin
```

- **GOOS=darwin**: This specifies that the target OS is macOS.
- **GOARCH=amd64**: This specifies the target architecture is 64-bit.
- **-o todoapp-darwin**: The output file will be named todoapp-darwin.

Running this command will generate a macOS-compatible executable that you can run on any macOS machine.

Example 4: Cross-Compiling for ARM Architecture (e.g., Raspberry Pi)

For ARM-based devices like the **Raspberry Pi**, you can cross-compile your Go application by targeting the **arm64** architecture:

bash

Copy

```
GOOS=linux GOARCH=arm64 go build -o todoapp-arm64
```

- **GOOS=linux**: Specifies that the target OS is Linux (as Raspberry Pi uses Linux-based OSes like Raspbian).
- **GOARCH=arm64**: Specifies that the target architecture is ARM 64-bit.
- **-o todoapp-arm64**: The output binary is named todoapp-arm64.

456

This command will generate an ARM64 binary that can be deployed and run on Raspberry Pi 4 or other ARM-based systems.

Example 5: Cross-Compiling for 32-bit Systems

If you need to compile your Go program for a **32-bit architecture** (e.g., old computers or specific embedded systems), you can use the 386 architecture:

bash

Copy

```
GOOS=linux GOARCH=386 go build -o todoapp-32bit
```

- **GOOS=linux**: Target OS is Linux.
- **GOARCH=386**: Target architecture is 32-bit.
- **-o todoapp-32bit**: The output binary will be named todoapp-32bit.

This is useful for targeting older machines or specific embedded systems that only support 32-bit architecture.

Verifying the Cross-Compiled Binary

Once you've cross-compiled your Go application for a target platform, you may want to verify that the executable is built for the correct OS and architecture.

To check the properties of a compiled binary, you can use the file command (on Linux/macOS) or inspect the file properties in Windows:

On Linux/macOS: Use the file command:
bash
Copy
```
file todoapp-linux
```

This will tell you the architecture and target OS of the binary. For example, you might see something like:

bash

Copy

todoapp-linux: ELF 64-bit LSB executable, x86-64, version 1 (SYSV), dynamically linked, interpreter /lib64/ld-linux-x86-64.so.2, for GNU/Linux 3.2.0, not stripped

- **On Windows**: Right-click the .exe file and select **Properties**. Under the **Details** tab, you can see the target architecture and other metadata.

Using Go Build Flags for Cross-Compilation

In addition to GOOS and GOARCH, Go's go build command supports several other **build flags** that can be useful when cross-compiling, including:

1. -ldflags (Linker Flags)

The -ldflags flag is useful for specifying additional settings during the build process, such as stripping debugging symbols to make the binary smaller. For example:

bash

Copy

GOOS=linux GOARCH=amd64 go build -ldflags="-s -w" -o todoapp-linux

- -s: Strips the symbol table, reducing binary size.
- -w: Strips DWARF debugging information, further reducing binary size.

2. -a (Force rebuilding everything)

By default, Go will only rebuild the code if it has changed. However, if you want to ensure everything is rebuilt (for example, when cross-compiling), you can use the -a flag:

bash

Copy

```
GOOS=linux GOARCH=amd64 go build -a -o todoapp-linux
```

This ensures that all dependencies are rebuilt, even if they haven't changed.

3. -v (Verbose output)

For troubleshooting or better visibility, you can use the -v flag to get verbose output during the build process:

bash

Copy

```
GOOS=linux GOARCH=amd64 go build -v -o todoapp-linux
```

This will show which files are being compiled and link to the final executable.

Go's **cross-compilation** feature is one of its standout capabilities, allowing you to build applications for multiple platforms and architectures from a single source code base. This flexibility is particularly useful when you need to deploy your application across different environments, such as servers, desktops, or embedded systems.

In this section, we've covered:

- How to set **GOOS** and **GOARCH** to compile for different operating systems and architectures.
- The process of cross-compiling for platforms such as **Windows**, **Linux**, **macOS**, and **ARM**-based systems.
- Useful **build flags** like -ldflags, -a, and -v to optimize and manage your builds.

10.2. Deploying a Web Application with Go

Go is an excellent choice for building web applications, thanks to its performance, ease of use, and built-in support for HTTP servers. In this section, we'll walk through the process of creating a simple web server in Go, followed by deploying your Go application to the cloud. This process will give you the knowledge and tools necessary to take your Go application from local development to production-ready deployment.

Creating a Simple Web Server in Go

Go's standard library includes the net/http package, which makes it incredibly easy to create a web server. Let's start by building a simple HTTP server that serves basic web pages and handles requests.

Step 1: Setting Up the Web Server

To create a simple web server, all you need is a Go file that imports the net/http package and defines a handler for incoming requests. Below is an example of a simple Go web server that responds to HTTP requests with a "Hello, World!" message.

go

Copy

```
package main

import (
```

```go
    "fmt"

    "net/http"

)


// Handler function to respond with "Hello, World!"

func helloHandler(w http.ResponseWriter, r *http.Request) {

    fmt.Fprintln(w, "Hello, World!")

}


func main() {

    // Set up the server to respond to requests at the root URL

    http.HandleFunc("/", helloHandler)


    // Start the server and listen on port 8080

    fmt.Println("Starting server on :8080...")

    err := http.ListenAndServe(":8080", nil)

    if err != nil {

        fmt.Println("Error starting the server:", err)

    }

}
```

Explanation of the Code:

1. **http.HandleFunc**: This function registers a URL pattern (in this case, the root /) and associates it with a handler function (helloHandler). This means that whenever a user visits the root URL of the server, the helloHandler function is called.

2. **helloHandler function**: This function takes two parameters: w (the http.ResponseWriter used to send a response back to the client) and r (the http.Request that represents the HTTP request from the client). It responds with the text "Hello, World!" using fmt.Fprintln(w, ...).

3. **http.ListenAndServe(":8080", nil)**: This line starts the server on port 8080. It listens for incoming HTTP requests and passes them to the appropriate handler. If there's an error while starting the server, the program will print the error message.

To run the web server, simply save the file as main.go, then execute the following command in your terminal:

bash

Copy

```
go run main.go
```

Now, open a browser and navigate to http://localhost:8080. You should see the message "Hello, World!" displayed in your browser.

Adding More Complex Routes

Once you have a basic server running, you can expand it by adding more routes. Go's http.HandleFunc allows you to map different URL paths to different handler functions.

go

Copy

```
func aboutHandler(w http.ResponseWriter, r *http.Request) {
```

462

```go
    fmt.Fprintln(w, "Welcome to the About Page!")
}


func main() {
    http.HandleFunc("/", helloHandler)
    http.HandleFunc("/about", aboutHandler) // New route for "/about"

    fmt.Println("Starting server on :8080...")
    err := http.ListenAndServe(":8080", nil)
    if err != nil {
        fmt.Println("Error starting the server:", err)
    }
}
```

In this example:

- /about route is added, and it returns a different message when accessed.
- You can visit http://localhost:8080/about to see the "Welcome to the About Page!" message.

This is the foundation for building more complex web applications using Go. You can build dynamic websites by expanding the handler functions to serve HTML pages, manage forms, interact with databases, and more.

Deploying Your Go Application to the Cloud

Now that we have a simple web server running locally, let's deploy it to the cloud. There are multiple ways to deploy Go applications, but for simplicity and popularity, we'll walk through deploying to **Heroku**, a cloud platform that simplifies app deployment.

Step 1: Preparing Your Application for Deployment

Before deploying your Go application, make sure it is production-ready. In a production environment, there are a few things you might want to do:

1. **Environment Variables**: Make sure sensitive information, like API keys or database credentials, are stored in environment variables rather than hardcoded into your code.
2. **Port Configuration**: Cloud platforms often assign a dynamic port to your application. Modify your application to use the port provided by the platform (Heroku, for instance).

Modify your code to listen on the correct port:

go

Copy

```go
package main

import (

    "fmt"

    "net/http"

    "os"

)


func helloHandler(w http.ResponseWriter, r *http.Request) {

    fmt.Fprintln(w, "Hello, World!")
```

```
}

func main() {

    port := os.Getenv("PORT")

    if port == "" {

        port = "8080"  // Default port if the environment variable is not set

    }


    http.HandleFunc("/", helloHandler)


    fmt.Printf("Starting server on port %s...\n", port)

    err := http.ListenAndServe(":"+port, nil)

    if err != nil {

        fmt.Println("Error starting the server:", err)

    }

}
```

Here, the application checks for the PORT environment variable (which is set by Heroku). If not set, it defaults to port 8080.

Step 2: Setting Up Your Heroku Account

1. **Sign Up for Heroku**: If you don't have a Heroku account, sign up at https://signup.heroku.com/.
2. **Install Heroku CLI**: Download and install the Heroku CLI. This tool allows you to interact with Heroku from your command line.

3. **Log into Heroku**: Open your terminal and log in to your Heroku account using the following command:

bash

Copy

```
heroku login
```

This will open a browser window for you to log in.

Step 3: Creating a New Heroku Application

1. **Initialize a Git Repository**: Heroku uses Git for deployment, so if you haven't already initialized a Git repository in your project, do so by running:

bash

Copy

```
git init
```

2. **Create a New Heroku Application**: You can create a new application on Heroku by running the following command:

bash

Copy

```
heroku create
```

This command will automatically create a new Heroku app with a random name and provide you with the app's URL (e.g., https://myapp.herokuapp.com).

Step 4: Deploying to Heroku

1. **Add Files to Git**: Add your Go files to the Git repository:

bash

Copy

```
git add .

git commit -m "Initial commit"
```

2. **Deploy to Heroku**: Now that you have everything set up, deploy your application to Heroku using the following commands:

bash

Copy

```
git push heroku master
```

Heroku will automatically detect that your app is a Go application, build it, and deploy it. The first deployment may take a little longer as Heroku sets up the environment.

3. **Open Your Application**: Once the deployment is complete, you can open your application by running:

bash

Copy

```
heroku open
```

This will open your default web browser and take you to your deployed Go web application.

Step 5: Monitoring and Scaling Your Application

Once your application is deployed, you can monitor its performance and scale it as necessary using the Heroku CLI.

Viewing Logs

To view the logs of your application, which can help with debugging or performance monitoring, run:

bash

Copy

```
heroku logs --tail
```

This will show real-time logs from your application, which can be helpful for debugging issues after deployment.

Scaling Your Application

Heroku allows you to scale your app, meaning you can add more web dynos (containers) to handle more traffic. To scale your application, run:

bash

Copy

```
heroku ps:scale web=1
```

This command sets the number of web dynos (workers handling HTTP requests) to 1. You can scale up or down depending on your app's traffic needs.

In this section, we've learned how to create a simple web server in Go and deploy it to the cloud. Here's a summary of the key steps:

1. **Creating a Web Server**: We used Go's net/http package to build a basic web server that responds to HTTP requests.

2. **Deploying to Heroku**: We prepared the Go application for deployment by ensuring it dynamically listens on the correct port and uses environment variables for configuration. Then, we deployed the app to Heroku using Git and the Heroku CLI.

3. **Scaling and Monitoring**: We explored how to monitor and scale the app on Heroku to handle more traffic.

Deploying Go applications to cloud platforms like Heroku is simple, thanks to Go's cross-platform nature and built-in tools for web development. With these steps, you can deploy production-ready Go applications to the cloud and scale them as needed.

10.3. Managing Dependencies and External Libraries

When building larger applications, it's common to use external libraries or packages to extend the functionality of your Go program. These libraries can save you time by providing pre-built solutions for common tasks like database interaction, web frameworks, or HTTP request handling. In this section, we'll explore how **Go modules** work for managing dependencies and how to **add external libraries** to your Go project.

Go modules provide a clean and effective way to manage the dependencies of your Go application. They track the versions of the libraries your project relies on, ensuring reproducibility across different environments. Let's walk through how to use Go modules for dependency management and how to add external libraries to your project.

Using Go Modules for Dependency Management

Go modules, introduced in Go 1.11 and made the default in Go 1.13, simplify the process of managing dependencies in Go applications. They allow you to specify the versions of the external libraries your project depends on, making it easier to share, deploy, and maintain your codebase.

Step 1: Initializing Go Modules

To get started with Go modules, you need to initialize a Go module in your project directory. This creates a go.mod file, which keeps track of your project's dependencies.

1. Navigate to the root of your project directory.

469

2. Run the following command to initialize the Go module:

bash

Copy

go mod init your_project_name

Replace your_project_name with the name of your project. For example, if you're building a To-Do List application, you might run:

bash

Copy

go mod init todo-app

This command creates a go.mod file in your project, which will look something like this:

go

Copy

module todo-app

go 1.18

The go.mod file defines the module path and the version of Go you are using. The file will also automatically be updated when you add or remove dependencies.

Step 2: Adding External Libraries to Your Go Project

Once you have initialized the Go module, you can start adding external libraries to your project. To add a new library or package, you simply import it into your code and run go get to download the dependency.

For example, let's say you want to add a popular third-party library for handling HTTP requests, such as the **Gin web framework**. Here's how to do it:

1. First, import the Gin package into your Go file (for example, main.go):

go

Copy

```go
package main


import "github.com/gin-gonic/gin"


func main() {

  router := gin.Default()


  router.GET("/", func(c *gin.Context) {

    c.JSON(200, gin.H{

      "message": "Hello, Go with Gin!",

    })

  })


  router.Run(":8080")

}
```

2. Run the following command to fetch the Gin package and its dependencies:

bash

Copy

```
go get github.com/gin-gonic/gin
```

3. This will download the Gin library and add it to your go.mod file as a dependency. You will also see a new file called go.sum, which keeps track of the exact versions of dependencies and verifies their integrity.

Your go.mod file will now look something like this:

go

Copy

```
module todo-app


go 1.18



require github.com/gin-gonic/gin v1.7.7
```

The require directive in go.mod indicates that your project depends on the Gin library at version v1.7.7.

Step 3: Managing and Upgrading Dependencies

As your project evolves, you may want to upgrade or change the versions of the external libraries you are using. Go makes it easy to manage and update dependencies.

1. **Upgrading a dependency**: To upgrade a package to its latest version, use the following command:

bash

Copy

```
go get github.com/gin-gonic/gin@latest
```

This will update the Gin package to the latest available version and update the go.mod file accordingly.

2. **Checking for outdated dependencies**: If you want to check which dependencies are outdated, you can use:

bash

Copy

```
go list -u -m all
```

This will display a list of all the dependencies in your go.mod file along with the versions that are available for updating.

3. **Removing unused dependencies**: Over time, you may accumulate dependencies that are no longer used in your project. To remove them, run:

bash

Copy

```
go mod tidy
```

This command cleans up your go.mod and go.sum files by removing any dependencies that are no longer required by your project. It also ensures that all the dependencies listed in go.mod are actually used in your code.

Adding External Libraries to Your Go Project

Now that we've learned how to manage Go modules, let's explore how to add some commonly used external libraries to a Go project.

Example 1: Adding a Logger

A logging library is often needed for production-grade applications to log errors, requests, and other important events. One popular library for logging is **Logrus**.

1. To install Logrus, use the following command:

bash

Copy

```
go get github.com/sirupsen/logrus
```

2. In your Go code, import the Logrus package and use it for logging:

go

Copy

```
package main

import (

    "github.com/sirupsen/logrus"

)

func main() {
    // Create a new logger instance
```

474

```
log := logrus.New()


// Set the log level

log.SetLevel(logrus.InfoLevel)


// Log an info message

log.Info("This is an info message!")


// Log an error message

log.Error("This is an error message!")

}
```

This will log messages with different levels of severity, such as Info, Warn, Error, etc.

Example 2: Adding Database Support with gorm

For applications that interact with a database, an ORM (Object-Relational Mapping) tool like **GORM** can simplify database operations. To add GORM to your project, follow these steps:

1. Install GORM:

bash

Copy

```
go get github.com/jinzhu/gorm

go get github.com/jinzhu/gorm/dialects/mysql  // For MySQL support
```

2. Import and use GORM in your Go code to interact with a database:

go

Copy

```go
package main

import (
    "fmt"
    "github.com/jinzhu/gorm"
    _ "github.com/jinzhu/gorm/dialects/mysql"  // Import MySQL dialect
)

func main() {
    db, err := gorm.Open("mysql", "user:password@/dbname")
    if err != nil {
        fmt.Println("Failed to connect to the database:", err)
        return
    }
    defer db.Close()

    // Use GORM to interact with the database
    var users []User
```

```go
db.Find(&users)

fmt.Println("Users:", users)

}


type User struct {

gorm.Model

Name  string

Email string

}
```

In this example:

- We import the GORM package and its MySQL dialect.
- We establish a connection to a MySQL database and retrieve data using GORM.

Example 3: Adding Middleware with Gin

If you're building a web application, you may want to add middleware for authentication, logging, or request validation. The **Gin** web framework is excellent for this, and it comes with built-in middleware support.

1. To add Gin, first run:

bash

Copy

```bash
go get github.com/gin-gonic/gin
```

2. Use Gin and its middleware to handle HTTP requests:

go

Copy

```go
package main

import (
    "github.com/gin-gonic/gin"
    "net/http"
)

func main() {
    r := gin.Default()

    // Use a middleware to log requests
    r.Use(func(c *gin.Context) {
        println("Request received")
        c.Next() // Call the next handler in the chain
    })

    // Define routes
    r.GET("/", func(c *gin.Context) {
        c.JSON(http.StatusOK, gin.H{
```

```
      "message": "Hello, world!",

   })

})


// Start the server

r.Run(":8080")

}
```

In this example, we use Gin's Default() function to create a new router that includes some basic middleware, and we define a route that responds with a JSON message.

Best Practices for Managing Dependencies

As your project grows and you start incorporating more libraries, it's important to follow best practices for dependency management:

1. **Keep Dependencies Minimal**: Only add external libraries when necessary. Go's standard library is extensive and well-documented, so prefer using it over adding dependencies when possible.
2. **Use Semantic Versioning**: Pay attention to the version of libraries you're using. Ideally, use the **latest stable version** to avoid bugs or breaking changes introduced in newer versions.
3. **Regularly Update Dependencies**: Regularly check for updates to the dependencies in your project. Tools like go list -u -m all or services like **Dependabot** can help you stay on top of updates.
4. **Use Go Modules Efficiently**: Always use Go modules to manage dependencies and ensure that your go.mod and go.sum files are properly maintained.

In this section, we covered how to manage dependencies and add external libraries to your Go project using **Go modules**. We learned how to:

1. **Initialize a Go module** to start tracking dependencies.
2. **Add external libraries** to the project using the go get command.
3. Use popular external libraries like **Logrus** for logging, **GORM** for database interaction, and **Gin** for building web applications.
4. Follow **best practices** for managing dependencies and keeping your project clean and up-to-date.

With Go's built-in dependency management and the ability to easily add and manage external libraries, you can build powerful, feature-rich applications while keeping your codebase clean and maintainable. In the next section, we will look at **optimizing** Go applications for performance and scaling them in production environments.

10.4. Practical Deployment Examples

Once your Go application is ready, it's important to ensure that it is deployed correctly in various environments such as **local development, staging**, and **production**. In this section, we'll explore how to deploy Go applications in different environments and provide practical examples for **cloud deployment, containerization with Docker**, and **server deployment**. These deployment methods will help you scale and manage your Go applications efficiently.

Running Go Apps in Different Environments

Local Development

During the development phase, you will typically run your Go application locally on your machine. This allows you to test, debug, and refine your application before deploying it to a production environment.

1. **Running a Local Web Server**: If your Go application is a web server, simply use the go run command to start it locally. For example:

bash

Copy

go run main.go

This command compiles and runs your application, allowing you to access it on http://localhost:8080 (or any other port you've specified in your code).

2. **Environment Variables**: In local development, you may want to set environment variables (such as API keys or configuration options) without hardcoding them in your Go code. You can set environment variables in your terminal:

bash

Copy

export MY_API_KEY="your_api_key_here"

Then, access the variable in your Go code using os.Getenv:

go

Copy

package main

import (

  "fmt"

  "os"

481

```
)

func main() {

  apiKey := os.Getenv("MY_API_KEY")

  fmt.Println("API Key:", apiKey)

}
```

3. **Configuration for Development**: In local development, you may want to use a local database or mock services instead of production systems. Make sure your application reads the configuration (e.g., database connections, API keys) from environment variables or configuration files, so you can easily switch between different environments.

Deploying to Cloud Providers

Once your application is ready, deploying it to the cloud is one of the most common approaches to scaling your Go application. The most popular cloud platforms include **Heroku, AWS, Google Cloud Platform**, and **Microsoft Azure**. Let's go through deploying a Go application to a **cloud platform** using **Heroku** as an example.

Step 1: Prepare Your Go Application for Deployment

For cloud deployment, ensure that your Go application is production-ready. This includes:

- Setting up environment variables.
- Handling errors gracefully.
- Ensuring that your application listens on a dynamic port (provided by the cloud platform) instead of a hardcoded one.
- Using logging libraries like **Logrus** for better production logging.

Here's a simple Go web application that will work well in any cloud environment, as it listens on the dynamic PORT environment variable:

go

Copy

```go
package main

import (
    "fmt"
    "net/http"
    "os"
)

func helloHandler(w http.ResponseWriter, r *http.Request) {
    fmt.Fprintln(w, "Hello, Cloud!")
}

func main() {
    port := os.Getenv("PORT")
    if port == "" {
        port = "8080" // Default port for local development
    }

    http.HandleFunc("/", helloHandler)
```

```go
fmt.Printf("Starting server on port %s...\n", port)

err := http.ListenAndServe(":"+port, nil)

if err != nil {

    fmt.Println("Error starting the server:", err)

}

}
```

Step 2: Deploying to Heroku

1. **Install the Heroku CLI**: First, you need to install the Heroku Command Line Interface (CLI). Follow the instructions from Heroku's official website to install it on your machine: Heroku CLI Installation.
2. **Login to Heroku**: After installing the Heroku CLI, log in to your Heroku account:

bash

Copy

```bash
heroku login
```

3. **Create a Git Repository**: Heroku uses Git to deploy applications, so you need to initialize a Git repository in your project directory if you haven't done so already:

bash

Copy

```bash
git init
```

4. **Create a Heroku App**: In your project directory, create a new Heroku app by running the following command:

bash

Copy

```
heroku create
```

This will create a new Heroku app and assign it a random name (you can also specify a custom name).

5. **Deploy Your Application**: Add all your changes to the Git repository, commit them, and deploy your app to Heroku:

bash

Copy

```
git add .
git commit -m "Initial commit"
git push heroku master
```

6. **Access Your App**: After Heroku finishes building and deploying your app, it will provide you with a URL (e.g., https://your-app-name.herokuapp.com). You can access the app using this URL in a web browser.

bash

Copy

```
heroku open
```

This will open your app in a web browser, and you should see the message "Hello, Cloud!" if everything is set up correctly.

Deploying to Docker

Containerization with **Docker** has become the standard for deploying applications due to its portability and consistency across different environments. Docker allows you to package your application along with all its dependencies into a container, ensuring that it runs exactly the same way on any system, whether it's your local machine, a staging server, or a production environment.

Step 1: Installing Docker

First, make sure Docker is installed on your machine. You can download it from Docker's website.

Step 2: Creating a Dockerfile

A **Dockerfile** is a script that contains instructions on how to build a Docker image for your application. Here's an example Dockerfile for a Go application:

Dockerfile

Copy

```
# Use the official Go image as the base image

FROM golang:1.18


# Set the Current Working Directory inside the container

WORKDIR /app


# Copy the Go Modules files and download dependencies

COPY go.mod go.sum ./

RUN go mod download


# Copy the entire Go application into the container
```

```
COPY . .
```

```
# Build the Go app inside the container

RUN go build -o todo-app .
```

```
# Expose the port the app runs on

EXPOSE 8080
```

```
# Command to run the executable

CMD ["./todo-app"]
```

Explanation of the Dockerfile:

1. **FROM golang:1.18**: This tells Docker to use the official Go image (with Go 1.18) as the base image.
2. **WORKDIR /app**: This sets the working directory inside the container to /app. All subsequent commands will be executed relative to this directory.
3. **COPY go.mod go.sum ./**: This copies the Go module files (go.mod and go.sum) to the container.
4. **RUN go mod download**: This downloads the dependencies inside the container.
5. **COPY . .**: This copies the rest of your Go application code into the container.
6. **RUN go build -o todo-app .**: This builds the Go application inside the container.
7. **EXPOSE 8080**: This tells Docker that the app listens on port 8080.
8. **CMD ["./todo-app"]**: This specifies the command that Docker should run when the container starts.

Step 3: Building the Docker Image

Once your Dockerfile is ready, you can build the Docker image using the following command:

bash

Copy

```
docker build -t todo-app .
```

This command builds the Docker image and tags it as todo-app.

Step 4: Running the Docker Container

After building the image, you can run the container:

bash

Copy

```
docker run -p 8080:8080 todo-app
```

This command runs the todo-app container and maps port 8080 on your local machine to port 8080 inside the container. Now, you can access your Go application by visiting http://localhost:8080 in your web browser.

Step 5: Pushing the Docker Image to a Registry

Once your image is ready, you can push it to a Docker registry (such as Docker Hub, Amazon ECR, or Google Container Registry) for easier deployment across different environments. To push to Docker Hub, first log in to your Docker account:

bash

Copy

```
docker login
```

488

Then, tag the image with your Docker Hub username:

bash

Copy

```
docker tag todo-app yourusername/todo-app:latest
```

Finally, push the image to Docker Hub:

bash

Copy

```
docker push yourusername/todo-app:latest
```

You can now pull and run this image from any machine with Docker installed by using the following command:

bash

Copy

```
docker run -p 8080:8080 yourusername/todo-app:latest
```

Deploying to a Virtual Machine or Server

In addition to deploying to cloud services or Docker containers, Go applications can also be deployed to traditional virtual machines (VMs) or bare-metal servers. This method involves manually copying the compiled Go binary to the server, setting up environment variables, and running the application.

489

1. **Copy the Binary to the Server**: Use scp (secure copy) or rsync to copy the Go binary to your server:

bash

Copy

```
scp todo-app user@yourserver:/path/to/destination
```

2. **Set Up Environment Variables**: On your server, set the environment variables needed for your application:

bash

Copy

```
export PORT=8080

export DB_HOST=your_database_host
```

3. **Run the Go Application**: On the server, execute the Go binary:

bash

Copy

```
./todo-app
```

This will start your Go web application on the server, and you can access it using the server's IP address or domain.

In this section, we've learned how to:

- **Deploy Go web applications** to cloud platforms like Heroku.

- **Containerize Go applications** using Docker, allowing for consistent deployment across environments.
- **Deploy Go applications** to virtual machines or traditional servers using basic file transfers and manual configuration.

By following these deployment practices, you can take your Go applications from local development to scalable, production-ready deployments.

Chapter 11: Next Steps and Advanced Topics

11.1. Exploring Go's Advanced Features

As you become more comfortable with Go, it's essential to explore its **advanced features**. Go is a simple yet powerful language, and it offers several advanced concepts that allow developers to write more robust, maintainable, and efficient programs. Two of the key features that distinguish Go are **interfaces** and **structs**. These concepts form the backbone of Go's object-oriented capabilities and allow you to design flexible and reusable code.

In this section, we will dive deep into **interfaces** and **structs**, examining how they work together to create powerful, modular applications.

Understanding Interfaces and Structs

In Go, the concepts of **interfaces** and **structs** serve as the primary building blocks for achieving polymorphism, data encapsulation, and abstraction. While Go does not have traditional classes as seen in languages like Java or C++, it provides alternatives such as **structs** (for defining data structures) and **interfaces** (for defining behavior). This enables you to create modular, extensible, and clean code in a way that maintains simplicity.

Structs: Defining Custom Data Types

A **struct** in Go is a composite data type that groups together variables (fields) under a single name. These fields can be of different types, allowing you to model more complex objects. Structs are similar to classes in other object-oriented languages but lack the notion of inheritance.

1. Defining a Struct

Here's a basic example of defining a struct in Go:

```
go
Copy
package main
```

492

```go
import "fmt"

// Define a struct named 'Person'
type Person struct {
    Name    string
    Age     int
    Address string
}

func main() {
    // Create an instance of 'Person'
    person := Person{Name: "John Doe", Age: 30, Address: "123 Main St"}

    // Access struct fields
    fmt.Println(person.Name)    // John Doe
    fmt.Println(person.Age)     // 30
    fmt.Println(person.Address) // 123 Main St
}
```

In this example:

- The Person struct is defined with three fields: Name, Age, and Address.
- We create an instance of the Person struct and initialize it with values using the struct literal syntax.
- The fields can be accessed using the dot notation.

2. Structs and Methods

Go allows you to associate methods with structs. Methods are functions that are defined with a receiver type, which is a reference to the struct.

go
Copy
```go
package main

import "fmt"

// Define a struct named 'Person'
```

493

```
type Person struct {
    Name    string
    Age     int
    Address string
}

// Define a method on the 'Person' struct
func (p Person) Greet() {
    fmt.Printf("Hello, my name is %s and I am %d years old.\n", p.Name, p.Age)
}

func main() {
    // Create an instance of 'Person'
    person := Person{Name: "Alice", Age: 25}

    // Call the Greet method on the instance
    person.Greet() // Output: Hello, my name is Alice and I am 25 years old.
}
```

In this case:

- The Greet method is associated with the Person struct.
- The method uses a **receiver** (in this case, p Person) to access the struct's fields.

Notice that methods in Go can be associated with **value receivers** (like the p Person above), meaning the method operates on a copy of the struct, or **pointer receivers** (when passed by reference), which we will cover in the next section.

Interfaces: Defining Behavior in Go

While structs represent the data in Go, **interfaces** define the behavior. An interface in Go specifies a set of methods that a type must implement. If a type implements all the methods in an interface, it automatically satisfies that interface—**no explicit declaration or inheritance** is required.

1. Defining an Interface

An interface is defined by a set of method signatures. Here's an example:

go
Copy

```go
package main

import "fmt"

// Define an interface named 'Speaker'
type Speaker interface {
    Speak() string
}

// Define a struct named 'Person'
type Person struct {
    Name string
}

// Define a method on the 'Person' struct
func (p Person) Speak() string {
    return fmt.Sprintf("Hello, my name is %s", p.Name)
}

func main() {
    // Create an instance of 'Person'
    person := Person{Name: "John"}

    // Assign 'person' to the 'Speaker' interface
    var speaker Speaker = person

    // Call the Speak method via the interface
    fmt.Println(speaker.Speak())  // Output: Hello, my name is John
}
```

In this example:

- The Speaker interface defines a single method Speak() string.

- The Person struct implements the Speak() method, so it automatically satisfies the Speaker interface.
- We can assign a Person instance to a variable of type Speaker and call the Speak() method via the interface.

2. Empty Interface and Type Assertion

Go also has an **empty interface** (interface{}), which is a special case of an interface that can hold values of any type. This allows you to work with arbitrary types and can be useful when you need generic functionality.

Here's an example of the empty interface:

go
Copy
```go
package main

import "fmt"

func printAnything(v interface{}) {
   fmt.Println(v)
}

func main() {
   printAnything("Hello, Go!")
   printAnything(42)
   printAnything(3.14)
}
```

In this example:

- The printAnything function accepts an argument of type interface{}, which means it can take any value.
- The function works with different types (string, int, float64) by accepting values of any type and printing them.

You can also use **type assertions** to retrieve the underlying value of an interface if you know the type.

496

```go
go
Copy
var x interface{} = "Hello, Go!"
s, ok := x.(string)
if ok {
    fmt.Println(s) // Output: Hello, Go!
} else {
    fmt.Println("Not a string")
}
```

In this case:

- We assert that x is a string, and if the assertion is successful, we print the value.

Combining Structs and Interfaces

One of the most powerful features in Go is the ability to combine **structs** and **interfaces** to achieve polymorphism—enabling different types to be treated interchangeably as long as they satisfy the same interface.

```go
go
Copy
package main

import "fmt"

// Define the 'Speaker' interface
type Speaker interface {
    Speak() string
}

// Define a struct named 'Person'
type Person struct {
    Name string
}

// Define another struct named 'Dog'
```

497

```go
type Dog struct {
    Name string
}

// Implement the 'Speak' method for 'Person'
func (p Person) Speak() string {
    return fmt.Sprintf("Hello, my name is %s", p.Name)
}

// Implement the 'Speak' method for 'Dog'
func (d Dog) Speak() string {
    return fmt.Sprintf("Woof! I am %s", d.Name)
}

func introduce(speaker Speaker) {
    fmt.Println(speaker.Speak())
}

func main() {
    person := Person{Name: "Alice"}
    dog := Dog{Name: "Buddy"}

    // Both Person and Dog satisfy the Speaker interface
    introduce(person) // Output: Hello, my name is Alice
    introduce(dog)    // Output: Woof! I am Buddy
}
```

In this example:

- Both the Person and Dog structs implement the Speak() method, so they satisfy the Speaker interface.
- We pass instances of both Person and Dog to the introduce function, which accepts any type that satisfies the Speaker interface. This demonstrates **polymorphism** in Go.

Go's Interface Composition: Embedding Interfaces

In Go, interfaces can also **embed** other interfaces, which allows you to create more complex behaviors by combining simpler ones. This approach enables **composition over inheritance**, one of the key principles of Go's design philosophy.

```go
go
Copy
package main

import "fmt"

// Define the 'Speaker' interface
type Speaker interface {
    Speak() string
}

// Define the 'Writer' interface
type Writer interface {
    Write() string
}

// Define the 'Person' struct
type Person struct {
    Name string
}

// Person implements both the 'Speak' and 'Write' methods
func (p Person) Speak() string {
    return fmt.Sprintf("Hello, my name is %s", p.Name)
}

func (p Person) Write() string {
    return fmt.Sprintf("I am writing a letter. - %s", p.Name)
}

// Define the 'WriterSpeaker' interface that embeds both 'Speaker' and 'Writer'
type WriterSpeaker interface {
    Speaker
```

499

```go
    Writer
}

func introduce(wrtskr WriterSpeaker) {
    fmt.Println(wrtskr.Speak())
    fmt.Println(wrtskr.Write())
}

func main() {
    person := Person{Name: "Alice"}

    // Pass 'person' to the 'WriterSpeaker' interface
    introduce(person)
}
```

In this case:

- WriterSpeaker embeds both Speaker and Writer, meaning it requires types that implement both Speak() and Write().
- The Person struct satisfies both interfaces, so it can be passed to introduce as a WriterSpeaker.

In this section, we've explored two of Go's most powerful features: **structs** and **interfaces**. We've seen how:

- **Structs** allow you to define custom data types and methods to operate on them.
- **Interfaces** allow you to define behavior, and how they enable polymorphism in Go.
- By combining structs and interfaces, you can create modular, flexible applications that are easy to extend and maintain.
- **Interface embedding** provides a powerful mechanism for composing behaviors, enabling clean and reusable designs.

As you advance in Go, these concepts will form the foundation of your programming skills, allowing you to write complex, efficient, and highly maintainable Go applications. Next, we will explore more advanced Go topics, including **concurrency patterns**, **error handling**, and **performance optimization**.

Working with Go's Powerful Standard Library

Go's **standard library** is one of its most powerful features, providing a comprehensive set of packages that allow you to handle a wide variety of tasks without relying on external libraries. The Go standard library is designed to be simple, efficient, and well-documented, making it an essential tool for building robust applications. Whether you're working with HTTP servers, databases, file systems, or concurrency, Go's standard library has built-in support to help you get the job done.

In this section, we'll explore some of the most commonly used packages in Go's standard library and demonstrate how to leverage them to simplify your Go applications.

---

1. Working with HTTP and Web Servers

Go's net/http package is powerful for building both **client** and **server** applications. With this package, you can create web servers, handle HTTP requests, and make HTTP requests to other services.

Creating a Basic Web Server

Here's a simple example of how to create a basic HTTP server using Go's net/http package:

go

Copy

```
package main


import (

    "fmt"
```

```go
    "net/http"
)


func helloHandler(w http.ResponseWriter, r *http.Request) {
    fmt.Fprintf(w, "Hello, World!")
}


func main() {
    // Register the handler function for the root route
    http.HandleFunc("/", helloHandler)

    // Start the server on port 8080
    fmt.Println("Starting server on :8080...")
    if err := http.ListenAndServe(":8080", nil); err != nil {
        fmt.Println("Error starting the server:", err)
    }
}
```

In this example:

- **http.HandleFunc**: Registers a handler for HTTP requests at the root path /.
- **http.ListenAndServe(":8080", nil)**: Starts the server and listens for requests on port 8080.

Once the server is running, you can open your browser and navigate to http://localhost:8080 to see the "Hello, World!" message.

502

Making HTTP Requests (Client-side)

Go also makes it easy to make HTTP requests to other services. For example, to send a GET request to a URL, you can use the http.Get function:

go

Copy

```go
package main

import (
    "fmt"
    "log"
    "net/http"
)

func main() {
    response, err := http.Get("https://jsonplaceholder.typicode.com/posts/1")
    if err != nil {
        log.Fatal(err)
    }
    defer response.Body.Close()

    fmt.Println("Response Status:", response.Status)
}
```

In this example:

- **http.Get**: Sends a GET request to the provided URL and returns a response object.
- **defer response.Body.Close()**: Ensures that the response body is closed once we're done with it.

Go's net/http package provides many other useful functions for making requests with different methods (POST, PUT, DELETE), handling response bodies, and dealing with headers, making it easy to interact with web services.

---

2. Handling Files and Directories with os and io/ioutil

Go provides excellent tools for working with files and directories through the os and io/ioutil packages.

Creating and Writing to a File

To create and write to a file in Go, use the os.Create function to create a new file and the io.Writer interface to write to it:

go

Copy

```
package main

import (

    "fmt"

    "os"

)


func main() {
```

```go
// Create a new file or open an existing file

file, err := os.Create("example.txt")

if err != nil {

    fmt.Println("Error creating file:", err)

    return

}

defer file.Close()


// Write to the file

file.WriteString("This is a test file written by Go.")

fmt.Println("File written successfully!")

}
```

In this example:

- **os.Create**: Creates a new file called example.txt. If the file already exists, it truncates it to zero length.
- **file.WriteString**: Writes the specified string to the file.

Reading from a File

Go provides several ways to read from files, including the ioutil.ReadFile function for reading the entire content of a file into memory:

go

Copy

```go
package main
```

```go
import (

    "fmt"

    "io/ioutil"

)


func main() {

    // Read the contents of the file

    content, err := ioutil.ReadFile("example.txt")

    if err != nil {

        fmt.Println("Error reading file:", err)

        return

    }


    // Print the file content

    fmt.Println(string(content))

}
```

In this example:

- **ioutil.ReadFile**: Reads the entire content of example.txt and returns it as a byte slice.
- We convert the byte slice to a string and print it to the console.

Working with Directories

Go also allows you to interact with directories. You can list files in a directory, create directories, or remove them:

go

Copy

```go
package main

import (
    "fmt"
    "os"
)

func main() {
    // Create a new directory
    err := os.Mkdir("my_directory", 0755)
    if err != nil {
        fmt.Println("Error creating directory:", err)
        return
    }
    fmt.Println("Directory created successfully!")

    // Remove a directory
    err = os.Remove("my_directory")
```

```
if err != nil {

    fmt.Println("Error removing directory:", err)

    return

}

fmt.Println("Directory removed successfully!")

}
```

In this example:

- **os.Mkdir**: Creates a new directory with the specified permissions (in this case, 0755).
- **os.Remove**: Removes the directory.

---

3. Concurrency with Goroutines and Channels

One of the defining features of Go is its built-in support for **concurrency** using **goroutines** and **channels**. These tools allow you to easily run multiple tasks concurrently, improving the performance and responsiveness of your applications.

Goroutines

A **goroutine** is a lightweight thread of execution managed by the Go runtime. You can create a goroutine using the go keyword:

go

Copy

```
package main


import "fmt"
```

```go
func printMessage() {

    fmt.Println("Hello from the goroutine!")

}


func main() {

    // Launch a goroutine

    go printMessage()


    // Wait for the goroutine to finish

    fmt.Println("Main function")

}
```

In this example:

- **go printMessage()** launches a goroutine that concurrently runs the printMessage function.

The output will be:
css
Copy
Main function

Hello from the goroutine!

Channels

Channels are used to communicate between goroutines. You can use channels to send and receive data between goroutines, ensuring safe concurrent operations.

Here's an example of using channels to communicate between two goroutines:

go

Copy

```
package main

import "fmt"

func sendData(channel chan string) {
    channel <- "Hello from the goroutine!"  // Send data to the channel
}

func main() {
    // Create a channel to communicate between goroutines
    channel := make(chan string)

    // Launch a goroutine to send data
    go sendData(channel)

    // Receive data from the channel
    message := <-channel
```

```go
	fmt.Println("Received:", message)
}
```

In this example:

- **channel := make(chan string)** creates a new channel that transmits strings.
- The sendData function sends a message to the channel, and the main function receives the message and prints it.

Channels provide a powerful way to coordinate and synchronize goroutines, making Go an excellent language for building concurrent systems.

---

4. Working with JSON: encoding/json

The encoding/json package in Go provides a simple way to encode and decode JSON data. It's extremely useful for working with web APIs, configuration files, or any application that needs to work with JSON.

Encoding Go Structs to JSON

You can easily convert Go structs into JSON data using json.Marshal:

go

Copy

```go
package main

import (

	"encoding/json"

	"fmt"

)
```

```go
type Person struct {
    Name    string `json:"name"`
    Age     int    `json:"age"`
    Address string `json:"address"`
}

func main() {
    person := Person{Name: "John", Age: 30, Address: "123 Main St"}

    // Encode the struct to JSON
    jsonData, err := json.Marshal(person)
    if err != nil {
        fmt.Println("Error encoding JSON:", err)
        return
    }

    fmt.Println(string(jsonData))
}
```

In this example:

- **json.Marshal** converts the person struct into a JSON string.
- The json:"name" tags specify the key names in the JSON output.

512

Decoding JSON to Go Structs

To decode JSON into Go structs, use the json.Unmarshal function:

go

Copy

```go
package main

import (
    "encoding/json"
    "fmt"
)

type Person struct {
    Name    string `json:"name"`
    Age     int    `json:"age"`
    Address string `json:"address"`
}

func main() {
    jsonData := `{"name":"John","age":30,"address":"123 Main St"}`

    var person Person
```

```go
// Decode the JSON string into the 'person' struct

err := json.Unmarshal([]byte(jsonData), &person)

if err != nil {

    fmt.Println("Error decoding JSON:", err)

    return

}


    fmt.Println(person)

}
```

In this example:

- **json.Unmarshal** is used to decode a JSON string into a Person struct.
- The struct fields must match the JSON keys (or be tagged with json tags).

Go's **standard library** is a powerful and essential resource that covers a wide range of functionality, from handling HTTP requests to working with files, concurrency, and JSON. By mastering the key packages in the Go standard library, you can efficiently build robust applications without needing to rely on external libraries for common tasks.

In this section, we explored:

- **Working with HTTP servers and clients** using the net/http package.
- **File and directory handling** using os and io/ioutil.
- **Concurrency** with **goroutines** and **channels**.
- **JSON encoding and decoding** using the encoding/json package.

By leveraging Go's rich standard library, you can streamline the development of your applications and ensure they are both powerful and efficient.

514

11.2. Writing Tests in Go

Introduction to Testing in Go

Testing is an essential part of software development, and Go makes it incredibly easy to write and run tests. Go's testing framework is built into the language itself, allowing you to write tests using a simple, clean, and intuitive approach.

Testing in Go is done using the testing package, which provides tools to define and run unit tests. Unit tests help ensure that your code functions as expected, making it easier to maintain, extend, and refactor your code. By writing tests, you can prevent future bugs and ensure that your application behaves as expected in different scenarios.

Go's testing framework supports:

- **Unit testing**: Testing individual functions or methods in isolation.
- **Test suites**: Grouping related tests together to test different parts of your code.
- **Test coverage**: Ensuring that all parts of your code are tested.
- **Benchmarking**: Measuring the performance of your functions.

Writing Unit Tests and Test Functions

In Go, **unit tests** are written in a separate file from the code being tested, usually with the suffix _test.go. The testing functions are designed to test the behavior of your code and check if it behaves as expected.

1. Writing Your First Unit Test

To get started, let's create a simple Go function and write a test for it. For example, consider the following function that adds two numbers:

go

Copy

```
package mathutils


// Add adds two integers and returns the result.
```

515

```go
func Add(a int, b int) int {

    return a + b

}
```

Now, let's write a unit test for this function. We'll create a new file named mathutils_test.go **in the same directory as** mathutils.go:

go

Copy

```go
package mathutils


import "testing"


// TestAdd tests the Add function.
func TestAdd(t *testing.T) {

    result := Add(2, 3)

    expected := 5


    if result != expected {

        t.Errorf("Add(2, 3) = %d; want %d", result, expected)

    }

}
```

Explanation of the Test:

1. **Test Function Naming**: The test function is named TestAdd because it is testing the Add function. Go's testing framework automatically recognizes functions that begin with Test as test functions.
2. **Testing Logic**:
   - We call the Add function with the values 2 and 3.
   - We define the expected result as 5.
   - We compare the result from the Add function to the expected result. If they don't match, we call t.Errorf to report a failure.
3. **t.Errorf**: This function is used to log the error. The test will fail if the result does not match the expected value, and the error message will include the values involved.

2. Running the Tests

To run your test, use the go test command:

bash

Copy

```
go test
```

This command will automatically detect all the _test.go files in your project, run the test functions inside them, and report the results in the terminal.

If everything is correct, you should see an output like this:

bash

Copy

```
PASS
ok      yourmodule/mathutils  0.002s
```

517

If the test fails (for example, if the Add function is incorrect), you'll see something like this:

lua

Copy

```
--- FAIL: TestAdd (0.00s)

    mathutils_test.go:10: Add(2, 3) = 6; want 5

FAIL

exit status 1

FAIL    yourmodule/mathutils  0.002s
```

This output helps you pinpoint where things went wrong.

3. Writing More Complex Tests

Go's testing framework is simple, but it also allows for more advanced testing scenarios. For instance, you can write tests with multiple cases or use setup and teardown logic.

Test with Multiple Cases

You can write a test that checks several different inputs for the same function using a **table-driven** approach, which is common in Go:

go

Copy

```
package mathutils


import "testing"


func TestAdd(t *testing.T) {
    tests := []struct {
```

518

```
    a, b, expected int
}{
    {2, 3, 5},
    {1, 1, 2},
    {5, -3, 2},
    {0, 0, 0},
}

for _, test := range tests {
    result := Add(test.a, test.b)
    if result != test.expected {
        t.Errorf("Add(%d, %d) = %d; want %d", test.a, test.b, result, test.expected)
    }
}
}
```

Explanation:

- We define a slice of test cases, each consisting of the input values (a and b) and the expected result (expected).
- We loop over the test cases, run the Add function with the input values, and check if the result matches the expected value.
- This approach allows you to test multiple scenarios with the same logic in a concise and efficient manner.

---

4. Test Setup and Teardown

In some cases, you may need to set up some initial conditions before running your tests (such as creating temporary files or initializing a database connection) and clean up after the tests run (such as closing connections or deleting files). Go's testing framework provides support for this through **setup** and **teardown** logic.

Example of Setup and Teardown:

go

Copy

```go
package main

import (
    "fmt"
    "os"
    "testing"
)

// Setup creates a temporary file for testing.
func Setup() (*os.File, error) {
    file, err := os.CreateTemp("", "testfile")
    if err != nil {
        return nil, err
    }
    return file, nil
}
```

```go
// Teardown removes the file after the test is completed.
func Teardown(file *os.File) {
    os.Remove(file.Name())
}


func TestFileOperations(t *testing.T) {
    // Setup
    file, err := Setup()
    if err != nil {
        t.Fatalf("Failed to set up: %v", err)
    }
    defer Teardown(file) // Ensure teardown happens after the test finishes


    // Perform the test: writing to the file
    fmt.Fprintln(file, "This is a test")


    // Check if the file exists (just as an example test)
    if file.Name() == "" {
        t.Errorf("Expected file to be created, but it wasn't")
    }
}
```

521

Explanation:

1. **Setup**: Before running the test, we create a temporary file using os.CreateTemp.
2. **Teardown**: After the test finishes, we use defer to call the Teardown function, which removes the temporary file.
3. **Test Logic**: In the test, we write to the file and check if it was created.

Using defer ensures that the cleanup happens even if the test fails, providing a robust way to manage resources.

---

5. Benchmarking Tests in Go

Go's testing framework also supports **benchmarking**, allowing you to measure the performance of your functions. Benchmark tests are useful when you want to ensure that your application maintains or improves its performance over time.

Example of a Benchmark Test:

go

Copy

```
package mathutils

import "testing"

func BenchmarkAdd(b *testing.B) {
  for i := 0; i < b.N; i++ {
    Add(2, 3)
  }
}
```

522

Explanation:

- b.N: The b.N value is automatically managed by the Go testing framework to determine how many times the benchmark should run.
- **Benchmark Loop**: The loop inside the benchmark function calls the Add function repeatedly to measure its performance.

To run the benchmark, use the following command:

bash

Copy

```
go test -bench .
```

This will run the benchmark and display the results, including the number of operations per second and the time taken for each operation.

6. Test Coverage

Go has built-in support for measuring **test coverage**, which helps you determine how much of your code is being tested. You can run tests with coverage reporting using the following command:

bash

Copy

```
go test -cover
```

This will display the percentage of code covered by your tests. For more detailed coverage information, you can use:

bash

Copy

```
go test -coverprofile=coverage.out

go tool cover -html=coverage.out
```

This generates an HTML report that you can view in your browser to see which lines of code were tested and which were not.

In this section, we've covered the basics of **writing tests in Go** using the built-in testing package. Here's a summary of the key concepts:

- **Unit testing**: Writing tests for individual functions or methods to ensure they behave as expected.
- **Table-driven tests**: Writing tests that handle multiple scenarios in a single test function.
- **Test setup and teardown**: Using functions to prepare and clean up test resources.
- **Benchmarking**: Measuring the performance of functions.
- **Test coverage**: Ensuring that all parts of your code are tested.

11.3. Contributing to Open-Source Projects with Go

Getting Involved in the Go Community

The Go programming language has a vibrant and active **community** of developers who contribute to a wide variety of open-source projects. Contributing to open-source projects can be a rewarding experience, both for personal growth and for helping improve tools and libraries that others rely on.

524

Go's community is built around the **Go Forum, Go GitHub repositories**, and other social platforms such as **Go Slack channels** and **Stack Overflow**. These platforms provide opportunities for developers to collaborate, share ideas, report issues, and contribute to the development of Go itself and the ecosystem surrounding it.

Before you dive into contributing, here's how you can get involved:

1. Join Go's Official Community Spaces

Go has several community spaces where you can connect with other Go developers, discuss ideas, and find opportunities to contribute:

- **Go Forum**: The Go Forum is a space for general discussion about Go. You can ask questions, share experiences, and learn from others.
- **Go Slack Channels**: The Go community has active Slack channels where developers from around the world communicate. You can join by signing up for an invite at the Go Slack.
- **Go Mailing Lists**: Go has various mailing lists (e.g., golang-dev, golang-announce) that discuss Go's development and new features.

Being involved in these spaces allows you to stay up to date with Go's latest developments, understand community needs, and contribute to discussions.

2. Follow Go's Official GitHub Repositories

Go is an open-source project maintained by **Google** and the Go community, and its source code is hosted on **GitHub**. The main Go repository can be found at https://github.com/golang/go. Contributing to this repository can include reporting bugs, submitting patches, or reviewing pull requests. Here are a few ways to get started with Go's GitHub repositories:

- **Explore Go's GitHub**: Look through the **Go GitHub repository** and familiarize yourself with the structure of the project. You'll find the main Go language code, tools, documentation, and resources.
- **Explore Other Go Repositories**: Beyond the Go language itself, there are many other open-source Go projects maintained by the community, including libraries, frameworks, tools, and utilities. These repositories are often open to contributions from new developers.

3. Attend Go Conferences and Meetups

Go has a global community, and developers frequently organize events and meetups to discuss the latest advancements in the language. You can attend these events, learn from experts, and connect with other contributors. Some notable Go events include:

- **GopherCon**: GopherCon is one of the largest Go conferences in the world. It is a great place to learn from industry leaders, contribute to the Go ecosystem, and meet like-minded developers.
- **Local Go Meetups**: Many cities host Go meetups where you can meet developers in your area. Platforms like **Meetup.com** can help you find events near you.

Open-Source Contribution Tips

Contributing to open-source projects, especially in Go, can be an incredibly rewarding experience. Whether you're contributing to the Go language itself, libraries, or other Go-based tools, your contributions help improve the ecosystem and allow you to grow as a developer. Here are some tips to help you get started with open-source contributions.

1. Start with Small Issues

When you're new to open-source contribution, it's helpful to start with small, manageable tasks. This helps you get familiar with the project's workflow, coding standards, and review process. Look for issues that are tagged with **"good first issue"** or **"beginner-friendly"**. These issues are often simpler and well-suited for newcomers.

To find such issues:

- Browse through the **Issues** section of the Go GitHub repository or other Go-based projects.
- Look for labels like **"help wanted"** or **"good first issue"**.
- Read through the issue discussions to understand the context and ask questions if necessary.

By starting with small issues, you can gradually increase the complexity of your contributions and build confidence in your ability to contribute to larger projects.

2. Understand the Codebase

Before making any changes to a project, take the time to understand the codebase. Here are some steps to follow:

- **Fork the Repository**: Fork the repository you want to contribute to, and clone it to your local machine.
- **Explore the Code**: Take time to read the documentation, explore the code structure, and understand the main components.
- **Run the Tests**: Before submitting any code, run the existing tests to ensure you haven't broken anything. Understanding the tests is essential for contributing code that integrates smoothly with the project.
- **Check the Contribution Guidelines**: Many projects, including Go, have contribution guidelines, code style rules, and a process for submitting pull requests. Make sure to read and follow these guidelines to ensure your contribution is considered.

3. Work on Documentation

One way to get started with open-source contributions is by improving the project's **documentation**. Go projects often need help with documenting code, writing tutorials, or improving existing documentation. A well-documented project is crucial for new contributors and users alike. Some potential documentation contributions include:

- **Improving code comments**: Help make the codebase more understandable by adding or refining comments.
- **Writing tutorials**: Contribute guides or tutorials to help new users get started with Go.
- **Fixing documentation typos**: Even small improvements, such as fixing typos in documentation, are highly valuable and welcome in the open-source community.

4. Submit Your First Pull Request

After making your changes or fixing a bug, it's time to submit a pull request (PR). Here's how to do it:

1. **Fork and clone the repository**: This creates a personal copy of the repository where you can make changes without affecting the original codebase.
2. **Create a new branch**: Always create a new branch for each set of changes. This helps keep your work organized and avoids conflicts with other contributions.

527

3. **Make your changes**: Implement the changes you want to contribute, and ensure that your code follows the project's style and guidelines.
4. **Run tests**: Run any existing tests to ensure your code works as expected and doesn't break any existing functionality.
5. **Submit the PR**: Push your branch to your forked repository and submit a pull request to the main repository. Be sure to provide a clear description of the changes you made and why they are needed.

Once the maintainers review your pull request, they may ask for changes or merge it into the main codebase.

5. Communicate Effectively

Effective communication is essential when contributing to open-source projects. Be clear and respectful when discussing issues or asking for help. Here are some tips for better communication:

- **Be respectful**: Open-source communities are made up of people from diverse backgrounds. Be polite, professional, and patient when interacting with others.
- **Describe the problem clearly**: When submitting an issue or a pull request, provide as much detail as possible. If you're fixing a bug, describe how to reproduce it, what the expected behavior is, and the steps you took to fix it.
- **Ask questions if needed**: If you're unsure about a piece of code or how to contribute, don't hesitate to ask for clarification. It's better to ask than to make assumptions that could lead to mistakes.

6. Learn from Code Reviews

When you submit a pull request, the project maintainers may provide feedback and ask for changes. Code reviews are an excellent opportunity to learn from experienced developers. Here's how to make the most out of a code review:

- **Be open to feedback**: Accept constructive criticism and use it as an opportunity to improve your coding skills.
- **Ask for clarification**: If something is unclear, ask for more details. Understanding why a change is requested can help you grow as a developer.
- **Iterate and resubmit**: After addressing feedback, make the necessary changes and resubmit your PR.

7. Contribute Regularly

Contributing to open-source projects is a long-term commitment. The more you contribute, the more experience you'll gain, and the more you'll learn from the community. Regular contributions can also help you build a strong portfolio, which is valuable for career growth.

Set a realistic goal for how often you want to contribute (e.g., a few hours per week) and gradually increase your involvement over time. Whether you're fixing bugs, adding features, or improving documentation, consistent contributions will help you build a reputation in the community.

Contributing to open-source projects with Go is a great way to improve your skills, collaborate with like-minded developers, and give back to the community. In this section, we've covered:

- **How to get involved** in the Go community through forums, GitHub repositories, and events.
- **Tips for contributing** to open-source Go projects, including starting small, understanding the codebase, improving documentation, and submitting pull requests.
- **Best practices for communication** and receiving feedback from code reviews.

By following these tips and engaging with the community, you'll be able to make meaningful contributions to Go and other open-source projects, further developing your skills while helping improve the tools and libraries that you rely on.

11.4. Additional Resources for Further Learning

As you continue to deepen your knowledge of Go, there are many valuable resources available to help you refine your skills, stay up-to-date with new features, and learn advanced topics. From books to online courses, tutorials, and active community involvement, the following resources will provide you with a wealth of information to continue growing as a Go developer.

Books, Online Courses, and Tutorials

While hands-on coding is the most effective way to learn, there are many educational resources that can guide you through the more intricate aspects of Go programming, ranging from beginner-friendly tutorials to advanced Go concepts.

1. Books for Learning Go

Books are an excellent way to dive deep into Go, whether you are just getting started or looking to expand your expertise in specific areas.

- **"The Go Programming Language" by Alan A.A. Donovan and Brian W. Kernighan**: This is considered one of the most authoritative books for learning Go. Written by the creators of the language, it covers Go's core concepts and idioms in detail. It's suitable for both beginners and those familiar with programming.
- **"Go in Action" by William Kennedy**: This book provides practical examples and real-world use cases of Go. It focuses on helping you build Go-based applications, manage dependencies, and dive into advanced Go topics.
- **"Go Programming Blueprints" by Mat Ryer**: This book teaches Go by building real-world applications, focusing on concepts like concurrency, testing, and deploying Go applications. It's great for intermediate developers looking to apply Go to real-world projects.
- **"Go Web Programming" by Sau Sheong Chang**: If you're specifically interested in web development with Go, this book is a great choice. It covers building web applications, handling HTTP requests, and integrating with databases and other services.
- **"Go Systems Programming" by Mihalis Tsoukalos**: This book dives into building performant and concurrent systems with Go. It's ideal for developers looking to optimize Go applications for system-level programming.

2. Online Courses and Tutorials

For more interactive learning, online courses provide a structured path with hands-on exercises and the opportunity to learn from expert instructors.

- **Udemy**: The platform offers many Go programming courses, including:
  - *Go: The Complete Developer's Guide* by Stephen Grider: This course covers the basics of Go and dives deep into its features, including Go's concurrency model.

- *Learn Go with Tests* by Cory LaViska: A great resource for learning Go while focusing on writing tests and adopting a test-driven development (TDD) approach.
- **Coursera**:
  - *Programming with Google Go* (University of California, Irvine): This beginner-level course covers the basics of Go programming and its concurrency model, taught by professors from UC Irvine.
  - *Cloud Native Development with Go* (University of Colorado): This advanced course is excellent for developers looking to build cloud-native applications with Go, focusing on building scalable and performant systems.
- **Go by Example**: This website offers a hands-on approach to learning Go through practical code examples. Each example covers a different aspect of the language, such as variables, slices, and concurrency.
- **Exercism**: Exercism provides interactive Go exercises that help you build real skills by solving coding challenges and receiving mentorship from the Go community.
- **Go Wiki**: The official Go Wiki on GitHub provides a treasure trove of links, tutorials, and learning resources directly from the Go community and contributors.

3. Go Documentation and Tutorials

- **Official Go Documentation**: The Go documentation is one of the most comprehensive resources available. The documentation covers everything from language fundamentals to advanced topics, and the Go blog often posts deep dives into language features and performance optimization.
  - Go Programming Language Documentation
- **Go by Example**: Go by Example offers simple, easy-to-follow examples to understand Go's syntax and how to use various features in real-world situations. It's perfect for both beginners and experienced developers.
  - Go by Example
- **Go Wiki on GitHub**: The Go Wiki on GitHub includes helpful resources and community-contributed tutorials, including best practices, advanced patterns, and guides for contributing to Go projects.
  - Go Wiki

Joining Go Programming Communities

One of the best ways to continue learning and growing as a Go developer is by becoming active in Go programming communities. These communities provide an opportunity to ask questions, share experiences, collaborate on projects, and learn from others.

1. Go Forum

The **Go Forum** is an online discussion platform where developers from around the world discuss all things Go. You can ask questions, offer solutions, and learn about Go-related topics.

- Go Forum

2. Go Slack

The **Go Slack** community is one of the most active places to chat with Go developers in real-time. It is a great resource for seeking help with coding problems or discussing Go features. You can join specific channels based on topics such as Go web development, concurrency, and testing.

- Go Slack

3. Stack Overflow

Stack Overflow is a well-known platform where developers ask and answer technical questions. You can find a vibrant community of Go developers there. Search for answers to common problems or post your questions to get help from the community.

- Go on Stack Overflow

4. Go Reddit Community

The **Go subreddit** is another popular community where Go developers share knowledge, ask questions, and discuss Go-related news. It's a great place to keep up with the latest trends and developments in the Go ecosystem.

- Go Reddit

5. Meetups and Conferences

- **GopherCon**: GopherCon is the largest annual Go conference, where you can meet fellow Go developers, learn from experts, and participate in workshops. It's a great place to deepen your understanding of Go and stay connected with the community.
- **Local Go Meetups**: Many cities around the world host Go meetups, providing an opportunity to network, collaborate, and learn from other developers in your area. Use platforms like **Meetup.com** to find a Go meetup near you.

6. Go Developer Mailing Lists

Go's official mailing lists are a valuable resource for staying updated with the language's development and contributing to discussions around Go's future. Subscribe to the **Go-Dev** mailing list to stay informed about Go-related news, new features, and changes in the language.

- Go Mailing Lists

7. Go GitHub Repository

The official **Go GitHub repository** is where the Go language itself is developed. You can contribute by submitting pull requests, reporting issues, or reviewing code. Contributing to the Go codebase is a great way to learn more about Go and its internals while giving back to the community.

- Go GitHub Repository

In this section, we explored some essential **resources** for furthering your Go programming knowledge. By utilizing these resources and actively engaging with the Go community, you can accelerate your learning and stay current with the latest developments in the Go ecosystem.

Key takeaways:

- **Books and online courses** offer structured learning paths for both beginners and advanced Go developers.

- **Go documentation** and practical **tutorials** provide in-depth knowledge of the language.
- **Go communities** like the Go Forum, Slack, Reddit, and Stack Overflow offer valuable opportunities for collaboration, networking, and problem-solving.
- **Contributing to open-source Go projects** helps you grow as a developer and make a real impact on the Go ecosystem.

With these tools and communities at your disposal, you'll be well-equipped to continue growing your Go skills and contributing to the thriving Go ecosystem.